The Art of Regulation

Dedicated to
Helen Joanne 'Jo' Cox
(22 June 1974 – 16 June 2016)
and
Sa and Sabine
for the joy of living while working

The Art of Regulation

Competition in Europe – Wealth and Wariness

Christian Koenig

Professor, Center for European Integration Studies, University of Bonn, Germany

Bernhard von Wendland

Directorate General for Competition, European Commission, Belgium

In collaboration with *Nora Bettina Braun*, *Center for European Integration Studies, University of Bonn, Germany*

Edward Elgar PUBLISHING

Cheltenham, UK • Northampton, MA, USA

Published by
Edward Elgar Publishing Limited
The Lypiatts
15 Lansdown Road
Cheltenham
Glos GL50 2JA
UK

Edward Elgar Publishing, Inc.
William Pratt House
9 Dewey Court
Northampton
Massachusetts 01060
USA

A catalogue record for this book
is available from the British Library

Library of Congress Control Number: 2016953927

This book is available electronically in the **Elgar**online
Law subject collection
DOI 10.4337/9781785367595

MIX
Paper from
responsible sources
FSC
www.fsc.org
FSC® C013604

ISBN 978 1 78536 758 8 (cased)
ISBN 978 1 78536 759 5 (eBook)

Typeset by Columns Design XML Ltd, Reading

Printed and bound by CPI Group (UK) Ltd, Croydon, CR0 4YY

Contents

Note from Bernhard von Wendland

The content of this book does not reflect the official position of the European Commission.

Responsibility for the information and views expressed lies entirely with the author.

Abbreviations

ACCL	Azienda Comunale Centrale del Latte
ACER	Agency for the Cooperation of Energy Regulators
AIFM	Alternative Investment Fund Managers
AIFMD	Alternative Investment Fund Managers Directive
AoA	Agreement on Agriculture
BCBS	Basel Committee on Banking Supervision
BEREC	European Regulators for Electronic Communications
BTS	Binding Technical Standards
CCP	Central Counterparties
CDS	Credit Default Swaps
CFI	Court of First Instance (now General Court of the European Union)
CJEU	Court of Justice of the European Union
CoR	Committee of the Regions (see Article 307 TFEU)
CRA	Credit Rating Agencies
CRD IV	Directive 2013/36/EU
CRR	Capital Requirements Regulation No 575/2013
DG COMP	Commission's Directorate-General for Competition
DG ECFIN	Directorate General for Economic and Financial Affairs
DRM	Digital Rights Management
DSM	Digital Single Market
DSU	WTO's Dispute Settlement Understanding
EBA	European Banking Authority
EC	European Community
ECB	European Central Bank
ECJ	European Court of Justice
ECON	Economic and Monetary Affairs Committee
ECR	European Court Reports

EDNA	European Data Networking Agency
EEA	European Economic Area
EEC	European Economic Community
EIOPA	European Insurance and Occupational Pensions Authority
EMIR	European Market Infrastructure Regulation
ENLR	European Networks Law & Regulation Quarterly
EP	European Parliament
ERGP	European Regulators Group for Postal Services
ESC	Economic and Social Committee (see Article 304 TFEU)
ESFS	European System of Financial Supervision
ESMA	European Securities and Markets Authority
EStAL	European State Aid Law Quarterly
EUSCRA	EU Supervisory Competition and Regulatory Authority
FTA	Free Trade Agreement
GATS	General Agreement on Trade in Services
GATT	General Agreement on Tariffs and Trade
GBER	General Block Exemption Regulation
GDP	Gross Domestic Product
HHI	Herfindahl-Hirschman Index
ICT	Information and Communications Technology
IPR	Intellectual Property Rights
ISO	Independent System Operator
ITO	Independent Transmission Operator
KET	Key Enabling Technologies
LRIC	Long-run Incremental Costs
MAR	Market Abuse Regulation
MCT	Mobile Call Termination
MEIP	Market Economy Investor Principle
MEIT	Market Economy Investor Test
MEOP	Market Economy Operator Principle
MiFID I/II	Revised Markets in Financial Instruments Directive
MiFIR	Markets in Financial Instruments Regulation
MPIfG	Max-Planck-Institut für Gesellschaftsforschung

MTF	Multilateral Trading Facility
NBER	National Bureau of Economic Research
NRA	National Regulatory Authorities
OECD	Organization for Economic Cooperation and Development
OJ	Official Journal of the European Communities
ONP	Open Network Provision
OTC	Over-the-counter
OTF	Organised Trading Facility
PCP	Pre-Commercial Procurement
PMBS	Private-label Mortgage-backed Securities
PPI	Public Procurement of Innovative Solutions
R&D	Research & Development
R&D&I	Research and Development and Innovation
REFIT	Regulatory Fitness and Performance
SAM	EU State Aid Modernisation
SCM/SCMA	Agreement on Subsidies and Countervailing Measures
SGEI	Services in the General Economic Interest
SME	Small- and Medium-sized Enterprises
SMP	Significant Market Power
SOE	State-owned Enterprise
SRF	Single Resolution Fund
SRM	Single Resolution Mechanism
SSM	Single Supervisory Mechanism
SSNIP	Small but Significant Non-transitory Increase in Price
SSR	Short Selling Regulation
SWD	Commission Staff Working Document
TEU	Treaty on European Union
TFEU	Treaty on the Functioning of the European Union
TRIP	Agreement on Trade-related Aspects of Intellectual Property Rights
TRIPS	Trade-Related Aspects of Intellectual Property Rights
TSO	Transmission System Operator
TTIP	Transatlantic Trade and Investment Partnership

UCITS	Undertakings for Collective Investment in Transferable Securities
WIOD	World Input Output Database
WRP	Wettbewerb in Recht und Praxis
WTO	World Trade Organization

1. Why regulation?

We found a continent scarce in natural but rich in human resources and their produce!

That or the like might be the first report of a discoverer of modern day Europe. No matter how glowing that earliest account might be – it would most likely disregard that humans are not 'resources' but 'the source' of well-being, and that human dignity is an end in itself. At first sight, our pioneer would also not notice the cultural, religious and philosophical roots of the old continent, and that it rose to wealth through centuries of wars, strife, revolutions and toil. Voyaging deeper into the continent, the discoverer would learn that most of its nations are united in a political and economic union which is founded on the assumption of the values of respect for human dignity, freedom, democracy, equality, the rule of law and respect for human rights. Our voyager's second and more enlightening report might then say that the essence of Europe's wealth is rooted, to a large extent, in intelligent supranational governance and public regulation.

'Regulation' is more tangible than 'governance': in the broader sense, it prescribes official methods and standards to which market and non-market behaviour must adhere. Since this book will focus on regulation in the pursuit of economic justice and welfare, we address regulation, in the narrower sense, as any state or supranational intervention in market allocations of resources in order to direct market behaviour towards the public interest. The knee-jerk reaction of economic players subjected to regulation is to ask for justification. Hence, justification of regulation is this book's guiding theme, its 'leitmotiv'. Justification implies legitimacy. After all, it is the citizen for whom regulation is made, namely to promote his or her welfare. Here, 'governance' comes into play. 'Governance' is an elusive concept: it encompasses both, the normative aspects of regulation as well as aspects related to public coordination, guidance, surveillance and transparency.[1] Governance is regulation's fashionable

[1] EU-law refers to 'Governance' as a principle only in specific contexts: The Treaty on the Functioning of the European Union (TFEU), Article 15, refers to 'Governance' in the context of an administrative and legislative transparency: 'In order to promote good governance and ensure the participation of civil society,

and capricious cousin. This lesser cousin, though, can still bring a tiny sense of legitimacy to regulation where fragmented political institutions, both national and supranational, fail to do so.

The art of successful national and supranational regulation to reach sustainable wealth under terms of economic justice and inclusiveness is invoked in Pope Francis' frequent exhortations to overcome an economy of exclusion. In his highly debated Apostolic Exhortation, Evangelii Gaudium (The Joy of the Gospel),[2] the Pope does not rely on any God-made or God-given terms of economic justice. By contrast, his Jesuit down-to-earth approach calls for better man-made regulation:

> In this context, some people continue to defend trickle-down theories which assume that economic growth, encouraged by a free market, will inevitably succeed in bringing about greater justice and inclusiveness in the world. This opinion, which has never been confirmed by the facts, expresses a crude and naïve trust in the goodness of those wielding economic power and in the sacralized workings of the prevailing economic system. Meanwhile, the excluded are still waiting. [Evangelii Gaudium, para. 54]

> While the earnings of a minority are growing exponentially, so too is the gap separating the majority from the prosperity enjoyed by those happy few. This imbalance is the result of ideologies which defend the absolute autonomy of the marketplace and financial speculation. Consequently, they reject the right of states, charged with vigilance for the common good, to exercise any form of control. A new tyranny is thus born, invisible and often virtual, which unilaterally and relentlessly imposes its own laws and rules. (…) The thirst for power and possessions knows no limits. In this system, which tends to devour everything which stands in the way of increased profits, whatever is fragile, like the environment, is defenseless before the interests of a deified market, which become the only rule. [Evangelii Gaudium, para. 56]

---

the Union's institutions, bodies, offices and agencies shall conduct their work as openly as possible.' 'Governance' in the context of 'EU Economic Governance' consists in monitoring, preventing and correcting problematic economic trends, see e.g. the EU's broad economic governance framework http://ec.europa.eu/economy_finance/economic_governance/index_en.htm, 06.07.2016; see also Conclusions of the European Council of 17.06.2010, points 9–13 on enhancing economic governance; and the Treaty on Stability, Coordination and Governance in the Economic and Monetary Union of 02.03.2012, i.e. 'to improve the governance of the Euro-area'. The European Commission considers regulation as 'an essential part of modern society and good governance', Communication of 02.10.2013 COM(2013) 685 final, Regulatory Fitness and Performance (REFIT): Results and Next Steps.

[2] Released on 26.11.2013.

Regulation is the key to overcoming the *tyranny of the marketplace* in the pursuit of economic justice and welfare: it can prevent the abuse of both capital and economic dominance. Such abuse undermines a functioning market as the economic motor to produce welfare, sustainability and inclusiveness. Pope Francis voices concern over a new tyranny of *private* capital, but does not appropriately address the *public* cause of abuse. Neither did Karl Marx before him. Those who criticise the public cause of abuse of capital are too often attributed to the dingy school of libertarianism. Abuse of *public* capital, however, is as omnipresent as the abuse of market dominance by *private* capital. The state has vast resources at its command and can use them to intervene in the market: it can make major investments or compete with the private sector, or pick winners and subsidise them. Such interventions may be necessary e.g. to provide infrastructure and services of general economic interest, or to give incentives to industry in situations where the market alone would not deliver a desired outcome. The wasteful allocation of public monies, however, can do immense harm: it can crowd out private investments, distort private incentives, and help foreclosing markets. In any case, it deviates scarce funds from those who need them most. The abuse of public capital thus undermines sustainability and inclusiveness, the very values the state shall protect. Examples of the abuse of public funds abound, ranging from idle airports out in the sticks and FIFA-standard mega stadiums where only third-league teams play, to operating aid to ailing industries that are plagued by overcapacity. Political *megalomania* may sink a mega-investment just to create a monument to the decision maker himself. The negative outcome of wasting public capital may be even more abusive and detrimental to welfare than the abuse of market dominance by private capital. Therefore, regulation of state aid and public procurement is just as essential as regulation against the abuse of market dominance by private capital.

States' monopolies have been another public cause of economic exploitation until the recent past. Besides poor quality of service, consumers' bondage within state monopolies used to entail much higher prices for services compared to liberalised markets in other jurisdictions. A quarter of a century ago, the liberalisation of telecommunication markets acted as an ice-breaker for the modernisation of other politically embattled network industries, such as energy, postal, and railway services. Only the grid-based water supply, still incarcerated in municipal monopolies in some EU Member States, is yet to be released. In particular, in one of the rainiest countries worldwide (Germany) water supply is among the most expensive in the world. Even taking high-quality and environmental standards into account, municipal monopolies of grid-based water supply tend to excessively exploit consumers.

After liberalisation though, complex and well-adjusted regulation is crucial to induce functioning competition and to allocate the welfare benefits from liberalisation. In concrete terms, those are higher quality of services at affordable prices. Following liberalisation, former monopolists, i.e. *incumbents*, tend to obstruct newcomer access to their network infrastructure. Hence, any newcomer to the market, or at least the financing of such an undertaking, would be deterred in the absence of a special regulatory regime. So an independent regulator is needed to ensure market entry via access to the incumbent's physical networks under non-discriminatory and fair terms. Otherwise the release of consumers from the monopolies' bondage would be foiled.

Another area where regulation serves as 'the' key to safeguard welfare is the financial sector. The global financial crisis was the perfect laboratory for refining the art of regulation: financial key players, above all big banks as lenders, are systemic pillars in the relevant financial markets and the economy as a whole. At the same time, they are subject to principles and dynamics of the market. Refined regulation does justice to both roles. Since the financial crisis, the universal lack of adequate *ex-ante* supervisory powers, regulatory rules and institutions has been remedied, in particular in the European Union. Europe has done a lot to counter reckless voracity, e.g. in derivatives markets, which had decoupled from the performance of the 'real' economy. The now established regulatory framework also allows remedying the most harmful effects from the pre-crisis absence of a seismic regulatory and supervisory system.

Even in the absence of a seismic *ex-ante* supervisory system, the Commission had powers – and used them – to instantly authorise state aid as the last resort to prevent financial institutions from collapsing. Imagining the effect of disparate state interventions in a Europe without a strong supranational competition regulator is gruesome.

This book will give an overview of the European Union's toolkit of regulation for sustainable and inclusive wealth in an internal market. That overview will at times go into detail, but endeavours to be comprehensible. It points to the strengths of European regulations and criticises its weaknesses. This discussion must be seen against the backdrops of failing markets, challenged regulators and economic globalisation. This book will cross the borders of the legal community and address the wider public, especially the 'Eurocritics' in and outside Europe. However, the authors tried to avoid a euro-centric perspective, striving to provide a narrative that contributes to the universal art of regulation instead.

2. Where are we coming from?

The political history of the European Union and its internal market is very short: it begins in the aftermath of World War II. Trade and competition in Europe, however, flourished 2000 years ago, when Roman law and order applied in large parts of today's EU. Already then, thousands of miles of excellent roads connected cities and regions, one language was spoken and a common currency existed. Since then, the European market, and regulation of that market, naturally underwent many developments. In this chapter, we are looking at the most significant decisive regulatory advancements. Briskly walking back through regulatory history, we will meet market effects and forces that are highly relevant today, albeit in different forms and contexts.

2.1 FROM THE DARK AGES TO THE MEDIEVAL GUILD SYSTEM

In the fifth century, at the peak of the Roman Empire's disintegration, Europe slipped into the 'dark age'. Epidemics and wars drastically decimated the population; cities lost more than half of their inhabitants. Aggregate demand for markets and labour division were not met. Maintenance of roads and other infrastructure was no longer financed and overseen by the state. Income per capita dropped drastically, attaining the level of the Roman Empire only in the thirteenth century. Slowly, the Latin language retreated behind the walls of monasteries and universities. Robber barons and countless toll stations made trade dangerous and foreign goods expensive. During that time, Europe was far behind the wealth standard of the Eastern Roman Byzantine Empire. One factor that helped Europe make it from that dark period was … competition. It flourished on what seems to be a massive weakness, namely utter territorial and political fragmentation: unlike China, the Mogul Empire, or the Byzantine Empire, Europe was divided into several hundred territories and city states. This resulted in constant competition, fast tracking development and, eventually, surpassing the other Empires.

Obviously, this was not competition between legitimate industrial policies and regulatory systems as we can observe in Europe today, nor was it competition between market operators as we know it today. Rather, until the advent of industrialisation and the concept of free trade, competition in the 'European market' was confrontational competition between dynasties or trades that protected their economic interests to the detriment of efficiency and therefore the consumer.

In the Middle Ages, the Roman legacy was not entirely lost, though. The Latin language had survived and still connected the intellectual and political elite. Trade roads had deteriorated but could be rebuilt. Trade picked up and cities started growing. Sovereigns knew that in order to ensure the existence of their dynasty and state, income had to be secured, not least to pay for military expenses. They knew that high taxes or restricting key industries would only result in workers and their knowledge relocating to neighbouring states.

In the cities, merchants and craftsmen organised themselves in guilds. Guilds set product standards, regulated prices and decided how many masters of the same profession were allowed to do business in a city. They took in apprentices who then lived with their masters for the duration of their learning. That system also guaranteed a minimum of social security, i.e. sickness insurance or taking care of the family of a deceased guild member. Guilds also wielded political power in local matters, as city councils usually represented the wealthy merchant middle class. Moreover, monarchs were always ready to grant cities wide-ranging economic privileges, in return for steady tax contributions, and as long as they did not interfere with imperial policy prerogatives. Thereby, the regulation of prices and market output was the very fabric of the medieval economy. On the one hand, of course, this gave rise to the textbook negative effects of cartels – less innovation pressure and higher prices due to a lack of competition. On the other hand, next to social security for guild members, positive effects would be seen in setting universal product standards. Today, these positive effects are legally recognised in cartel exemptions of standardisation (see Article 101(3) Treaty of the Functioning of the European Union).

2.2 THE STATE DISCOVERS REGULATION – MERCANTILISM

Growing military expenditures though, combined with growing administrations and the insatiable demands of absolutist courts required new sources of state revenue. Hence, the European dynasties embraced mercantilism in its various forms. The idea underlying this concept is that the state centrally interferes in the market and regulates it. The objective was to increase the state's income by maximising exports of manufactured goods and minimising imports from other nations. England, especially, pursued a policy of strict regulation of imports and tariffs, and enforced an export ban on bullion, which was believed to be the main driver of a nation's wealth.

In France, Jean-Baptiste Colbert as finance minister regulated industry by granting monopoly and concession rights. He accelerated innovation by encouraging immigration that brought technical know-how. A similar model was adapted by Frederick II, King of Prussia, who to a large extent subsidised industry in sectors he deemed important, and who supported companies in difficulties. One example of Frederick II's very comprehensive mercantilist approach to regulation is his silk industry policy. In order to become independent of raw material imports, the state provided operating aid to plantations, provided them with silkworm eggs, and then guaranteed to purchase the silk; moreover, export subsidies, tariff protection or tax exemptions were granted.[1] Other companies were granted a monopoly and the works were overseen by the state. Today's EU state aid rules stigmatise operating aid as the form of state aid with the greatest potential to distort competition – it may help to perpetuate inefficient structures and over-capacities, and to deter innovation, to the detriment of both competitors and the taxpayer/consumer. EU state aid rules allow investment aid where the market alone would fail to deliver a desired outcome and where the aid does not create inefficient structures. Already 250 years ago, however, Frederick II's contemporaries understood fairly well that unnecessary state aid cannot promote welfare. In his monography on the Prussian monarchy, the French Count Mirabeau wrote in 1788:

> The King of Prussia recently gave six thousand écus for the establishment of a watch factory at Friedrichswalde. Such a small project was not worthy of this gift. It is easy to foresee that if this factory is not continually fed with further benefits, it will not sustain itself. Of all useless accoutrements, there is none more useless than a bad watch.[2]

---

1 Clarke, The Iron Kingdom – The Rise and Downfall of Prussia, 175, 176.

2 Honoré-Gabriel Riquetti, Comte de Mirabeau, De la Monarchie Prussiennne sous Frédéric le Grand, vol. 3, 191; cited from Clarke, The Iron Kingdom – The Rise and Downfall of Prussia, 179.

Today, the European Commission, in charge of regulating state aid, would have come to the same conclusion.

2.3 MODERN CAPITALISM UNFOLDS

There was no big bang to mark the end of mercantilism and the dawn of modern capitalism. Mercantilism had drawn criticism from its contemporaries on many different points. Already in 1624, England made the first step from mercantilism towards capitalism when she limited the Crown's power to grant monopolies based on patents.[3] Later, the industrial revolution was about to unfold. Building on that development, Adam Smith in 1776 presented an entire new theory of an economic system in his book *Inquiry into the Nature and Causes of the Wealth of Nations.* Smith delivered explanations of modern economic phenomena. He shed a bright light on the idea of obtaining larger production returns through the interplay of division of labour and free market concepts. Holders of resources (labour, land, and capital) are driven under competition, in the belief in free, basically non-regulated markets, to use resources most efficiently. It was Smith's market theorem which laid down the foundation of concepts such as free trade, competition and their regulatory limits based on sovereign jurisdictions.

However, unregulated markets resulted in the inherent options of abuse, so vividly described by Karl Marx in response to Adam Smith. According to his Hegelian influenced terms of dialectics in history, Marx reasoned in 'Das Kapital' that workers become exploited by any capital accumulation. According to his labour theory of value, the value of a good or service is directly connected to the amount of labour required for its production. However, the proletarian working class lacks any effective means to get a fair recompense for labour. Thus, the proletariat is necessarily driven to revolt to remedy this core problem. For Karl Marx, neither law nor regulation are options. For Marx, both are mere manifestations of the capital's will.

2.4 POST-WAR SOCIAL MARKET ECONOMY AND THE REDISTRIBUTION OF WEALTH IN EUROPE

Marx' analysis turned out to be a mere snapshot of the Industrial Revolution and capitalism as he perceived them in his times; the true

---

[3] Statute of Monopolies of 1624.

dialectics in history, and in particular European history, have refuted their German author. Indeed, his vision of a new communist social order as a synthesis emerging from the dialectics of economies of scale proved to be a failure. To the contrary, after periods of wars, strife and toil, Europe's states have embraced the concept of social market economy. The EU is, at last, approaching an equitable distribution of inclusive wealth by virtue of the rule of law and regulation. That policy is marked by one of the many schools of capitalism that have developed since Smith: Ordoliberalism. This European approach in the pursuit of inclusive wealth has become more and more apparent, e.g. in regional development policy, or research and innovation funding to tackle societal challenges such as social exclusion and job insecurity, or the coordination of national social security schemes.

3. Tempering the tyranny of market powers

3.1 BOON AND BANE OF MARKET POWERS IN THE EU

Effective competition is the main driver to achieve inclusive wealth. To protect competition, sustainable regulation has to balance market forces threatened by anti-competitive behaviour. At the same time, competition is not a goal in itself. Effective and well-targeted regulation therefore interferes where necessary, steering competition to achieve fundamental societal goals such as social progress. The latter translate into measurable strategic goals, such as universal broadband coverage under affordable and user-friendly terms, or the protection of the environment.

A competitive environment fosters the individual's inherent driving energies and forces to strive for wealth. Where the driving energies of individuals interact, resources are allocated to where they are needed and desired. As a consequence, society at large profits.

The individual entrepreneur strives to reduce his costs in order to maximise his own benefit. This seemingly self-serving desire for prosperity, once deemed 'greed' in Christian philosophy, is for the benefit of society at large in a competitive setting. Faced with competition, the individual, aiming at fulfilling his own goals of wealth, needs to set his products off from the competition in order to be attractive on the market and to continue generating profit. The individual is therefore challenged to sense what kind of product is most desired, be it particularly innovative or simply cheaper than a competing product.

One way to offer cheaper goods is to take advantage of *economies of scale*. By maximising production, entrepreneurs are able to spread their investments (e.g. in research and development or marketing) over a large quantity of items: costs per unit of output are generally decreasing with increasing scale while fixed costs are spread out over more units of output, leading to lower variable costs. The entrepreneur who leverages economies of scale will be able to offer his goods at a cheaper price than his competitor offering same-quality goods while not profiting from economies of scale. For this very reason, we will often observe larger market participants superseding smaller competitors, or absorbing them altogether.

Within a competitive market, individual entrepreneurs will pass on the gains of large-scale production to their consumers: if they did not, consumers would choose a cheaper competitor. If, however, competitive incentives are non-existent, entrepreneurs can exploit the efficiency of large-scale production without passing on the benefit to consumers. The need to innovate disappears, too: why should entrepreneurs invest in research when no competitor challenges them to offer a superior product? This example shows the opportunities of abuse and the bane of market power, present whenever competitive pressure is reduced, be it through a monopoly, cartel, or through state intervention.

The internal market can be challenged in two significant ways: first, by anti-competitive behaviour of market participants on either the supply or demand side; and secondly, distortions of competition can be caused by Member States' public interventions in the market, in particular by state aid selectively favouring companies. The fundamental tools of European regulation to remedy the abuse of capital and market power are anchored in the experience that economies of scale and maximisation of profits have to be tempered under the rule of law by general competition law and, in particular, by sector-specific regulation in areas like health, housing, telecommunications, digital and postal services, energy supply, railways, etc.

Furthermore, modern regulation has to cope with new challenges of market power based on network effects, often present on digital markets, which have overtaken the traditional economies of scale. These network effects became visible with the emergence of telecommunications services and networks: the more people had a telephone, the more valuable the service was to each connection holder (more people could be reached via phone) and, in particular, to the network owner. Following this dynamic, positive externalities are created because users purchase network access without intending to create value for other users, but do so automatically in any case. Social networks such as Facebook or LinkedIn become more attractive as more users join; online marketplaces like eBay depend on a substantial number of sellers and buyers. The more users a computer or smartphone operating system has, the more attractive that platform becomes for third-party app developers, thus making the platform more attractive for other users too. Another prominent example for network effects is the tremendous success of search engines. With more users submitting searches comes more information on which search results are relevant. This helps improve algorithms, drawing in even more users. Value and power of a company leveraging network effects are proportional to the number of users as opposed to labour input. These new economies of digital network effects have created tremendous options of growth as well as a number of regulatory challenges, in particular for consumer and cultural protection. The EU is constantly adjusting its tools of regulation to meet these challenges.

EU regulation is set within the framework of the internal market; achieving it is a fundamental goal of the Union. The internal market is an area where market participants are afforded the greatest possible degree of economic freedom of action subject to regulatory limits to safeguard a sustainable and social market economy. European law establishes an internal market in which market participants can engage in supply and demand in countless geographic and industrial markets within the EU without being hindered by trade barriers. The competition rules on trade contained in Articles 101–109 TFEU (Treaty on the Functioning of the European Union) serve to further develop and protect this economic space against distortions of competition. The Union's aims, in particular social progress and a high level of protection of the environment, are of equal importance and therefore influence the interpretation of competition law. The general competition rules as well as the regulations relating to specific sectors aim to guarantee a system of sustainable competition in order to achieve economic and social justice. The Treaty's spirit reverberated in Pope Francis' words, when he stated that we should not trust in 'trickle-down theories which assume that economic growth, encouraged by a free market, will inevitably succeed in bringing about greater justice and inclusiveness in the world'.[1]

3.2 THE CORE INSTRUMENTS OF REGULATION

3.2.1 Prohibition of Cartels

Instead of competing with each other at arms' length, members of a cartel act according to agreed behaviour patterns, removing the uncertainty inherent in any competition. The incentive to surpass competitors with better products or lower prices is reduced. Such an effect occurs if the coordinated behaviour either limits the competitive freedom of the undertakings involved (the independence postulate) or affects competition

---

1 Evangelii Gaudium, para. 54.

in the market, for example increasing costs to consumers or damaging market structure.

To prevent such effects, Article 101 TFEU prohibits agreements or concerted practices between undertakings that distort or prevent competition. Below the level of agreements, 'concerted practices' pass the cartel threshold under Article 101(1) TFEU when market behaviour is coordinated between undertakings, inter alia, by the exchange of business secrets, e.g. internal cost structures or preliminary information about an upcoming announcement of price increases. Thereby, the concerting undertaking anticipates that other undertakings will adapt to the changes in the market (e.g. through concerted price increases). However, mere parallel behaviour is not caught by the prohibition under Article 101(1) TFEU due to the inherent competitive right of any undertaking to adapt themselves intelligently to the existing or anticipated conduct of their competitors. Nevertheless, such freedom to adapt does not extend to permitting direct or indirect contact between undertakings, the object or effect of which is to influence the conduct on the market of an actual or potential competitor, or to disclose to such a competitor the course of conduct which an undertaking has decided to adopt on the market. Concerted practices only fall within the prohibition contained in Article 101(1) TFEU if they will remove a significant degree of uncertainty.

3.2.2 Controlling the Abuse of Market Power

Undertakings with a particularly strong market power may abuse this power to secure their position by hindering competitors in the same relevant market or restricting competition in neighbouring markets. Regulatory abuse control combats such behaviour.

An introductory example could be a scenario where an undertaking with dominant market power offers products at a loss-making price. While the customers will rejoice in the face of low prices, competitors will have to follow suit. Their pockets are likely not to be as deep as those of the dominant player so they will not be able to finance these losses for long. Once this low-price-strategy has controlled or even eliminated the competitors (or prevented a potential competitor from entering the market), the dominant undertaking is free to act in the market as it pleases. This example illustrates the vulnerability of markets where one undertaking is significantly stronger than its competitors and shows that basic principles of competition might need to be tweaked when dealing with dominant undertakings. Generally, competition through price reduction is an inherent part of healthy competition and should not be punishable. However, as illustrated above, low-pricing-strategies practiced by a dominant undertaking can be detrimental to competition in the long run. Regulators thus have to tread a fine line in order to not discourage effective and successful undertakings but also to protect the structure of competition. If an undertaking can lower its prices through passing on efficiency gains, this does not constitute an abuse. The ECJ does however presume an abuse when prices are set below the average variable costs or when prices are below the average total costs and are part of a specific strategy to eliminate competitors.

Abuse control is situated in Article 102 TFEU, which prohibits dominant undertakings from abusing that position to distort competition:

> Any abuse by one or more undertakings of a dominant position within the internal market or in a substantial part of it shall be prohibited as incompatible with the internal market in so far as it may affect trade between Member States.
>
> Such abuse may, in particular, consist in:
>
> (a) directly or indirectly imposing unfair purchase or selling prices or other unfair trading conditions;
> (b) limiting production, markets or technical development to the prejudice of consumers;
> (c) applying dissimilar conditions to equivalent transactions with other trading parties, thereby placing them at a competitive disadvantage;
> (d) making the conclusion of contracts subject to acceptance by the other parties of supplementary obligations which, by their nature or according to commercial usage, have no connection with the subject of such contracts.

Article 102 TFEU only applies to undertakings holding a dominant position. Dominance can only be determined with a clear view of with whom the undertaking is competing. Therefore, the precise relevant market needs to be defined first.[2] Once the relevant market is defined, dominance can be assessed. An undertaking is considered to be dominant in a relevant market if it can behave largely independently of its competitors and customers. The undertaking therefore has a position so strong, that the usual balancing powers of competition are feeble. There are certain indications for a dominant position; a starting point is the market shares of the dominant undertaking. Market shares over 50 per cent constitute a rebuttable presumption for dominance. Other indications

---

2 For the market definition, see later Chapter 3.5.

are the strength of the competitors, market entry barriers and potential competition, and the strength of the other market sides.

If dominance is assessed, the undertaking's behaviour can be scrutinised under Article 102 TFEU. A conduct is abusive if the conduct is only possible because of the dominant position and if it weakens competition. It is important to note that a dominant position in itself is not abusive. Dominant undertakings are however assigned a special responsibility to not allow their conduct to distort genuine competition.

Article 102 TFEU lists examples of what constitutes an abuse, but the list is not exhaustive. Through case law, specific case groups were developed. A few select examples will be given:

- Exclusive contracts: In a recent case, Intel abused its dominant position by contractually obliging Media Saturn, an outlet, to only sell products with Intel's central processing units (CPUs). Since Intel held a dominant position with 70 per cent of market shares, Media Saturn was reliant on Intel products and could not refuse. These contracts threatened to force Intel's main competitor, Advanced Micro Devices, Inc. (AMD), out of the market as AMD could not lay off its products. The same foreclosure effect can ensue if the dominant undertaking refuses to supply stores that also sell products of competitors.
- Loyalty rebates: A more hidden form of abuse with the same foreclosure effect are loyalty rebates. These rebates are not based on economic reasoning (e.g. size advantages) but are constructed in a way to eliminate competitors (e.g. rebate offered only if 90 per cent of all of the items sold in an outlet are from the dominant undertaking).
- Essential facility doctrine: More complicated cases occur when a dominant undertaking is vertically integrated and owns facilities, access to which is necessary in order to participate in a downstream market. A refusal to allow access to or the use of certain products can be abusive if that conduct is likely to eliminate all of the undertaking's competition. This applies to physical constructions, e.g. a port or a newspaper distribution system, as well as intellectual property rights. To illustrate with an example: Microsoft had held a near-monopoly position in the market for personal computer operating systems. It also sold work group server operating systems. In order to compete with the work group servers of Microsoft, competitors needed interface information which Microsoft withheld from them. The ECJ found this to be an abusive behaviour and Microsoft was ordered to disclose the interface information.

The structural changes caused by digitalisation pose a new challenge for the established abuse control: digitalisation is fast-paced, former strong market players like MySpace were driven out within a few years by Facebook, which is now facing competition from Instagram and WhatsApp (which, in turn, have been acquired by Facebook) as well as from Snapchat and LinkedIn. Competition authorities might be alarmed by the near-monopoly-like positions although the market might regulate itself within a short while.

3.2.3 Merger Control

Merger control shares with the other competition instruments the aim of preventing distortions of competition in the internal market. Merger control prevents the unnatural accumulation of market power through mergers and acquisitions that are likely to pose a significant impediment to effective competition in the future. It thereby takes an *ex-ante* view and seeks to protect the structure of the market. In comparison, the prohibitions on abuse of a dominant position and cartels focus on infringements of competition law which have already occurred. Merger control is hence necessarily more speculative as decisions must be taken on the basis of forecast information rather than the evidence of what has already occurred.

3.2.4 Fighting Distortive Market Interventions by Member States: Regulating State Aid and Public Procurement

Above, we discussed how private behaviour, and in particular the abuse of private capital, can distort competition. State intervention through public resources can however also have significant distortive effects. The EU's regulatory response is found in the so-called state-directed competition provisions in Articles 107–109 TFEU.

State aids (Chapters 4 and 5) are, in principle, prohibited under Article 107(1) TFEU:

> Save as otherwise provided in the Treaties, any aid granted by a Member State or through state resources in any form whatsoever which distorts or threatens to distort competition by favouring certain undertakings or the production of certain goods shall, in so far as it affects trade between Member States, be incompatible with the internal market.

The Member States' purchase of goods or services in the marketplace must also comply with European competition law. The EU directives on public procurement harmonise and standardise national procedures relating to the Member States' purchase of goods or services. European public procurement law aims to ensure that the purchasing activities of the state adhere to market economy principles and do not distort competition: Member States must not discriminate against any economic actor and must ensure the allocation or bidding process is transparent. Public procurement directives set out precise procedural rules on the award of public contracts. The requirements provide, in particular, for a European-wide standardisation of tenders avoiding discrimination and encouraging transparency (public procurement will be dealt with in Chapter 5.2).

3.2.5 Sector-specific Regulation versus General Competition Law

EU competition rules on the prohibition of cartels, abuse of market power and state aids (Articles 101–109 TFEU) apply regardless of the nature of the goods or services offered in the relevant market. They primarily apply on an *ex-post* basis, i.e. after a contravention has occurred. A conceptual distinction exists between such general rules and the rules that apply to a specific sector which take into account the particular features of the concerned markets, e.g. health, telecommunications, postal services, energy supply, railways. While general competition rules apply equally to all economic actors, sector-specific rules apply only to certain operators, e.g. to those holding a natural (or historical) infrastructure monopoly such as an electricity or gas transmission/distribution grid or railway network. Additionally, a key difference between general and sector-specific competition regulation is the competence of national regulatory authorities to intervene *ex ante* in well-defined markets of certain sectors (for example, to impose network access as well as access price regulation). These *ex-ante* regulatory instruments, which are widely harmonised in the EU, prescribe from the very start of service (e.g. network) operations official methods and standards to which market behaviour must adhere. *Ex-ante* intervention by sector-specific regulation is intended to allow for a comprehensive, future-oriented influence on the sector.

European merger control can be said to occupy a hybrid position between general competition law and sector-specific regulation. On the one hand, merger control is applicable to all sectors of the economy; on the other, authorisation requirements and merger approval are subject to threshold tests, which resemble sector-specific *ex-ante* regulation.

General (non-sector-specific) competition law is insufficient to liberalise traditionally monopolistic or state industries and to ensure sustainable competitive access to liberalised markets. In particular, in the case of grid-based network industries (e.g. telecommunications, gas and electricity grids, transportation networks, etc.), it is not possible for new competitors in downstream service or supply markets to establish (i.e. duplicate) the necessary networks upstream and to maintain the necessary domestic and off-shore physical infrastructure. For example, construction of competing gas pipelines by new market entrants, especially at the distribution grid level (closer to the final consumer than the long-distance transmission grid) would be next to impossible to finance given the high 'sunk costs' involved (i.e. expenses which a company cannot recoup at market prices upon exiting the market). Hence, any newcomer to the market, or at least the financing of such an undertaking, would be deterred in the absence of a special regime supporting market entry via e.g. access to physical networks. Furthermore, grid duplications are, as a matter of principle, environmentally negative due to their external effects on the environment.

If an ex-monopolist, e.g. the 'incumbent' telecommunications or postal services provider, refused a competitor access to its network infrastructure, which was built up in times of monopoly, this could constitute an abuse of market power (prohibited under Article 102 TFEU). However, if only *ex-post* competition control were available, in the time frame in which competitive justice is established a newcomer would have suffered death by insolvency. It is precisely in this sort of situation that EU sector-specific directives and regulations in the fields of telecommunications, gas, electricity, postal services and railway network infrastructure have created a harmonised *ex-ante* access regime regulated by national regulatory authorities in Member States under the supervision of the European Commission. Such authorities are authorised by sector-specific competition rules and by special *ex-ante* regulatory competence to monitor network access conditions and terms of use and to approve compensation access fees for use of the incumbent's network.

3.3 THE MANTRAS OF EU COMPETITION LAW

3.3.1 Consumer Protection

The European rules of competition place particular importance on the idea of consumer protection.[3] Therefore in considering whether a certain

---

[3] See Commission, Guidance on the Commission's enforcement priorities in applying Article 82 of the EC Treaty to abusive exclusionary conduct by dominant undertakings, OJ EU 2009 C 45/7, para. 5.

behaviour infringes competition rules, such behaviour is assessed not only in technical terms, but also on the basis of whether it produces negative effects on final consumers. Such negative effects can include, for example, artificially high prices, the availability of products to consumers which are quantitatively inadequate or qualitatively insufficient, or economically undesirable production which precludes the optimum allocation of resources, resulting, in the long term, in disadvantages for consumers. A detriment to consumers can also lie in the giving away of information where the consumer is not aware of the consequences. In recent years, protecting consumer data has come into focus as data has become a key feature of digital business models. Instead of paying with money, consumers pay with data (consumers' preferences profiles), which in turn are then commercialised by the online service providers, inter alia, on advertising markets. Here, consumer data protection can obviously not rely on general competition rules. Whereas the US jurisdiction quarrels much less with consumer data protection if consumers pay with their data instead of their money, the European Union keeps a rather jealous watch over such digital data transactions. It may appear exaggerated, but these markets of digital (personal) data transactions may reveal a clash of regulatory civilisations in the near future. Anyway, by contrast to the US jurisdiction, the EU has established a comprehensive legislative privacy framework aimed at protecting data pertaining to individuals. The EU is permanently adapting its data protection legislation to the information society. The EU General Data Protection Regulation, which is directly binding within the Member States, provides for large responsibilities for controllers (providers). Supervision and enforcement by independent supervisory authorities are subjected to the principle of '*one stop regulatory shops*' for citizens and business alike. Above all, in order to meet universal challenges, like those caused by the network effects driven '*GAEFAs*' (Google, Apple, eBay, Facebook, and Amazon), the territorial scope of the General Data Protection Regulation covers undertakings that are operating on the European internal market from an establishment elsewhere in the world.

3.3.2 Freedom of Action

An important key aspect of European competition law and competition ethics is the 'independence postulate' – the idea that every undertaking's business policy should be determined independently.[4] EU competition law is based on the principle that every competing undertaking is entitled to determine its behaviour independently, and that any restriction of that freedom of action – for example, as a result of agreements or concerted practices (cartels) between companies – constitutes an infringement. However, in infrastructure markets with high sunk costs, e.g. broadband telecommunications infrastructure investments, which cannot really be recovered in the event of a market exit, European and national competition authorities tend to accept that infrastructure sharing between competing undertakings reduces investment risks and they therefore permit – under strict proportionality conditions – a well-balanced compromise between such practices and the 'independence postulate'.

3.3.3 Efficiency Through Competition and the 'More Economic Approach'

The advantages of (cost) efficient competition lie, in simple terms, in lower prices, with demand matching the supply of qualitatively and quantitatively optimal products, sufficient choice and the most efficient means of production. In contrast to monopolistic markets, competition leads, according to the models of the Chicago School of economic thought, to the best possible allocative efficiency. This optimum is achieved in an economy if no individual can be made better off, without at the same time another person being made worse off, i.e. no change in the existing situation is conceivable which benefits one person yet damages no one else ('*Pareto efficiency*'). If such a state were to be reached, an optimal balance would be created in which every individual produces and experiences the best possible efficiency. Additionally, inherent in the best possible productive efficiency is that the necessary factors of production, such as labour and raw materials, are used by market participants without avoidable losses.

In the pursuit of economic welfare efficiency, the Commission in recent years has undertaken a comprehensive modernisation of competition law, in general aiming at a '*more economic approach*'. Previously, European competition law was characterised by a more formalistic approach, which focused on identifying the kinds of behaviour which usually result in negative effects on competition, with very little analysis of the negative effects in an individual case. Today, the question of the

---

4 ECJ, judgment of 16.12.1975, joined cases C-40/73 to C-48/73, C-50/73, C-54/73 to C-56/73, C-111/73, C-113/73 and C-114/73 – *Suiker Unie*, para. 173.

economic effects of the relevant behaviour is paramount: whether an infringement of competition law exists is determined first and foremost on the basis of the economic effects of the relevant behaviour rather than on the existence of a technical or structural violation of competition provisions. Thus, EU supranational competition regulation has adopted a clear '*substance over form approach*'.

On the basis of the more economic approach to positive effects of what seems on the surface to be an anti-competitive cartel (Article 101(1) TFEU), industry-wide cooperation for technical advancements, automotive security or industrial standardisation might be considered legal under the terms of Article 101(3) TFEU, if such cooperation (cartel):

> contributes to improving the production or distribution of goods or to promoting technical or economic progress, while allowing consumers a fair share of the resulting benefit, and which does not:
>
> (a) impose on the undertakings concerned restrictions which are not indispensable to the attainment of these objectives;
> (b) afford such undertakings the possibility of eliminating competition in respect of a substantial part of the products in question.

Likewise, the Commission now considers that predatory pricing[5] by a dominant undertaking is not necessarily abusive under Article 102 TFEU if it leads to efficiency advantages which, at least in the long run, are passed down to consumers, and any negative effects are offset by positive ones.[6]

This adjustment to competition policy focuses on a stronger inclusion of economic standards of assessment in competition control, including a paramount analysis of the real effects of a behaviour, supplemented by empirical data, and resulting in a quantitative appraisal of the effects of this behaviour on the welfare aims pursued by the Union. The use of models which have been economically tested makes it easier for the

---

[5] The offer of goods for a price below the variable costs of such goods' production and distribution (known as predatory pricing) can be abusive under Art. 102 TFEU if a market-dominating company uses such goods to edge out its competitors over the medium to long term. An abuse is constituted in these cases when a company is prohibited from taking part in market competition even though it is as efficient as the market-dominating company, but, e.g. cannot withstand the pressures of competition due to a lack of financial power.

[6] Commission, 'Guidance on the Commission's enforcement priorities in applying Article 82 of the EC Treaty to abusive exclusionary conduct by dominant undertakings' (Communication), OJ EU 2009 C 45/7, para. 30.

priorities set out in Union policy to be achieved, and increases the transparency of competition and welfare related decisions.

However, dynamic and ongoing academic discussions are indicative of the unending nature of the development of economic knowledge. The analysis of competition law with the help of economic models and data remains therefore inevitably selective and must be carried out on a case-by-case basis. A higher conceptualisation of economic matters (e.g. the use of mathematical econometric methods) in the application of competition law can only increase the transparency and efficiency of the decision-making process if the application of such economic criteria is open to permanent scrutiny and consistent with prevailing law. Additionally, focusing on short-term effects should not prevent a consideration of the long-term consequences of business behaviour.

3.4 THE ADDRESSEES OF EU COMPETITION LAW AND REGULATION

3.4.1 Undertakings

Before some selective areas of EU competition law and regulation are discussed in more detail, we will first consider the addressees caught by those rules. The concept of an 'undertaking' includes more than the common conception of companies operating on a market, which means that a broader range of entities is caught by the Articles 101–109 TFEU and sector-specific regulation than might initially be expected.

An undertaking in European competition law is 'every entity engaged in an economic activity, regardless of the legal status of the entity and the way in which it is financed'.[7] Under this *activity-based* approach, the activity allegedly constituting a competition infringement is considered in isolation and analysed as to whether it constitutes an economic activity. If it does, the entity is an 'undertaking', regardless of the legal or corporate status, profit orientation and of whether the entity is a public or private undertaking. Because of this *functional* approach, certain state behaviour may fall within the definition of an undertaking even though the state in its entirety would not be considered an undertaking.

The concept of an 'economic activity' is functional and broad. An *economic activity* is any activity consisting of the offering of goods or

---

[7] Established in ECJ, judgment of 23.04.1991, C-41/90 – *Höfner and Elser v Macrotron*, para. 21.

services on a given market.[8] Purchasing only constitutes an 'economic activity' if the product is then subsequently used in exercise of an economic supply activity in a certain market (possibly after i.e. further processing). Monetary compensation for the goods or services offered is not required. So-called 'free of charge' streaming services or social networks are therefore 'economically active', especially if consumers pay with their data. In fact, even an intention to make a financial profit is not necessary, which means that charitable organisations can be 'undertakings' within European competition law. Certain areas however remain outside the realm of economic activity – for example, the exercise of state powers or the purchase of goods solely for the purposes of private consumption.

After identifying the operating entity and after analysing whether it is an undertaking under European law, the legal organisation of the entity comes in as the unit or the person to whom the Commission's sanction of an offending behaviour must be addressed. Therefore, the examination of an infringement follows a two-step-approach: first, the operating undertaking (the unit of 'real economic behaviour') must be identified, and second, the legal entity, i.e. the unit to whom any decision or sanctions should be addressed, must be identified pursuant to corporate law in the relevant jurisdiction.

3.4.2 The Member States

To ensure the practical effectiveness of the provisions, Member States are likewise bound by EU competition law.[9] Article 4(3) TEU (Treaty on European Union) refers to Member States' 'sincere cooperation' and obliges them to refrain from any measure which could jeopardise the attainment of the Union's objectives. Member States must not actively support breaches of competition law, or transfer legislative competence to private economic participants so that the Member State is effectively 'authorising' the infringement of Article 101 or 102 TFEU.

If national regulations permit, promote or simplify anti-competitive behaviour, undertakings still remain responsible for their own behaviour. They infringe Article 101 or 102 TFEU independently and therefore cannot rely on their trust of the state in the area of national law as regards their conformity with EU law.

---

8 ECJ, judgment of 19.02.2002, C-309/99 – *Wouters*, para. 47.
9 ECJ, judgment of 29.01.1985, C-231/83 – *Cullet v Leclerc*, para. 16.

3.5 THE LEVEL PLAYING FIELD OF COMPETITION: RELEVANT MARKETS

In order to examine whether a certain action distorts competition, it is necessary to first analyse which products and which undertakings are competing with each other. The market where the competition takes place is called the relevant market.

3.5.1 Why it is Necessary

Only when the relevant market is identified can it be determined whether competition in the relevant market has been distorted by an agreement between undertakings (*cartel*). Market definition is also a key aspect in investigating whether an undertaking has a market-dominating position and is therefore subject to *abuse control*. Under a wider market definition covering more products, the influence an undertaking has in that market is likely to be smaller and therefore an undertaking might not be seen as dominant whereas a narrower definition makes market-dominance more likely. In order to identify whether a *merger* will have harmful effects on competition, it is necessary to define the relevant market so that it may then be analysed, how much competition the merged undertaking would still be subject to.

3.5.2 How it is Done

The most relevant question to define the product market is the question which products (or services) are interchangeable in the consumer's view due to similar characteristics of these products (price, intended use etc.). This is called demand substitutability. The relevant market encompasses all actual alternative products or suppliers to which a consumer can easily swap.[10] Demand substitution is the most important factor in determining the relevant market, as it constitutes the most immediate and effective disciplinary force on the suppliers of a particular product.

An intuitive example is defining the relevant market for beverages. Different beverages might be used in different situations, for example soft drinks as a refreshment, sport drinks after or during an exercise and milk for breakfast. To the consumer wanting to buy a specific soft drink, a different soft drink with a similar flavour and in the same price range

---

10 Cf. Commission Notice on the definition of the relevant market, para. 13.

would probably be a reasonable substitute and the two beverages would be in the same market.

Different methods and approaches to the concept of demand substitution have developed over time. An initial analysis considers the characteristics and intended use of a product. At the next stage, the 'SSNIP test' and various quantitative tests are undertaken to define the relevant market in further detail. The 'SSNIP test' ('Small but Significant Non-Transitory Increase in Price') is a thought experiment asking a hypothetical question: if the price of a product was raised permanently by 5–10 per cent, would consumers of this product change to another product?[11]

If the answer is yes and the increase in price cannot compensate for the resulting loss of sales, then both products belong to the same market. If a small price increase would drive consumers to other products, then these products are substitutable, and therefore in the same market. The SSNIP test is repeated with other products until a set of products is identified where a permanent price increase would be profitable, as there are no further substitutes available.

Market data used for the SSNIP test can be historic[12] or it can be gathered through questionnaires given to customers asking how they would act in the event of a permanent price increase.

However, this method is only really effective where the price of a product is of determining significance – it loses its effectiveness, for example, in the medical market where price may not be the determining factor in consumption.[13]

Another approach to market definition considers supply rather than demand side substitution. This test is useful when a change in the selling price of a product would make it worthwhile for a supplier of a similar but not interchangeable product to alter its production and now also produce the relevant product. An example might be the paper industry. For the consumer, normal writing paper is not generally interchangeable with high-quality paper used for reproductions of art. However, on the manufacturing side, it is relatively straightforward to swap to production of a different type of paper as this can be done simply by changing the settings on production machinery.

---

11 Ibid., para. 15.
12 Ibid., para. 38.
13 Cf. Morse, Product Market Definition, 638.

3.6 THE NEW FRONTIER: BIG DATA AND DIGITALISATION

Some economists have voiced the opinion that freely sourced user data is non-rivalrous and therefore not qualified as a source of market power.[14] However, if the same data is processed and accumulated, it turns into a non-ubiquitous and rivalrous good which is able to strengthen market power. Even non-rivalrous online data such as search query data can nourish market power in search and search advertising.[15]

Furthermore, it is the ubiquitous open access to online data which drives more and more users into connectivity, thereby producing valuable network effects and increasing the power of providers who exclusively own the tools to exploit big data. Meanwhile under these connectivity effects the big data pool is inexorably expanding and it is becoming increasingly valuable, yet in asymmetrical terms in favour of the owners of proprietary data mining tools. The world of big data has to be analysed most carefully and attentively, free from conditioned patterns of classical 'one-fits-all economics' in the old offline world.

Unprejudiced understanding of big data economics enables regulation to incentivise good data protection and privacy as tradable quality features while at the same time providing a safety net of law against violations. In order to make informed choices on which services to use, consumers need to understand what type of personal data service providers will keep track of. Currently, access to that information is often non-obvious, cumbersome, or outright impossible for the individual user. Due to said information asymmetries between providers and consumers with regard to the precise nature and use of data, regulatory sanctions against violations of well-adjusted data protection rules are necessary.

Big data is used to trace and to foresee business potentials and risks on the basis of predictive models. Currently unknown relationships between patterns of economic behaviour contained in big data are explored and processed by virtue of machine learning techniques, inter alia by support vector machines, neural nets, deep learning, or decision tree techniques, which help model predictive algorithms. Thereby data analysis and the underlying econometrics enable producing, in essence, four groups of valuable intermediate products: prediction, summarisation, estimation, and hypothesis testing.[16]

---

14 Lerner, The Role of 'Big Data'.

15 Cowen, Big Data as a Competition Issue, 15.

16 Varian, Big Data.

For instance, whereas Amazon ads are produced by virtue of predictive algorithms on preferred items (e.g. books) individual consumers might ask for, Google's search or news engines apply predictive algorithms to users' information preferences with regard to particular websites in order to classify their relevance and thereby their business priorities. Credit card companies rely on predictive algorithms of default risks derived from consumers' behavioural data, for instance indicating excessive purchasing or gambling activities, in order to improve their contract terms, risk management, and pricing. Similar risk score patterns are applied by life or health insurances. The list of economic potentials of big data is endless since computing is nowadays involved in most economic transactions. Thus, big data will get bigger and bigger with each click. Machine learning is therefore a permanent revolution in mining and processing huge datasets. Business strategists, economists, welfare policy agents, and regulators are well advised to understand at least the very basics by learning the intellectual patterns of these techniques in order to perceive the potentials and risks of big data mining.

By contrast, public regulation and economic welfare policy are at the very beginning of realising the potentials of big data. For instance, government agencies may, subject to data protection, provide open datasets to researchers, market players, or altruistic 'wiki-citizens' in order to enable informed business decisions or to improve new technologies (think connected cars) or non-commercial collaborative knowledge projects (think Wikipedia, OpenStreetMap). Intelligent processing of big data may enable economic welfare policy as well as regulators to measure and predict economic effects of any public intervention in markets. The processing of big data by the state bears the potential to provide a new basis for future oriented economic research on consequences of economic policies and regulatory techniques.[17]

Lesson to be learned: consumers as well as citizens expect vendors, governments, and regulators to exploit technological progress in order to improve everyday life. Just tightening laws, be it data protection, competition, or intellectual property rules, without understanding the new data economy will erode business and welfare opportunities. Lawmakers, governments, and regulators are well advised to be open-minded with regard to innovation potentials instead of sticking with established industrial and regulatory practices.

---

[17] Einav/Levin, The Data Revolution and Economic Analysis, 13.

Big data and digitalisation challenge regulators and legislators alike to let go of preconceived rules and ideas about mechanisms of competition. In the digital world, quasi-monopolies are rather common but, in contrast to traditional markets, do not pose the same threats and thus need to be scrutinised differently. Fugacious (near) monopolies are typical due to low market entry barriers, short innovation cycles, and vibrant competition which keeps the monopoly-holder from lazily leaning back and demanding monopolistic prices. Network effects do apply but they are not as big a barrier to new entrants as traditional network effects – it is no problem to entertain more than one social network for instance and thanks to smart phones, competing apps can often be used in parallel (WhatsApp, Skype, Viber, iChat, SMS), making transitions possible. In fact, the competitive pattern seems to be that major players supersede each other instead of dividing market shares between each other over a longer period of time. Competitive pressure therefore stems from the danger of being replaced in the future rather than from the competing product in the next shelf.

Consider the still-predominant social network Facebook, which is being replaced by mobile-centric apps like Instagram (for photo sharing) and WhatsApp (for messaging). Facebook saw the signs of the times early enough and acquired WhatsApp and Instagram, thus bringing potentially lethal competitors under its own roof. The Commission decision on the Facebook/WhatsApp merger[18] serves for interesting talking points:

On the one hand, it showed the limits of the legal framework in the context of digital markets: merger control at the European level only applies when the companies involved surpass certain turnover thresholds. At the point of the takeover by Facebook, WhatsApp had 600 million users and thus EU-wide relevance but only $ 10.2 million in turnover, thereby falling below the EU merger control threshold. If the national competition authorities had not voluntarily directed the case to the European Commission, the case would have been decided at national level, although being relevant at EU level.

In its decision in the matter, the Commission adapted its analyses to the realities of big data markets concerning the potential of data aggregation for online advertising, stating that Facebook only had a market share of 6.39 per cent and that WhatsApp's market share was

---

[18] European Commission, decision of 03.10.2014 in Case M.7217 – *Facebook/WhatsApp*; see also the corresponding press release: http://europa.eu/rapid/press-release_IP-14-1088_en.htm, 06.07.2016.

negligibly small. The Commission also argued that due to low market entry barriers, a merged Facebook Messenger/WhatsApp will still face competitive pressure from smaller services such as Line, Viber, or Google Hangouts.

What the Commission did not consider, though, was Facebook's ability to unilaterally change its data standards, leaving consumers the choice either to consent or quit the network altogether. Prior to the merger, users that were unhappy with such unilateral change could exert pressure by switching from Facebook Messenger to WhatsApp. Now with both major messaging apps belonging to the same company, the consumer cannot exert that pressure anymore as Facebook could lower data protection standards for both products. As there is currently no alternative messaging app with a similar reach, Facebook has a lot more leeway for changing its terms of use against consumers' will than before the acquisition.

During the merger proceedings, some jealous European incumbents who feared further erosion of their services had voiced concerns against Facebook's acquisition of WhatsApp. Merger control, like any kind of regulation, must not be abused as a pretext to shield industries failing to adapt their business models from innovative global competition. The failure of former national or European 'champions' to compete with Silicon Valley's user-centric digital services does not constitute a concern relevant to competition law.

4. The public cause of exploitation

> Our modern life is so infinitely wide and complex, indeed, that we may go great distances in any field of enterprise without receiving either direct aid or check from government; but this is only because every field of enterprise is vastly big nowadays, not because government is not somewhere in it: and we know that the tendency is for governments to make themselves more and more conspicuously present.[1]

4.1 EXPLOITATION AND COMPETITION – ABOUT UNFAIR DISTRIBUTION OF STATE RESOURCES

The fair distribution – or rather redistribution – of resources in the public interest is one of the principal functions of the state. The underlying idea of 'public interest' is constantly interpreted by policy preferences and stakeholder demands. However, since politicians are only human and state pockets are blindingly deep, state resources are every so often used contrary to the public interest. Misallocated public resources can distort competition by creating market power that would not exist under normal market conditions. Thereby, individual groups of citizens are better off while society at large is exploited.

Fair competition, the driving power for wealth, cannot persist if the state distorts competition. With unfair competition between *private* companies in mind, Wilson wrote:

> It is not competition that kills but unfair competition, the pretence and form of it where the reality and substance of it cannot persist.[2]

Wilson's above-cited view is highly relevant for *public* capital, too, on both sides of the Atlantic. Only the state can levy taxes and may exceed its debt limits and thus is richer and potentially stronger than any private market operator. When the state uses its resources to intervene in the market, efficient competitors may be driven out of the market, or state

1 Wilson, The State: Elements of Historical and Practical Politics, 1245.
2 Ibid., 1271.

subsidies may crowd out private investment or distort markets upstream the subsidised product. Hence, *'the reality and substance of competition'* cannot persist if the state, the very guardian of the civil (and economic) society and its values, distorts competition. At the same time, of course, the state needs to use its resources to sustain the welfare standard and support industry where this is necessary for the welfare standard, e.g. to establish societal goals of infrastructure or environmental protection. This is where the Art of Regulation comes into play.

Supranational regulation can *prevent* competitive harmful interventions, *limit* spending where it is needed to the necessary, and *steer* the resources to accomplish the common goals of all Member States.

In principle, state aid is prohibited under Article 107(1) TFEU (Treaty on the Functioning of the European Union in the EU). This means that supranational regulation does not allow governments to bestow a selective economic advantage on undertakings. Article 107(3) c) TFEU is the most frequently applied exception to that general prohibition. It implies that in order to qualify for an exception, an aid's positive effects in the common interest must outbalance distortions of competition. 'Common interest' can be interpreted as 'social welfare' in the EU and thereby includes the welfare of consumers and producers as well as fair distribution of welfare across groups of society and regions. Objectives in the common interest are thus the efficiency of markets as well as equity in the EU, i.e. the redistribution capacity of Member States and the supranational body.

Balancing the positive effects of aid in the common interest against its negative effects means that the impact that state aid has on the welfare of the recipient, its competitors, consumers and input suppliers must be measured by an authority that is in charge of the entire internal market and not only a national segment of it.

This chapter explores the *public* causes of exploitation – i.e. the state's intended or unintended 'grasping selfishness that has thrust out free competition'[3] – and EU-supranational regulation to fight exploitation. We will look at specific roles in which the state may have a cause to 'exploit' and into the EU's supranational legal instruments to counter any such tendency. The division of powers in the EU, between Member States and the supranational level, will be a recurring theme in that discussion. First of all, though, we will look into the concepts of 'state' and 'state resources'.

---

[3] Ibid.

4.2 THE CONCEPT OF 'STATE' AND 'STATE RESOURCES' IN EU COMPETITION LAW

Before looking into 'the cause of public exploitation', one must define the legal concepts of 'state' and the resources it has at hand. What is the 'state' in the sense of EU state aid rules? What is that entity that has access to public monies and can use them to interfere in the competition mechanisms, increasing market power or crowding out private investment?

It is not an abstract nation state that interferes, but its multiple emanations in the form of governments at the central, regional or local level as well as administrative bodies that are vested with state power. That is why EU state aid law applies wherever public authorities are involved, in one way or another, in the granting of an advantage through state resources.

The concept of 'state' and 'state resources' for the purposes of state aid law is thus quite broad: it includes 'government' and its treasury and beyond. It extends to any entity that has close enough relations with public authorities so that the entity when using funds has to take public policies or government instructions into account. The concept of 'state resources' includes any resources that are constantly under public control and thus are within reach of state authorities. The underlying idea is to track any actions in the market that show traces of state decision, as those carry the danger of being made not according to market logic and hence distort competition and therefore need to be reviewed under state aid rules. The concept of state and state resources, for the purposes of EU state aid law, is good regulation in so far as it is broad enough to prevent Member States from circumventing state aid rules with complex structures and financial engineering.

FURTHER READING – 'STATE' AND 'STATE RESOURCES' IN EU COMPETITION LAW

There are many situations where the decision to use resources to support an undertaking cannot be easily attributed to a public body, e.g. where government exerts only indirect control through intermediaries with various degrees of autonomy. In the *Stardust Marine* landmark judgment, the European Court of Justice (ECJ) dealt with the concept of 'state resources' and 'imputability of a measure to the state'. In that case, a subsidiary of the publicly owned French bank Crédit Lyonnais had repeatedly recapitalised one of its subsidiaries, a loss-making pleasure-boat chartering company – *Stardust Marine*. The Court found that the term 'state resources' in Article 87(1) EC [now 107(1) TFEU] covers all the financial means by which the public authorities may actually support undertakings, irrespective of whether or not those means are permanent assets of the public sector. Therefore, even if the sums corresponding to a state aid measure are financial resources of public undertakings and are not permanently held by the state treasury, the fact that they constantly remain under public control, and therefore available to the competent national authorities, is sufficient for them to be categorised as 'state resources'. That is the case where the state is perfectly capable, by exercising its dominant influence over public undertakings, of directing the use of their resources in order, as occasion arises, to finance specific advantages in favour of other undertakings. (see paras 37–38 of Case C-482/99 *France v Commission (Stardust)* [2002] ECR I-4397).

The Court also established a non-exhaustive set of indicators of imputability to the state of an aid measure that was taken by a public undertaking: its integration into the structures of the public administration; the nature of its activities and the exercise of the latter on the market in normal conditions of competition with private operators; the legal status of the undertaking (in the sense of its being subject to public law or ordinary company law); the intensity of the supervision exercised by the public authorities over the management of the undertaking; or any other indicator showing, in the particular case, an involvement by the public authorities in the adoption of a measure or the unlikelihood of their not being involved, having regard also to the compass of the measure, its content or the conditions which it contains. (paras 51–52, 55–56 ibid.)

The concept of state resources reaches far but there are limits. The mere non-committal and vague announcement, e.g. in a speech given by a minister, to provide financing to a company does not constitute state aid if it is not followed by any action, even if the announcement alone has a markedly positive effect on that company's rating and thus its refinancing conditions on the financial markets (Joined Cases T-425/04, T-444/04, T-450/04 and T-456/04, *French Republic and Others v Commission (France Télécom)*, paras 215–297).

EU state aid rules distinguish between two functions of the state: First, the state in the form of public authorities (exercising public powers) or any entity under public control as a potential granter of aid to an undertaking. This function is the *visible* hand, pulling the strings of the market, thus consciously and overtly promoting, or at least pretending to promote, public welfare. Second, the state may act as an entrepreneur who competes with private entrepreneurs through public companies. The state's right to compete with private business is enshrined in the principle of property neutrality of the EU Treaties: Article 345 TFEU stipulates that 'The Treaties shall in no way prejudice the rules in Member States governing the system of property ownership.' The state's right to operate on the market however entails that the state is bound by the same EU competition rules as any private market operator. Where is the borderline between economic and non-economic activities of a public authority?

As a rule, public entities provide services, many of them in the remit of public powers, e.g. the military, police, firefighting or air traffic control, to name just a few.

The state can of course also compete with private industry in a clear-cut market environment, e.g. where public universities carry out contract research, where regional governments operate airports, or where municipalities provide waste management services.

Public undertakings also provide services in areas that are not so overtly an exercise of public powers, in particular because the market environment has changed over time and private operators have entered, e.g. in education or health care. In the latter areas, the question of whether a market for a service, and thereby competition that can be distorted, exists, can only be answered in the context of the political choices and the regulatory environment in the individual state. Hence, as there is no EU-level uniform 'market environment', EU competition law can only be applied after a case-by-case market assessment. Such supranational assessment must be done in a changing environment that is subject to national political choices. We will discuss later in this chapter if the state entrepreneur can be guided at all by the invisible hand, i.e. leave aside political considerations and solely pursue an entrepreneur's interests.

FURTHER READING – THE CONCEPT OF 'UNDERTAKING' IN EU COMPETITION LAW

What is an 'undertaking' in the sense of EU law? That concept is not defined in the Treaties but the European Courts have constantly defined it as any entity engaged in an economic activity, regardless of its legal status and the way in which it is financed.[4] Hence, public entities such as public-service undertakings, research organisations, universities or non-profit organisations may, at least as concerns certain activities, qualify as an undertaking. Consequently, public financing of those 'economic activities' is subject to state aid rules, just as any state aid to private undertakings.

EU jurisprudence has also defined a broad concept of 'economic activity': This is any activity consisting in offering goods and services on a given market (Constant jurisprudence, e.g. Case 118/85 *Commission v Italy* [1987] ECR 2599, paragraph 7; Case C-35/96 *Commission v Italy* [1998] ECR I-3851, paragraph 36; Joined Cases C-180/98 to C-184/98 *Pavlov and Others*, paragraph 75).

---

4 E.g. ECJ, judgment of 12.09.2000, joined cases C-180/98 to C-184/98 – *Pavlov and others*, para. 74.

AN INEVITABLE EXCURSION

Further above we dubbed the aid granting function of the state 'the visible hand'. For the sake of completeness, we need to point to Smith's second, less worn out concept of the 'visible hand', namely the one depicted in his 'Theory of Moral Sentiments'. That distinct concept implies a state or other polity that redistributes wealth:

> The rich only select from the heap what is most precious and agreeable. They consume little more than the poor, and in spite of their natural selfishness and rapacity, though they mean only their own conveniency, though the sole end which they propose from the labours of all the thousands whom they employ, be the gratification of their own vain and insatiable desires, they divide with the poor the produce of all their improvements. *They are led by an invisible hand to make nearly the same distribution of the necessaries of life*, which would have been made, had the earth been divided into equal portions among all its inhabitants, and thus without intending it, without knowing it, advance the interest of the society, and afford means to the multiplication of the species.[5] (emphasis added)

Today, and in particular in European social market economies, this 'public' hand is quite visible, though, and thus contrasts with Smith's metaphor.

At this point, it is also important to discuss the relation between the national state and the supranational entity. This relation is characterised by tension between national sovereign and political integration in the European project. The EU is a community of sovereign nation states with democratic constitutions. In a constitutional setting based on the limitation of sovereignty or a transfer of powers from the states to the supranational level, the TEU stipulates that: 'the Union shall respect the equality of Member States before the Treaties as well as their national identities, inherent in their fundamental structures, political and constitutional, inclusive of regional and local self-government' (Article 4(2) first sentence TEU). That political community has seen a steady process of integration – i.e. transcending the sovereignty of Member States and transferring powers to central EU institutions in a federal setting of shared competences. That process has slowed down. The fact that a single currency is used in the absence of a single fiscal policy is symbolic of the deficits of European integration. While this book was being written, the very objective of political integration of advancing European

[5] Smith, Theory of Moral Sentiments, IV.I.10.

political integration has been put into question, by one of the EU's most important Member States, the United Kingdom.

EU competition rules in the area of state aid encapsulate the dichotomy between state powers and supranational objectives 'in the common interest': on the one hand, state aid control is an exclusive competency of the EU, with the objective to create a functioning internal market.[6] On the other hand, Member States enjoy full competency in areas such as industrial and fiscal policy, and they can organise markets for public services in a way that keeps the public financing of such services clear of EU state aid rules. Hence, state aid rules are constantly seeking a balance between the 'common interest' – that is the interest of the Union as a whole – on one hand and 'distortions of competition and trade' – through individual state intervention – on the other hand. State aid rules are thus positioned on the fault line between national policy objectives and the integrative overall objectives of the European project.

4.3 STATE POWER IN THE MARKET – TEMPTATIONS FOR THE VISIBLE HAND

In this section, we will look into the various direct and indirect forms of state intervention and their potential to distort competition. There are three overarching objectives for the state to intervene in the market: first, policy objectives such as employment, regional development, industrial policy, provisions of services in the general interest, or national security; second, fiscal objectives (revenue generation); third, economic objectives, in particular correcting market failures in situations where the private sector does not provide goods or services at optimal levels, where the private capital base is insufficient, or where only public monopolies can provide goods or services at optimal levels.[7]

In principle, each of these objectives seems a good reason for the state to intervene. However, problems and dangers occur when these objectives are used to justify state intervention and to hide that such intervention may be rather in the singular political interest of a certain politician or

---

6 Article 3(1) b) TFEU: 'The Union shall have exclusive competence in the following areas: […] the establishing of the competition rules necessary for the functioning of the internal market; […]'.

7 Discussion of legal and natural monopolies and state ownership as a means to deliver outcomes that come closer to social optimality as compared to unregulated, or poorly regulated, private ownership in Kowalski et al., State-Owned Enterprises: Trade Effects and Policy Implications, 12.

government but not in the long-term public interest. For instance if a company is facing bankruptcy but is a large employer, politicians might ride to the rescue, opening the spigots of public support to secure the jobs and thereby votes. Once on the lifeline of taxpayers' money, the company has little incentive to push for innovations. It will most likely be in the same dire situation a few years later while millions of Euros of support money have vanished. Or an in fact non-existent market failure is cited to justify state intervention, thereby reducing incentives for the private enterprises to invest, to innovate and to reduce their operating costs. The harmful fallout from such misallocation is that benefitting sectors will retire to their comfort zone and wait until state funding replaces their business risk. The public funds are lost and cannot be used in fields where the market really fails to deliver a desirable outcome 'in the public interest'.

The visible public hand may also carry out the desired commercial activity itself, e.g. as a market operator or an investor. In that context, the power of the 'political sublime' to drive large public investments should not be underestimated: it is politicians who in public justify the course of action of a public enterprise, e.g. a new costly investment, and it is high-ranking officials and other agents who take decisions that ultimately may be in the public interest – or not, and who may allocate resources inefficiently and thus may not fully achieve an objective in the public interest. The political sublime is 'the rapture politicians get from building monuments to themselves and for their causes, and from the visibility this generates with the public and media'.[8] These monuments may come in the form of airports, conference buildings, concert halls, sports stadiums and much more. There are a number of reasons, though, why public investors are less likely than private ones to bear the consequences of bad investments: the vote of stockholders or shareholders is less relevant for public enterprises and as ownership of strategic public enterprises cannot readily be transferred, hostile takeovers are not a serious threat. Moreover, public enterprises can sustain losses for extended periods of time if they are benefitting from hidden advantages or if the state helps with capital increases or soft loans. It is only through elections that the general public as 'shareholders' of public enterprises can influence, albeit indirectly, the operations of public enterprises.[9]

---

[8] Flyvbjerg, What You Should Know About Megaprojects And Why: An Overview(2014) 45(2) *Project Management Journal* 6 (8).

[9] See Capobianco, Competitive Neutrality and State-Owned Enterprises: Challenges and Policy Options, 9, in the context of a discussion of corporate governance weaknesses as a source of anticompetitive behaviour.

Distortive economic advantages granted by the state can take on various forms as financial instruments and transfer channels are manifold and permanently evolving. Distortive state measures could thus be concealed by financial engineering. Transparency is the principal answer to this threat. In the EU, a Transparency Directive provides for a non-exhaustive illustrative list of transfers that are a charge on the public budget: the setting-off of operating losses; the provision of capital; non-refundable grants or loans on privileged terms; the granting of financial advantages by forgoing profits or the recovery of sums due; the forgoing of a normal return on public funds used; compensation for financial burdens imposed by the public authorities.[10]

Another example for non-transparent state financing is implicit state guarantees to public enterprises.[11] Such 'implicit guarantees' may be based on long-standing national legislation and are difficult to track. They can constitute massive advantages, though, in particular as regards creditworthiness: for example, national legislation could provide that entities are immune from seizure of assets in the event of insolvency and bankruptcy, or that the state has last-resort liability for the debts of such legal entities, or that debts will be transferred to the state in the event of the winding up of such entity, or that the public entity enjoys preferential access to state treasury imprest accounts. Any such advantage can distort competition if the public entity is engaged in economic activities. Therefore, it is state aid and is in principle prohibited under EU state aid rules.

Soft budget constraints are also an issue, for example, in the European airport sector, where many airports are owned by public entities.[12] In this case, the regulatory response of EU state aid law aims at incentivising efficient airport management: the amount of operating aid must, in principle, be established *ex ante* as a fixed sum covering the expected operating funding gap (i.e. the amount of operating costs not covered by

---

[10] Article 3 of Commission Directive 2006/111/EC.

[11] Commission decision of 29.06.2011, in C 35/08 (ex NN 11/08), state aid granted by France to the Institut Français du Pétrole, OJ EU 2012 L 14/1.

[12] In particular, loss-making regional airports that often do not handle the critical passenger number to be profitable are publicly owned or under state control: in Germany, almost all such airports are in public ownership, Deutsche Bank Research (2015), Regionalflughäfen politisch und wirtschaftlich unter Druck, 9. In the EU, smaller airports display the greatest proportion of public ownership and most often rely on public support to finance their operations: European Commission, 2014, Staff Working Document – Impact Assessment accompanying the document 'Communication from the Commission – Guidelines on state aid to airports and airlines', 28.

revenues) determined on the basis of an *ex-ante* business plan during a transitional period from 2014 until 2024. Airports that receive operating aid must have a plausible business plan that paves the way towards full operating cost coverage at the end of that ten-year period.

Operating aid in its various overt and veiled forms has an even greater distortive effect as it is not only unavailable to private enterprises but may also sustain operating costs of inefficient public enterprises. So instead of reallocating their resources to more profitable activities or exiting the market, inefficient public enterprises could maintain or strengthen their market position, while competitors have less incentive to invest. As the public pocket is deep, and as inefficiencies and losses in the public sector can be politically justified, the distortion may be long lasting. Such hidden advantages are not easily detected and controlled by competition law enforcement. They may prevent structural change, and in particular efficiency improvements, or the opening of markets to private enterprises.

This problem will persist as long as there is sufficient incentive for politicians to place their own interest above the general interest. Therefore, it is on the supranational level where public spending needs to be regulated. The first step is to catch hidden advantages with the supranational radar.

This leads us to the question: What is a state intervention or, in legal terms, what action is 'imputable' to the state?

Any transfer of state resources to an undertaking is imputable to the state if a public authority, even an independent regional or local authority, carries out such transfer or orders a private or public body to do that.[13] The term 'public authority' is as multifaceted as is public administration in 28 EU Member States, ranging from federalist to unitary, some with largely autonomous regions. This concept allows for determining if an entity provides aid on behalf of the state, in particular in complex transactions involving multiple intermediaries. Interestingly, where the state orders one private party to transfer resources to another private party, such transfer is not 'state aid' under EU competition rules as long as there is no cost to the government.

---

[13] ECJ, judgment of 14.10.1987, C-248/84 – *Germany v Commission*, para. 62-68; and ECJ, judgment of 12.12.1996, T-358/94 – *Air France v Commission,* para. 62.

FURTHER READING – NO UNLAWFUL CIRCUMVENTION OF COMPETITION RULES IF THE STATE DECIDES THAT RESOURCES MUST BE TRANSFERRED BUT THAT SUCH TRANSFER MUST BE FINANCED BY PRIVATE UNDERTAKINGS

The 'Preussen-Elektra' landmark judgment of the European Court of Justice, case C-379/98, [2001] ECR I-2099:

(the following emphases added)

In that case, the ECJ looked into the question of whether the legal obligation imposed on private electricity supply undertakings to purchase electricity produced from renewable energy sources at fixed minimum prices does involve any direct or indirect transfer of state resources to undertakings which produce that type of electricity. The objective of that German Law on feeding electricity from renewable energy sources into the public grid, *Stromeinspeisungsgesetz*, obviously was to promote the production of 'green' electricity.

The Court notes first of all that the legal obligation to purchase electricity produced from renewable energy sources at minimum prices indeed confers a *certain economic advantage* on producers of that type of electricity, since it guarantees them, with no risk, higher profits than they would make in its absence. (para. 54)

Hence, there was an advantage and its *granting was ordered by the state* by virtue of a law.

The Court then recalls the concept of state aid and the prohibition of state aid pursuant to the Treaty: any aid granted by a Member State or through state resources in any form whatsoever which distorts or threatens to distort competition by favouring certain undertakings or the production of certain goods is, in so far as it affects trade between Member States, incompatible with the common market. (para. 57)

Then, the Court explains that only *advantages granted directly or indirectly through state resources* are to be considered 'state aid' within the meaning of Article 92(1) [now Article 107(1) of the TFEU] According to the Court, the distinction made in that provision between aid granted by a Member State and aid granted through state resources does not signify that all advantages granted by a state, whether financed through state resources or not, constitute aid. Rather, that provision would be intended merely to bring within that definition both advantages which are granted directly by the state and those granted by a public or private body designated or established by the state (with reference to further case law, para. 58).

Having said that, the Court briefly states that in this case, the obligation to purchase green electricity at fixed minimum prices does not involve any direct or indirect transfer of state resources to the producers of that type of electricity. (para. 59)

Moreover, the allocation of the financial burden arising from that obligation for those private electricity supply undertakings as between them and other private undertakings cannot constitute a direct or indirect transfer of state resources either. (para. 60)

The Court then concludes that the fact that the purchase obligation is imposed by statute and confers an undeniable advantage on certain undertakings is not capable of conferring upon it the character of 'state aid' within the meaning of Article 92(1) [now 107 (1)] of the Treaty. (para. 60)

Even the fact that the financial burden is likely to have negative repercussions on the economic results of the undertakings subject to that obligation and therefore entails a diminution in tax receipts for the state cannot undermine that conclusion. Rather, such a consequence would be an inherent feature of such a legislative provision and could not be regarded as constituting a means of granting to producers of electricity from renewable energy sources a particular advantage at the expense of the state (para. 61 with further reference to case law).

In essence, the state aid concept and the prohibition of state aid in Art. 107 of the TFEU refer directly to measures emanating from the Member States. Hence, that Article is in itself sufficient to prohibit the conduct by states referred to therein.

Previously, we have said that the state can be a market operator who competes with private operators; we also defined the notions of 'imputability to the state' and of 'undertaking'. Yet, we have to gauge the notion of 'public sector'. What is a public enterprise and is it identical with a state-owned enterprise?

The concept of 'state-owned enterprise' (SOE) is widely used in literature. Its definition is problematic, though, due to various forms of state ownership and multiple SOE-definitions across countries.

FURTHER READING – 'STATE-OWNED ENTERPRISES'

Kowalski et al. discuss the SOE-concept: The state can either hold various levels of equity in enterprises incorporated according to normal corporate law, or pass enabling legislation to create a statutory corporation governed by a status outlining its objectives and formal requirements. Multiple definitions of SOEs are applied across countries, which complicates formulation of a meaningful uniform definition of SOEs that would cover the full extent of government control and enable cross-country comparison (p. 11).

Christiansen also refers to 'uneven data definitions and methodologies'; he leaves it to reporting countries '*to ensure a full coverage of all enterprises that may be properly characterised as SOEs.*' (p. 5).

Price Waterhouse Coopers mentions the factors on which both form and name of SOEs depend: the level of government that owns the enterprise; the way in which the enterprise was founded; its position in the public administration hierarchy; its purpose; the status of the privatisation process; other variations such as full, majority or minority ownership by the government; listing (or not); government shareholdings through vehicles such as government pension funds, asset management funds, restructuring corporations and development lenders;

state-enabled enterprises (e.g. through exclusive rights) as opposed to state-owned enterprises (p. 8).

The OECD broadly defines SOEs as 'enterprises where the state has significant control, through full, majority, or significant minority ownership'.[14] This is a rather narrow concept as it merely reposes on ownership and does not take into account other forms of control, namely through supervision and through instructions given by governmental bodies.

The fact that an undertaking is state owned obviously means that the state is pursuing economic activities and in that respect is subject to EU competition rules.

The concept of 'public undertaking': the TFEU refers to the term 'public undertaking' when clarifying the relation between those undertakings and competition law in Article 106, but it does not define the term. This is done in a secondary legal text, the EU Transparency Directive, which defines 'public undertakings' as 'any undertaking over which the public authorities may exercise directly or indirectly a dominant influence by virtue of their ownership of it, their financial participation therein, or the rules which govern it'. The Directive then defines 'dominant influence' (the Directive will be discussed further below).

The Directive's definition of 'public undertaking' is based on 'dominant influence' by public authorities, namely when they hold the major part of the undertaking's subscribed capital, or control the majority of the votes attaching to shares issued by the undertakings, or can appoint more than half of the members of the undertaking's administrative, managerial or supervisory body.[15]

This book will use the term 'public undertaking' in the broadest sense possible. The term will thus include not only SOEs and 'public undertakings' in the sense of the Transparency Directive, but also private undertakings or any other entity that pursues, be it even partially, an economic activity *and* that has to take state instructions into account when taking decisions in relation to their economic activities.

---

[14] In their Guidelines on Corporate Governance of State-Owned Enterprises, OECD 2005.

[15] Article 2(b)i–iii of Commission Directive 2006/111/EC on the transparency of financial relations between Member States and public undertakings as well as on financial transparency within certain undertakings, OJ EU 2006 L 318/17.

The EU has supranational legal tools at hand to spot hidden advantages in the area of state investments in public enterprises: the EU's Transparency Directive[16] aims at making the financial relations between public authorities and public undertakings more transparent. A Directive is a specific legal instrument: it binds Member States to achieve a certain result but leaves the choice of form and methods to achieve that objective up to them.[17] In essence, the Transparency Directive obliges EU Member States to adopt legislation that makes the financial relations between public authorities and public undertakings transparent and publicly available. Moreover, Member States must ensure that public undertakings keep separate accounts in relation to, on the one hand, public services, as well as, on the other hand, other economic activities. Accordingly, public funds made available directly or through the intermediary of public undertakings or financial institutions, and the use to which these public funds are actually put, must 'emerge clearly'.[18]

The EU Commission also addresses inefficiency and soft budget constraints: where undertakings receive compensation for delivering services of general economic interest, the Member State concerned must incentivise efficiency improvements. Moreover, as will be discussed further below (Chapter 4.5.1.), EU rules prescribe a quite robust methodology to avoid overcompensation beyond actual net cost of discharging the public service obligations, including a reasonable profit.[19]

EU competition rules are good regulation in so far as they address possible hidden advantages (Article 106 of the TFEU): First, they prohibit any measure contrary to the EU-Treaties' antitrust and state aid rules in the case of public undertakings and undertakings to which Member States grant special or exclusive rights. Secondly, they subject to EU competition rules undertakings entrusted with the operation of services of general economic interest or having the character of a revenue-producing monopoly, in so far as this does not obstruct the

[16] Commission Directive 2006/111/EC on the transparency of financial relations between Member States and public undertakings as well as on financial transparency within certain undertakings, OJ EU 2006 L 318/17.

[17] Article 288 TFEU.

[18] Article 1 of Commission Directive 2006/111/EC.

[19] Communication from the Commission of 11.01.2012, European Union framework for state aid in the form of public service compensation, OJ EU 2012 C 8/15; 15. Decision of 20.12.2011 on the application of Article 106(2) of the Treaty on the Functioning of the European Union to state aid in the form of public service compensation granted to certain undertakings entrusted with the operation of services of general economic interest, OJ EU 2012 L 7/3.

performance of their particular tasks; the development of trade must however not be affected to an extent contrary to Union interests.

The question arises: Does EU governance and regulation prevent unfair distribution – 'exploitation' – by the visible hand?

4.4 STATE AID OR MARKET INVESTMENT?

4.4.1 Is the State Acting like a Private Investor? – The Market Economy Operator Principle

EU state aid law had long looked into the question of whether an economic transaction – for example, an investment, a loan, a guarantee or a privatisation – carried out by a public body distorts competition because it confers an advantage on an undertaking. In that process, the European Commission's state aid controllers investigate whether the behaviour of the public investor or creditor etc. is comparable to that of a private economic operator. If a private market participant would have made the same investment in the same market conditions, then the specific transaction, although transferring *public* resources, is presumed to not confer any advantage that the counterpart would not have obtained under market conditions. Rather, a *hypothetical* private investor of a comparable size could have been prompted to make the same investment in similar circumstances.[20] EU competition law refers to the overall concept as the 'Market Economy Operator Principle' (MEOP).

In other words, the state's visible hand ... dissolves. What remains is the state that, with a specific entrepreneurial action, seeks profit and leaves it up to the invisible hand to properly distribute wealth.

Accordingly, EU state aid control makes a very clear distinction between, on the one hand, the state as the political body, which through its government or authorities takes political decisions to promote common goals, and, on the other hand, the rational, politically indifferent private investor who acts solely on the basis of economic considerations.

---

[20] Constant jurisprudence, e.g. ECJ, judgment of 21.03.1990, C-142/87 – *Belgium v Commission*, para. 29; and ECJ, judgment of 21.03.1991, C-305/89 – *Italy v Commission*, paras 18–19; ECJ, judgment of 30.04.1998, T-16/96 – *Cityflyer Express v Commission*, para. 51; ECJ, judgment of 21.01.1999, joined cases T-129/95, T-2/96, T-97/96 – *Neue Maxhütte Stahlwerke and Lech-Stahlwerke v Commission*, para. 104; ECJ, judgment of 06.03.2003, joined cases T-228/99, T-233/99 – *Westdeutsche Landesbank Girozentrale and Land Nordrhein-Westfalen v Commission*.

The European Commission, after the European Court of Justice had developed the MEOP, produced a number of papers which explain how it applies that principle to specific transactions: state guarantees,[21] risk finance investments,[22] R&D-collaboration between public research organisations and industry, R&D-services and contract research by public research organisations on behalf of industry,[23] public financing for broadband deployment,[24] public airport financing,[25] and public land sales.[26]

The Commission has very recently managed to consolidate in a single paper the multiple facets of the MEOP as developed by jurisprudence as well as its own view of that principle.[27]

The principal weakness of such well-intended interpretational guidance is that it is lagging behind market developments. This can be illustrated by the MEOP-application in the field of public risk finance investments to promote innovative start-ups: there, the Commission presumes that a public investment does not involve any advantage for both private co-investors and start-up enterprises if public and private investors share the same risks and rewards, the same level of subordination, intervene simultaneously and if funding provided by independent private investors is 'economically significant'.

Pursuant to the currently applicable EU state aid rules in that field,[28] private investment is presumed to be 'economically significant' if it constitutes at least 30 per cent of the overall investment. In the previously applicable rules, though, the Commission demanded that private investors should provide at least 50 per cent of the funding of the measure so that

---

[21] Commission Notice on the application of Articles 87 and 88 of the EC Treaty to state aid in the form of guarantees, OJ EU 2008 C 155/ 10.

[22] Guidelines on state aid to promote risk finance investments, OJ EU 2014 C 19/34.

[23] Framework for state aid for research and development and innovation, OJ EU 2014 C 198/1.

[24] Guidelines for the application of state aid rules in relation to the rapid deployment of broadband networks, OJ EU 2013 C 25/1.

[25] Guidelines on state aid to airports and airlines, OJ EU 2014 C 99/3.

[26] Commission Communication on state aid elements in sales of land and buildings by public authorities, OJ EU 1997 C 209/3.

[27] Website of the Commission's Directorate General for Competition, paper not published in the EU's Official Journal, http://ec.europa.eu/competition/state_aid/modernisation/notice_aid_en.html, 06.07.2016, not dated; the accompanying press release dates from 19.05.2016.

[28] Guidelines on state aid to promote risk finance investments, OJ EU 2014 C 19/34.

the overall public-private measure does not distort competition. The new, more relaxed 30 per cent requirement is obviously not based on any risk-finance specific considerations – the Commission's corresponding Impact Assessment Report does not contain any reference to the quite significant drop from the 50 per cent to the 30 per cent threshold. Rather, the current legal text, by way of example, merely refers to a single Commission decision.[29] Hence, the assumption that a public-private co-investment where the public stake is 70 per cent is market based is standing on a shaky foundation: no account is taken of EU Member States' corporate law, no account is taken of the necessary coherence of interests between the investor and the project. The rule does not seem to effectively ensure that private investors who co-invest with the state pursue a genuine strategic interest instead of benefitting from reduced risks on a short-term horizon. Most importantly, the public investor's possible influence, with its 70 per cent stake, i.e. even more than two-thirds, on the company, is not at all discussed in the Commission's legal text.

In conclusion, the European Commission stretches the MEOP too far as regards public risk finance investments. That approach seems to be motivated by the EU's priority to improve affordable access to finance for small- and medium-sized enterprises (SMEs). In order to allow Member States to address a market failure, the Commission has veered away from the MEOP. Thereby it encourages Member States to secure a strong market position for public investors and to confer considerable advantages on private co-investors.

Nevertheless, in the small-scale field of SME and start-up risk financing, market terms and market failures can be gauged with reasonable effort. The market impact, in terms of crowding out of private investment and also in terms of market power through public financing, is certainly limited in that specific field.

4.4.2 The Problem with Megaprojects – a Rational Public Investor Test?

The situation is quite different, though, where the scale and complexity of the state's investments is such that in reality, no private investor would undertake such a venture. This is the case with so-called megaprojects, in particular in the field of infrastructure, where, as a rule, public

---

[29] On a public investment in a local glass fibre communication network, Commission Decision in state aid C 53/2006 – the Netherlands, Citynet Amsterdam, OJ EU 2008 L 247/27, paras 96–100.

investors have a stake: 'Megaprojects are large-scale, complex ventures that typically cost USD 1 billion or more, take many years to develop and build, involve multiple public and private stakeholders, are transformational, and impact millions of people.'[30] The effect of such intervention in terms of distortions of competition could be enormous, all the more so as the EU's internal market is becoming increasingly integrated and liberalised. How to ensure that in such exceptional situations, the state does not unduly strengthen the market power of its own public operators or of the recipient of the financing?

Examples of situations abound where, in reality, only the state would intervene in the market, so that comparing such intervention with the behaviour of a comparable private operator is extremely difficult:

Throughout decades of uncontested market power, state monopolists, for example in the telecoms or postal service, had used public resources to build infrastructure. In a liberalised market they could be tempted to lease out or sell such infrastructures, at very favourable conditions to public enterprises that are competing with private sector entrants. When dealing with the issue of such possible cross-subsidisation in the context of the French *La Poste* case, the EU's Courts had great difficulty carving out the hypothetical private operator and what level of remuneration such an operator would have charged for the provision of postal infrastructure – after all, private industry would certainly not have established such infrastructure in the first place.[31] What emerged was the awareness that comparing the situation of French *La Poste* with a private market operator was impossible. Consequently, purely hypothetical market conditions had to be used as a benchmark to assess the market rationale of the state enterprise's behaviour. For that purpose, only the objective and verifiable elements available can be used. This implies, though, that non-transparent cross-subsidisation cannot be prevented, namely subsidisation through the spill-over of non-quantifiable advantages arising from the public financing of the existing and fully amortised ex-monopolist's infrastructure.

Further examples can be found in the airport sector: in the EU, 77 per cent of airports are fully publicly owned while only 9 per cent are completely privately owned.[32] Public financing of a new airport is a

---

[30] Flyvbjerg (n. 8).

[31] ECJ, judgment of 03.07.2003, joined cases C-83/01 P, C-93/01 P, C-94/01 P – *Chronopost v Ufex and others*; ECJ, judgment of 07.06.2006, T-613/97 – *Ufex and others v Commission*.

[32] European Commission, Impact Assessment Accompanying the document Communication from the Commission 'Guidelines on state aid to airports and

megaproject with high technical and coordination risks and a long-term return. So as a rule, such projects are not undertaken by private operators alone but rather by public investors. Nevertheless, as there is competition between airports and as the creation of overcapacity must be avoided in order to ensure overall efficiency, EU state aid rules apply to public financing for EU-airports. What if the state makes an airport investment, allegedly at market terms? What would the comparable private operator be like?

The scandal-ridden new Berlin-Brandenburg airport illustrates the limits of the MEOP: the operator of that new airport is fully state owned. Construction started in 2006. Overall construction costs were estimated to be 3.56 billion. A first round of state aid, i.e. financing that was incommensurate with market terms, was allowed under EU state aid rules in 2009. Later on, in 2012, an equity increase to the tune of €1.2 billion became necessary, due to serious engineering and coordination flaws as well as inadequate noise protection. Then, the European Commission found that this new investment could not be linked to the previous state aid, that the reasons why the new equity increase became necessary were unforeseeable and that the investment satisfied the MEOP – in other words, a hypothetical private investor would have made the same investment, as it was the most profitable alternative and increased the equity value of the company. The sunk costs of the previous state aid, which clearly had no commercial logic, were not taken into account, though. In 2016, further cost overruns and the delayed opening of the airport required another substantial financing package, this time €2.2 billion. The Commission will again have to determine if a hypothetical private investor would make the same investment, if the completion of the airport would be the most profitable option and if the equity value would be higher than both the previous and the new investment.

The question arises: Should the Commission be prudent enough to take both the previous and the new investment into account when applying the MEOP? Indeed, failure to invest would most probably result either in the abortion of the project and thus in an utter economic and political disaster, or in a new airport that is in all likelihood economically less burdensome. In other words, the value of the state's invested capital would likely be either lost or seriously reduced. When this book was completed, the Commission had not yet decided the matter.

---

airlines', 2014, 11, http://ec.europa.eu/smart-regulation/impact/ia_carried_out/docs/ia_2014/swd_2014_0042_en.pdf, 06.07.2016.

Some critical issues remain, though, and this applies to all cases where the state invests in enterprises where it already has a stake: as explained above, the state is less sensitive to losses and can justify sub-optimal investments with equity-arguments, e.g. regional development. Moreover, a *private* investor cannot grant *state aid* for the same project and, after the lapse of a certain period, could then claim that these costs are sunk and do not any longer have to be taken into account. Lastly, the state, for political reasons, is less at liberty to pull the plug on a megaproject and walk away. Most importantly, unlike the situation of a real private market operator, there is no alternative 'investment' which the state would have to consider in order to find out whether e.g. a large infrastructure is the most profitable investment. After all, it is not the state's mandate to maximise profits on public resources which society entrusted to state authorities. Rather, the mandate is to make investments that are necessary and that are not undertaken by private operators or at least not without some state commitment.

This situation is best illustrated by borrowing from Surrealism: one of René Margritte's most famous paintings, *La trahison d'images* (The Treachery of Images), shows what quite obviously is a pipe. Below the pipe is written: '*Ceci n'est pas une pipe*' ('This is not a pipe.'). The MEOP is quite similar: There is a very visible hand. Still, if the MEOP is satisfied, we write – *Cette main n'est pas visible*.

ANOTHER INEVITABLE EXCURSION

This analogy was of course too nice not to seize, in particular as this author is writing in Belgium, a country with a certain penchant for surrealism. René Margritte, one of the great surrealists, was Belgian and Brussels is not only home to sprawling EU office buildings but also to the Margritte Museum.

Nevertheless, and for the sake of honesty, it must be said that Margritte was of course right – the mere image of a pipe is indeed not 'a pipe'. As regards the MEOP, the 'surrealist' analogy holds: state aid analysts in the EU competition authority are looking at 'images', produced by Member State governments, and not at the real rationale behind decision-making processes somewhere in a Member State.

Good competition regulation is facing a dilemma: on the one hand, it is obvious that major state interventions in the market – and actually any state intervention, at least in polities where state interventions must strictly be made in pursuit of the public interest – are absolved from the market logic. The authors suggest that the receiving end of any transaction that involves state resources is receiving an advantage that it would not have obtained under normal market conditions. So this must be taken into account when regulating the impact of state intervention in the market.

On the other hand, a functioning market as the basis of sustainable wealth and development must be in the very interest of the state. Moreover, it is the state – or, in the EU, the super-state – which has defined the notion of state aid, and it is the state that prohibits state aid if it unduly distorts competition. Hence, by the principle '*tu patere legem quam ipsi fecisti*' ('you are bound by the law you have made yourself'), the state as the guardian of a functioning internal market should, in the absence of any comparable market operator standard, be subject to a very strict test.

The unique position and capability of the public investor necessitate a unique market operator standard to gauge the distortive effect of that investor's actions.

How strict should that test be? A strict approach would resolve the dilemma that no comparable private investor can be defined and that the state is by nature in a situation that is outside the functioning of the market. Applying a strict MEOP to the overall state investment means that previous investments and also previous state aid (e.g. direct grants or soft loans) are considered as 'the stake' the state has in the venture in question. This would allow taking past 'sunk' investments into account. Otherwise, the state could sink multiple alleged 'market-economy' investments in one venture, e.g. a large infrastructure and each time again claim that the investment is necessary to avoid loss or reduction of the existing stake. The problem is, though, that public projects, as a rule, are large and have long-term prospects so that convenient business plans could be produced for each new intervention to support the argument that eventually, the venture will be profitable. This is the high-gloss image of the venture the European Commission as the state aid control authority would see.

Such long-term character is however difficult to reconcile with the plausibility of business plans: first of all, the very long-term nature makes business plans highly speculative, for instance, foreseeing air traffic development on a 25-year scale and its implications in public airport projects. This issue is perfectly illustrated by Flyvbjerg, who has analysed megaprojects' failures to be on time and on budget and has discovered the misrepresentation of cost/benefit ratios as a root cause:

> Underestimating costs and overestimating benefits for a given project (which is the common pattern [...]) leads to a falsely high benefit–cost ratio for that project, which in turn leads to two problems. First, the project may be started despite the fact it is not financially and economically viable. Or, second, it may be started instead of another project, which would have shown to yield higher returns than the project started had the real costs and benefits of both projects been known. Both cases result in Pareto inefficiency; that is, the misallocation of resources and, for public projects, waste of taxpayers' money. Thus, for reasons of economic efficiency alone, the argument must be rejected that cost underestimation and benefit overestimation are justified for getting projects started.[33]

Taking an *existing* public ownership or shareholding into account when assessing the economic rationale of a *new* public investment, however without enquiring if the state makes that new investment still with the same market operator spirit as the earlier one, has a quite significant consequence: one 'leaves entirely the wider framework of "normal market conditions" and passes to the particular, self-referential framework of the public investor in question and considers not whether its actions offer an advantage to the undertaking, but whether the investor's behaviour is rational from its perspective'.[34] In other words, the fact that a public intervention makes economic sense in itself does not preclude an advantage to the recipient outside normal market conditions. Such critique saw that the:

> state is not subject to the same disciplines as the real private investor and accepting that the MEOP is satisfied when investments are made on the basis that they represent the least worst course of action is liable to engender a form of moral hazard, where good money will be thrown after bad and capital inefficiently allocated, the state being less likely than the private investor to cut losses.[35]

The conclusion was that, to avoid such hazard, the MEOP should be applied from the perspective of the detached, profit maximising investor who has no pre-existing commitment to the undertaking in question that can influence its investment decision.

While that critique is right in recognising that the state is not comparable to real private investors, it errs in assuming that applying the

---

33 Flyvbjerg (n. 8) (14).

34 Khan/Borchardt, The Private Market Investor Principle: Reality Check or Distorting Mirror?, in *EC State Aid Law*, 109, (123).

35 Ibid.

rationale of the detached, profit-maximising investor who has no pre-existing commitment to the undertaking in question, would do the trick and thus make the state's investment comparable to a market investment. Consider the Berlin Airport case: with the 'detached investor logic', each new investment in this seemingly never-ending megaproject would seem profitable, at least from the view of a long-term strategic investor. Previous sunk investments, be they alleged 'market economy' investments or outright state aid, would not have to be considered – after all, megaprojects are by nature unpredictable, so there are enough reasons to keep them on the lifeline. Thus, moral and economic hazard materialises.

So it is submitted that competition law, in particular state aid law, should apply the concept of the 'rational public investor'. That investor is distinct from the elusive and hypothetical private market operator that state aid regulators are struggling to define case-by-case, to compare it with the public investor who, as was explained above, is remote from normal market operations: the public investor rather intervenes precisely when the market fails to intervene. This is its mandate. It is true that the market failure argument is the standard argument for justifying state aid to industry, and thus overt distortions of competition. It is however also true, as was explained above, that the state should only intervene when market forces fail to deliver a desirable outcome and this applies not only to overt state aid but also to state investments that formally correspond to market operator standards. The postulated 'rational public investor' is thus distinct from both the private market operator and the aid granting authority. It is an operator who follows its own investment philosophy. That philosophy is not guided by the dogma of profit maximisation as an end in itself but by an objective that is rooted in a democratic constitution, namely that services and goods must be delivered efficiently, sustainably and equitably to society. The rational public investor would certainly pursue industrial policy objectives – but these are not necessarily the sector development objectives which the postulated very large, long-term oriented private operator is assumed to pursue.

Moreover, the rational public investor is not at liberty to use its capital as advantageously as possible. Its capital is locked up – either in the form of a pre-existing stake in a public venture or in the form of a legal obligation to use it in the common interest. So, in the grand design of economic activities, the state has only three options: use its capital in the form of state aid and thereby overtly distort competition, and thus to be subject to competition law; or act as a rational public investor; or grant aid as a general measure that does not distort competition.

Applying the distinct concept of 'rational public investor' would once and for all do away with attempts to square the circle by artificially separating policy considerations from profit considerations, in order to find out if the state has either intervened with a strict market logic or has distorted competition. The following illustrates the ambiguity of such separation: while the commercial logic of state investment, in order to be deemed in line with market conditions, must be assessed leaving aside all policy considerations, private investors may of course not only seek profit maximisation but may also pursue exclusively altruistic objectives, e.g. promoting charity, health care, care for the elderly, the young, culture, environmental protection, consumer protection, sports and the preservation of monuments.[36]

The rational public investor would certainly pursue policy objectives, and legitimately so! Let it nevertheless be an investor *sui generis* that does not distort competition!

How to limit abuses of the 'rational public investor concept'? The answer is found in the legal and ethical reasons for due diligence to be carried out in state investments: first, the risks and revenues of a project must be disclosed to legislators, the general public and industry; secondly, a business plan must pave the way for at least full cost coverage and take previous 'sunk' investments – be they with a 'commercial' logic or a 'state aid' political logic – into account; and lastly, the failure of the market to deliver the outcome alone and the necessity of state investment must be ascertained. Recall that this is not about justifying state aid that is clearly an advantage for the receiving end of the transaction. This is about justifying a rational public investment, the investment *sui generis* that cannot reasonably be compared to a private investment under normal market conditions.

In a complex federation of sovereign nation states, characterised by shared and exclusive competencies, effective control of the rational public investor principle can be ensured at various levels: at the supranational executive level by a competition authority that constantly develops and codifies assessment principles applicable in all Member States – the European Commission in the EU; at the legislative level, by parliaments that control and supervise public investors; and at the national supervisory level by authorities such as courts of auditors that ensure the proper legal frameworks for due diligence procedures and for the accountability of non-elected public managers.

---

[36] E.g. a German private bank, Commission decision of 11.01.2008, state aid N 836/2006 – Mittelstandsfonds Schleswig-Holstein, recitals (23), (33), (34) and (150).

4.5 SERVICES IN THE GENERAL ECONOMIC INTEREST VS UNDISTORTED COMPETITION

A paradoxical situation occurs when the pursuit of the 'general economic interest' collides with the general interest to preserve fair competition. The EU supranational regulator's challenge here is: How to prevent distortions of competition (supranational competence) while at the same time safeguarding quality services in the 'general economic interest' (national competence)? The salient characteristic of such services is that while being in society's general interest, they are of an economic nature because they are provided in a market environment, contrary to e.g. defence or public education.

Services of general economic interest can be, for example, public transport, waste management, large commercial postal services, energy supply, electronic communication services, health care or education. They are usually referred to as SGEI. In these sectors, the market alone may not produce outcomes that meet the needs and standards of society, making public interference necessary. Public interference in the market, in the 'general economic interest', might seem harmless – after all, it is in the interest of the community. However, also in this 'public service' context, competitors may be crowded out and monies wasted when market participants rest on comfortable subsidies and, often exclusive, rights. SGEIs can be provided by both public and private enterprises. Public financing for the discharge of those services can crowd out private initiative and investment in situations where the market actually would be ready to deliver a service but the state, for political reasons, continues financing either public or private service providers. Moreover, in certain sectors, public or publicly financed enterprises may be the incumbent.

The art of regulation can limit distortions to the minimum.

4.5.1 Who Defines 'General Economic Interest'?

The necessary precondition is the awareness that any state intervention on a market, even with the sole intention of acting in the general economic interest, can distort the market. This is especially true since the operator of an SGEI is often granted an exclusive right (e.g. only *one* public bus operator in one city) and since competition, after a procurement procedure, is excluded. In the EU, it took many years and a number of landmark Court-rulings to create a basis for good regulation in the area of SGEI.

The ECJ resolved the challenge to incorporate the paradox – 'functioning competition vs satisfactory SGEI' – when it developed criteria to assess the absence of any advantage through public compensation for SGEI.[37] In essence, the Court found that four cumulative conditions have to be satisfied in order to exclude any undue advantage through public compensation:

- first, an entrustment act must clearly define the public service obligation;
- second, the parameters for calculating the compensation must be established in advance in an objective and transparent manner;
- third, overcompensation must be avoided, i.e. the compensation must not exceed the relevant costs plus a reasonable profit;
- fourth, the service provider must either be chosen through a public procurement procedure or the level of compensation is determined based on an analysis of the costs of an average 'well-run' undertaking in the sector concerned.

FURTHER READING – EU PUBLIC PROCUREMENT RULES AND THE ENTRUSTMENT OF AN UNDERTAKING WITH THE PROVISION OF SGEI

Where a public authority chooses to entrust a third party with the provision of a service, it is required to comply with national law that transposes EU law governing public procurement, namely the Union Directives on public procurement which refer to Arts 49–56 of the Treaty. Also in cases where these public procurements are wholly or partially inapplicable (for example, for certain service concessions and service contracts), the award may nevertheless have to meet Treaty requirements of transparency, equality of treatment, proportionality and mutual recognition.

Further reading: EU website on public procurement rules http://ec.europa.eu/growth/single-market/public-procurement/index_en.htm?cookies=disabled; ECJ judgment on the obligation to nevertheless meet certain transparency etc. requirement in Case C-324/98 *Telaustria Verlags GmbH and Telefonadress GmbH v Telekom Austria AG* [2000] ECR I-10745, para. 60; Commission interpretative communication on the Community law applicable to contract

[37] That case at issue was the entrustment of a bus company, Altmark Trans, with regional public transport in Germany; the criteria that the Court developed are usually referred to as the 'Altmark criteria' in European legal texts and were the basis for secondary legal texts in EU competition (State aid) law, ECJ, judgment of 24.07.2003, C-280/00 – *Altmark Trans and Regierungspräsidium Magdeburg*.

awards not or not fully subject to the provisions of the Public Procurement Directives (OJ C 179, 1.8.2006, p. 2; http://eur-lex.europa.eu/legal-content/EN/TXT/?uri=uriserv:OJ.C_.2006.179.01.0002.01.ENG&toc=OJ:C:2006:179:FULL).

Before applying these criteria, though, comes the correct definition of a specific service as SGEI. The division of powers in the EU's constitutional frame leaves to individual Member States the prerogative to define objectives in the economic interest of their citizens. EU Member States enjoy wide discretion to define services of general economic interest and thus to finance them.

Consequently, the relation between state aid and SGEI must be clarified. In its Communication on the relation between SGEI and state aid rules, the Commission says that 'SGEI are not only rooted in the shared values of the Union but also play a central role in promoting social and territorial cohesion'.[38] This programmatic statement encapsulates core values of the EU but it also marks a tectonic fault line: on one side of that line are Member State's governments which, according to the EU's subsidiarity principle,[39] are close to the interests of their citizens and have the competency to define and finance SGEI. On the other side is the EU's exclusive competency in the field of state aid control. The second sentence of that Communication recognises that fact: 'The Union and the Member States, each within their respective powers, must take care that such services operate on the basis of principles and conditions which enable them to fulfil their missions.'

The fault line is mainly due to the principle of subsidiarity in a constitutional setting of shared and exclusive competencies: the EU accordingly does not define the scope of SGEI at supranational level, but Member States have a wide margin of discretion in defining a given service as a SGEI and in granting public compensation to the service provider. The Commission's competence in this respect is limited to checking whether the Member State has made a manifest error when defining the service as an SGEI and to assessing any state aid involved in the compensation.[40] Indeed, the interest of citizens, markets and policies

[38] First sentence of the first point of the European Commission's Communication on EU state aid rules and compensation granted for the provision of services of general economic interest.

[39] Article 5 TEU.

[40] ECJ, judgment of 15.06.2005, T-17/02 – *Olsen v Commission*, para. 216; ECJ, judgment of 12.02.2008, T-289/03 – *BUPA and others v Commission*, paras 166–169 and 172.

are subject to permanent change. The '*special characteristics*' of SGEI as compared with other economic activities is the one stable principle.[41]

FURTHER READING – SERVICES IN THE GENERAL ECONOMIC INTEREST (SGEI)

EU competition law distinguishes between 'services of general economic interest' and 'non-economic services': the former are of particular importance to citizens and in all likelihood would not be supplied (or would be supplied under different conditions) if there was no public intervention. The latter consist in the exercise of state prerogatives, e.g. police or fire fighting, in public education or solidarity-based social-security schemes.

Services in the general economic interest are offered in a market environment. Hence, they are of an economic nature and specific EU state aid rules apply to their public financing (a somewhat complex collage of rules, consisting of two Communications, one Commission Decision and a Regulation[42]). On the one hand, the purpose of those rules is to give individual Member States flexibility to finance services they believe are important for society, and on the other hand ensure that public compensation to undertakings – public or private – for delivering the services is not excessive.

Article 14 TFEU refers to 'the place occupied by services of general economic interest in the shared values of the Union as well as their role in promoting social and territorial cohesion' and obliges both the Union and the Member States, each within their respective powers and competences, to ensure the proper operation of such services; this however applies without prejudice to competition rules set out in Articles 106 (public undertakings and competition rules) and 107 (state aid) TFEU.

---

[41] Developed by the Court: ECJ, judgment of 10.12.1991, C-179/90 – *Merci convenzionali porto di Genova v Siderurgica Gabrielli*, para. 27; ECJ, judgment of 17.07.1997, C-242/95 – *GT-Link v De Danske Statsbaner*, para. 53; and ECJ, judgment of 18.06.1998, C-266/96 – *Corsica Ferries France v Gruppo Antichi Ormeggiatori del porto di Genova and others*, para. 45.

[42] Communication from the Commission on the application of the European Union state aid rules to compensation granted for the provision of services of general economic interest, OJ EU 2012 C 8/02 of 11.01.2012, 4; Commission Decision on the application of Article 106(2) of the Treaty on the Functioning of the European Union to state aid in the form of public service compensation granted to certain undertakings entrusted with the operation of services of general economic interest, OJ EU 2012 L 7/3 of 11.01.2012; Communication from the Commission, European Union framework for state aid in the form of public service compensation, OJ EU 2012 C 8/03 of 11.01.2012, 15; Commission Regulation on the application of Articles 107 and 108 of the Treaty on the Functioning of the European Union to *de minimis* aid granted to undertakings providing services of general economic interest, OJ EU 2012 L 114/8 of 26.04.2012.

The Commission then developed, within its margin of discretion, rules for keeping the distortive potential of public funding for SGEI at bay.

As for the vast majority of sectors, Member States have full discretion and the European Commission as the supranational competition authority, in turn, has the prerogative to check for 'manifest errors'. Hence, the Member State's power to define SGEI is not unlimited and cannot be exercised arbitrarily, e.g. to remove a particular sector or undertaking from the application of the competition rules.

In that legal situation, the aforementioned European Commission's Communication on the application of state aid rules to compensation for SGEI cannot attempt to define the concept of genuine SGEI. It rather explains the relevant concepts of EU state aid, in particular the concepts of 'economic activity' vs 'non-economic activities' such as the exercise of public powers, education or health care. It rather 'aims at facilitating the application of State Aid rules for national, regional and local authorities as well as public service providers'.[43]

Distortion of competition is about 'exclusive rights'. This was true in the early seventeenth century when the Crown had the power to grant exclusive rights until the Parliament of England enacted the Statute of Monopolies in an attempt to curtail that privilege, and it is true today, when the European Court of First Instance finds that:

> a distinction must be drawn between a special or exclusive right conferred on an operator and the SGEI mission which, where appropriate, is attached to that right (…). The grant of a special or exclusive right to an operator is merely the instrument, possibly justified, which allows that operator to perform an SGEI mission.[44]

The granting of exclusive or special rights to undertakings can indeed only be justified if this is necessary to deliver an SGEI.

---

[43] European Commission, Staff Working Document – Guide to the application of the European Union rules on state aid, public procurement and the internal market to services of general economic interest, and in particular to social services of general interest, Brussels, 29.04.2013, SWD(2013) 53 final/2, 28.

[44] *BUPA and others v Commission* (n. 40), para. 179.

EXCURSION – SGEI IN SECTORS THAT HAVE BEEN 'HARMONISED' AT EU-LEVEL ARE EXEMPT FROM THE MEMBER STATE PREROGATIVE TO DEFINE OBJECTIVES IN THE ECONOMIC INTEREST OF CITIZENS – TELECOMMUNICATIONS, POSTAL SERVICES AND ENERGY

It is true that these exceptions do not help making the legal situation less complex. They are however the corollary of necessary supranational regulation where nation states failed to invite competition and innovation and provide adequate services at affordable prices. Further on, in Chapter 6, we will discuss supranational harmonisation that aims at safeguarding good, accessible and affordable postal, railway, energy, and telecommunication services, through the instrument of 'universal service'. In essence, where EU supranational regulation sets forth universal service obligations, Member States nevertheless have discretion to go further, by defining additional SGEI.

Today, manifest errors are still likely to occur purposefully and exclusive rights may still be granted. Again, the question arises: In whose interest does the state intervene in the market? On whose behalf is exploitation legitimised? Examples of a clash of social and economic interest and of difficulties to define the 'general economic interest' can be found in many sectors.

4.5.2 The Issue with Exclusive Rights and 'Manifest Error': Case Examples

CASE EXAMPLE – DOCK WORKERS

One Italian case[45] shows that overstretching the notion of SGEI, in an effort to protect the interests of workers, can paradoxically result in the abuse of a dominant position, or bluntly spoken exploitation. In Italy, in 1990, the loading, unloading, transhipment, storage and general movement of goods or material within the port of Genoa were by law reserved to dock-work companies whose workers had to be of Italian nationality. Moreover, Italian law granted to dock-work undertakings the right to organise dock work on behalf of third parties. For the performance of dock work such undertakings, which were, as a general rule, companies established under private law, had to rely exclusively on the dock-work companies. Hence, in the Port of Genoa, a shipping company had to call upon dock-work company *Merci Convenzionali Porto di Genova*, which

[45] *Merci Convenzionali Porto* (n. 41), para. 27; ECJ, judgment of 27.11.2003, joined cases C- 34/01 to C-38/01 – *Enirisorse*, para. 33.

enjoyed the exclusive right to organise dock work in the Port of Genoa, for the unloading of a ship's cargo, even if the ship's crew could have performed the unloading alone with on-board equipment. The Court found that this Italian legislation facilitated abuse of a dominant position: undertakings enjoying exclusive rights under that law were induced either to demand payment for services which had not been requested, to charge disproportionate prices, to refuse to have recourse to modern technology, which involved an increase in the cost of the operations and a prolongation of the time required for their performance, or to grant price reductions to certain consumers and at the same time to offset such reductions by an increase in the charges to other consumers. The Court further found that dock work is not of a general economic interest: it does not exhibit special characteristics as compared with the general economic interest of other economic activities. Even if it were, an undertaking entrusted with dock-work services could still not be exempt from Treaty rules on competition and freedom of movement as these rules would not obstruct the performance of such a task (the Court referred to the exemption in the current Article 106(2) of the TFEU).

CASE EXAMPLE – MILK PRODUCERS

Another case, also in Italy, concerned the SGEI-character of the production and selling of milk and dairy products.[46] The Municipality of Rome had established *Azienda Comunale Centrale del Latte* (ACCL) and wrote off all that company's operating losses. ACCL bought fresh milk from local producers, processed and packaged it and sold it on the local market, comprising about four million consumers. ACCL was loss making. The Municipality defined the collection, processing and marketing of milk for human consumption through ACCL as a 'public service' and thus was obliged to settle the 'social costs' of providing the service. The Commission found that producing and marketing agricultural products could not be regarded as undertakings entrusted with the operation of SGEI. Moreover, another point is interesting: although the Commission's initial doubt that ACCL would have purchased milk above market price and that public loss coverage would channel state aid to local milk producers was dispelled, it is still obvious from the facts described in the decision that the entire ACCL scheme was an extremely expensive and inefficient measure to keep up local agriculture. The taxpayer paid the price – €111 million in written-off operating losses from 1992–97. The Commission ordered Italy to recover the aid from ACCL.

46 Commission decision of 11.04.2000, state aid C 28/1998 on the aid granted by Italy to Centrale del Latte di Roma, OJ EU 2000 L 265/15.

CASE EXAMPLE – BUSINESS PARKS

The state may also try to declare the provision of infrastructure as an SGEI, in order to escape state aid rules in cases where such infrastructure does not even serve the general public but only a small number of enterprises: in a decision concerning aid for a broadband infrastructure that only served some business parks,[47] the European Commission rejected such an argument. It found that in some cases, electronic communication networks are SGEI but that such networks were accessible to all private individuals, enterprises and public entities in the region. The network at issue however was not a service in the general economic interest but rather a form of service for certain enterprises.

The Commission recalled that despite the large discretion Member States enjoy in defining SGEI, such services in essence should serve the interest of citizens or, as the decision was written in French language, '*citoyens*' – a somewhat weightier term.

The state may even attempt to restore lost market power in areas where it has privatised SGEI that previously were provided by public companies that enjoyed exclusive rights. This might be the case e.g. in waste collection or public transport where service providers are selected in open public tender procedures. There, the state could be tempted to put public service providers back on the map by cross-subsidising them from other public entities within large public holdings.[48] To date, though, neither the Commission nor the Court have looked into such cases. Nevertheless, the pull to maintain market power seems obvious in the utilities sector, which at a global level has not yet seen the privatisation rate of other sectors: almost half of the estimated total state owned enterprises employment in 2009 [...] was found in the power and transportation sectors.

It seems that justified cases of public support for SGEI are the mere tip of an entire iceberg of public operations that can distort competition, despite the actual public-interest objective. Below the waterline, though, no excuse at all can be found for measures that protect the interests of a small group at very high cost, at the expense of competitors and consumers. So, prodding under the waterline can only yield a selective and rather illustrative sample of cases. Fortuity and these authors' limited

---

[47] Commission decision of 10.07.2007 in state aid N 890/2006 – France, Aide du Sicoval pour un réseau de très haut débit, para. 35.

[48] Discussion of cross-subsidisation in Gesterkamp/Hellstern/Koenig, Wettbewerberschutz gegen Quersubventionen im Rahmen von Rekommunalisierungsstrategien am Beispiel des Abfallrechts, WRP 8/2011, 1047–51.

deep-diving capability bring to the surface another Italian case example, *Capital injections into SEA Handling SpA*.[49]

CASE EXAMPLE – AIRPORT GROUNDHANDLING SERVICES

That case is established in the 'airport groundhandling' sector, that is passenger handling, baggage and cargo handling and a number of related services for airlines at an airport. Interestingly enough, the case has its very origin in a supranational legislative initiative to open up markets and thereby reduce the operating costs of airline companies and improve the quality of service provided to airport users.[50] We will see, though, that the state responded to that initiative with an attempt to maintain its economic activity and defend the interests of a small group of stakeholders precisely against … efficiency and therefore the interest of the wide 'travelling public'. SEA, the public operator of two large Italian airports, Milan Malpensa and Milan Linate, established SEA Handling, following the entry into force of Italian legislation that transposed an EU Directive which aimed at opening up market access to ground handling at European airports and i.e. imposed the requirement to keep separate accounts for airport service activities. SEA-Handling started operations in 2002. From that very first year until 2010, its total losses amounted to € 339,784 million. Its public mother company SEA therefore kept it afloat with multiple capital increases, totalling € 359,644 million. For the purposes of this discussion, four points are interesting. First, the Commission found evidence that the loss coverage was at the request of the Municipality of Milan, which was the majority shareholder of SEA Handling's public mother company, especially with a view to maintaining employment levels. In that context, the Commission found that 'the Municipality's role went beyond that of a normal shareholder'.[51] Second, regarding labour costs, the Commission observed that the unit cost of labour rose nearly 10 per cent between 2003 and 2010. Third, the public mother company SEA claimed that it had limited capacity to achieve significant reductions in its operating costs since 'the power of the unions in collective bargaining negotiations and their political role in Italy restricted its room to manoeuvre in the short term'.[52] Fourth, the capital increases did not satisfy the market economy investor test since they were not based on financial analyses and business plans comparable to those that a private investor would have requested. In light of all this, the Commission ordered Italy to recover the capital injections from SEA-Handling, as these were incompatible with the internal market. In this decision, the Commission recalled

[49] Multiple Commission Decisions and press releases in state aid case SA.21420, http://ec.europa.eu/competition/elojade/isef/case_details.cfm?proc_code=3_SA_21420, 06.07.2016.

[50] Council Directive 96/67/EC of 15.10.1996 on access to the groundhandling market at Community airports, OJ EU 1996 L 272/36.

[51] Commission decision of 19.12.2012 in state aid case SA.21420 (C 14/10 etc.) regarding injections of capital by SEA SpA into SEA Handling SpA, para. 210.

[52] Ibid., para. 304.

that 'the very purpose of liberalising the sector is to stimulate competition so that the suppliers with the most competitive business models can establish themselves on the market, to the benefit of users, airlines and, ultimately, users'.[53]

Still, the need to retain its own groundhandling service operator and thus employment of approximately 1 800 workers prompted the public mother company, instead of recovering the aid – which anyway, given its oppressing amount of € 360 million plus interest, would have sunk the company, to liquidate it instead and set up a new groundhandling company, to transfer most of the previous company's workers and to inject capital, to the tune of € 25 million ... Again, two points are interesting. First, the transfer of workers was again orchestrated by the public mother company under agreements with trade unions. Second, this time the capital injections were based on business plans and financial analyses. The Commission decision in that follow-up case is interesting:[54] it finds that the new company does not benefit from previous aid to its predecessor and that the recent capital injection is commensurate with the market economy investor principle. The concern remains, though: both the predecessor that had been kept afloat by public loss-coverage and the new company were public enterprises; both had, respectively still have, a market share of around 70 per cent; at the same time, numerous competing ground handling competitors were structurally profitable and 'the market trend in the period in question was towards an end to investment by airport managers in ground handling services, and operators that had subcontracted ground handling services were generally more profitable than vertically integrated operators'.[55] In essence, this case is an example of labour specificity's 'strong, positive and consistently significant impact on subsidy disbursement'.[56]

4.5.3 State Services and EU State Aid Rules and Actual Numbers

Public funding for economic activities, even if they are in the general interest of society, can distort competition – so the EU has rules for keeping this distortive potential under control. The EU's so-called 'SGEI' package has a two-fold objective: first, to explain where public services of general interest are 'economic activities' that are subject to EU state aid law; and secondly, to set out rules to keep the public financing of SGEIs within the limitations of EU state aid control. Despite its aim to

53 Ibid., para. 311.

54 Commission decision of 05.07.2016 in state aid SA.21420 (2016/C etc.), Setting up of Airport Handling.

55 Commission decision of 19.12.2012 in state aid case SA.21420 (C 14/10 etc.) (n. 52), para. 312.

56 Discussion in Zahariadis, State Subsidies in the Global Economy, 128 *et seq*. That author demonstrates that 'higher specificity, that is lower movement of workers across industries in search of higher wages leads to more successful demands for a greater number of subsidies'.

provide simpler and clearer rules, the package consists of multiple legal texts of various legal statuses:

- Commission Communication – explains the principles of state aid in relation to SGEI.[57]
- Commission Decision – grants automatic approval of state aid within certain limits for the provision of certain SGEI-categories.[58]
- Commission Framework – sets out rules for individual assessment of large state aid for SGEI, being more than € 15 million annually. Such large cases have to be notified to the Commission for approval.
- Commission Regulation – stipulates that very small public support (not more than € 500.000 over any period of three fiscal years) for SGEI does not fall under EU state aid rules.[59]
- Commission 'Staff Working Document'[60] – explains the application of these rules.
- Moreover, the Commission has published a document on frequently asked questions on state aid and SGEI, which was published even before all parts of the legislative package had been adopted.[61]
- To add to this patchwork of legislative and explanatory texts, an electronic information service for further questions contains links to other Commission guides and websites on SGEI.[62]

---

57 Communication from the Commission on the application of the European Union state aid rules to compensation granted for the provision of services of general economic interest, OJ EU 2012 C 8/02, 4.

58 Commission Decision of 20.12.2012 on the application of Article 106(2) of the Treaty on the Functioning of the European Union to state aid in the form of public service compensation granted to certain undertakings entrusted with the operation of services of general economic interest, OJ EU 2012 L 7/3.

59 Commission Regulation (EU) No 360/2012 on the application of Articles 107 and 108 of the Treaty on the Functioning of the European Union to *de minimis* aid granted to undertakings providing services of general economic interest, OJ EU 2012 L 114/8.

60 European Commission, Staff Working Document – Guide to the application of the European Union rules on state aid, public procurement and the internal market to services of general economic interest, and in particular to social services of general interest, Brussels, 29.04.2013, SWD(2013) 53 final/2, 28. http://ec.europa.eu/competition/state_aid/overview/new_guide_eu_rules_procurement_en.pdf, 06.07.2016.

61 A memo dated 20.12.2011, http://europa.eu/rapid/press-release_MEMO-11-929_en.htm?locale=en, 06.07.2016.

62 http://ec.europa.eu/services_general_interest/registration/form_en.htm, 06.07.2016.

So overall, the legislative approach is extremely diverse while the efforts to explain are well intentioned yet chaotic. Calling this a clear and simple rulebook may be misleading.[63] The Commission 'Staff Working Document' illustrates the path to assessing the applicability of EU state aid rules to SGEI as shown in Figure 4.1 below.

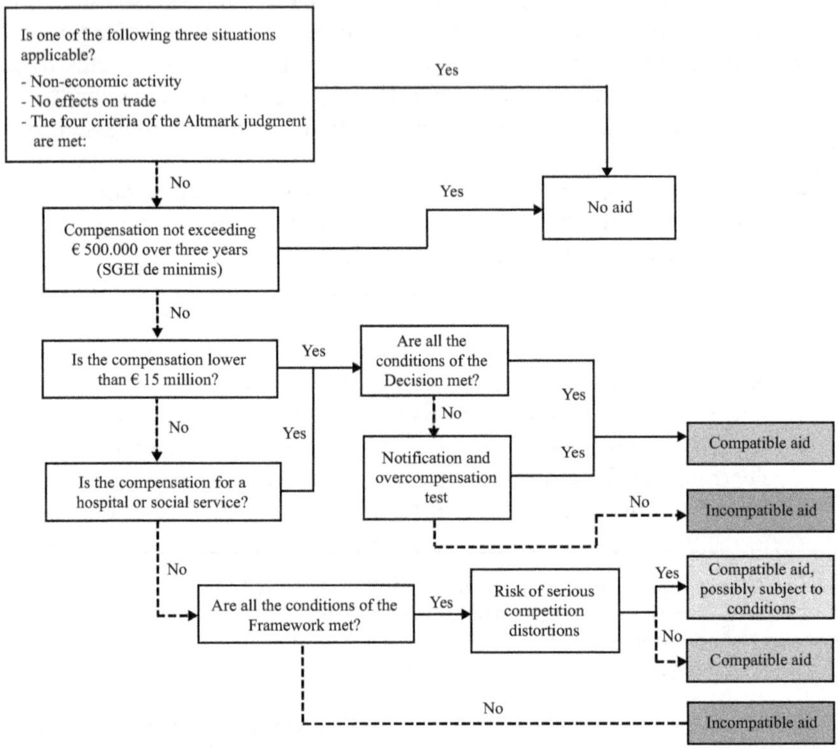

Source: European Commission, Staff Working Document – Guide to the application of the European Union rules on state aid, public procurement and the internal market to services of general economic interest, and in particular to social services of general interest, p. 29.

Figure 4.1 Applicability of EU state aid rules to SGEI

[63] The European Commission's then Vice-President in charge of competition policy, Joaquín Almunia, called the *newly adopted SGEI package a clearer and more flexible framework for supporting the delivery of high-quality public services, press release of 20.11.2011,* http://europa.eu/rapid/press-release_IP-11-1571_en.htm?locale=en, *06.07.2016.*

SGEI can give an idea of the magnitude of public or publicly financed services that potentially compete with private companies, also beyond the area of public interest services. Even if the volume of public investments and operations in the EU in total is largely under the waterline and one cannot see the whole iceberg of distortive state intervention, one could judge its size by its tip sticking out of the water.

When reviewing its state aid rules applicable to SGEI in 2012, the European Commission found:

> The direct contribution of SGEIs to the GDP is of great importance. It can be expressed as value-added for the services of economic nature, or on the basis of expenditure for health and social services. Statistics show that this expenditure in health and social services accounts for as high as 9,4% of GDP. The sectors of infrastructure networks have a contribution of 4,8% of GDP, while research and recruitment have a contribution of 0,9% of GDP. However, it is unclear how much of the sector of research and recruitment concerns SGEIs and how much non-economic SGIs. In any case, using these statistics, the average direct contribution of SGEI providers to the EU GDP can be estimated at around 15%. Moreover, there are important investments carried out by SGEI providers. For example, in the sectors of infrastructure networks and research, investments were of more than 150 billion Euros, which accounted for 6,4% of total EU investment. These investments are above average in the 10 Member States from Central and Eastern Europe, most likely because of the modernisation period they undergo.[64]

That finding reveals both the size of state intervention and the methodological lack of precision – this is particularly alarming for the research sector, where public and private interests interact, overlap and sometimes compete.

4.5.4 Intermediate Conclusion

If not properly balanced, the tension between national prerogatives to define public services and the supranational prerogative to protect competition can produce harm: on the one hand, EU Member States may overstretch the concept of SGEI, in order to please particular interests, or over-compensate a service provider which even may be an incumbent public company. On the other hand, overly demanding criteria to exclude

[64] European Commission, Reform of the EU rules applicable to state aid in the form of public service compensation, Impact Assessment, 20.12.2011, SEC(2011) 1581 final, 12, 13.

state aid, or to limit SGEI state aid, may prevent Member States from delivering quality public services where the market does not deliver them on its own initiative.

The proper balance can only be achieved by setting the right priorities: first, particular economic interests must be subordinated to the general interest in functioning competition; second, limited distortions of competition must be accepted where the market cannot deliver an SGEI on its own initiative; third, the system of the procurement of, the entrustment with, and the compensation for delivering SGEI must be sufficiently transparent so as to allow effective control, both by the market and the executive.

That system may be effective but it comes at a price: it means supranational interference with a core concern of national, often regional or local politics. However, the supranational prerogative to check for manifest error and applicable state aid rules ultimately moves control away from national legislative and judicial systems to the European Commission in Brussels respectively to the ECJ in Luxemburg.

4.6 THE EU PREROGATIVES TO CREATE MARKET POWER – SUPPORTING SECTORS AND TECHNOLOGIES BY ALLOWING STATE AID – PICKING WINNERS, SUSTAINING LOSERS

In the previous section, we looked at the ins and outs of abuse of *public* market power and ways to counter such abuse with supranational regulation. In the following section, we will look at policies that have the potential to strengthen *private* market power and at supranational regulation to limit that potential.

The question is: How to balance the strengthening of market power against the necessity to provide incentives to deliver an outcome in the interest of society?

We will start on the premise that the policy instrument for strengthening private market power is state aid in its various forms.

The main reason for national states to strengthen the market power of domestic industries has a protectionist background. Such protectionist motivation conflicts with the EU's common policy – entrusted to the EU supranational executive – to create and protect an efficiently functioning internal market. The challenge of transcending national motivations can be illustrated by the EU's strategy for sustainable economic growth: in the aftermath of the global financial and economic crisis, and just when the storm of the Eurozone sovereign debt crisis was gathering, the European Commission, in its 'Europe 2020' strategy paper stressed:

> A stronger, deeper, extended single market is vital for growth and job creation. However, current trends show signs of integration fatigue and disenchantment regarding the single market. The crisis has added temptations of economic nationalism. The Commission's vigilance and a shared sense of responsibility among Member States have prevented a drift towards disintegration.[65]

Economic nationalism within a common internal market is possible where the division of powers allows single-handed action: it is true that Article 5 TFEU demands that Member States '*coordinate*' their economic policies within the Union and that, to this end, the EU Council shall adopt measures, 'in particular broad guidelines for these policies' Title XVII – 'Industry' of the TFEU contains a sole article – Article 173:

> 1. The Union and the Member States shall ensure that the conditions necessary for the competitiveness of the Union's industry exist.
>
> For that purpose, in accordance with a system of open and competitive markets, their action shall be aimed at:
>
> - speeding up the adjustment of industry to structural changes,
> - encouraging an environment favourable to initiative and to the development of undertakings throughout the Union, particularly small and medium-sized undertakings,
> - encouraging an environment favourable to cooperation between undertakings,
> - fostering better exploitation of the industrial potential of policies of innovation, research and technological development.
>
> 2. The Member States shall consult each other in liaison with the Commission and, where necessary, shall coordinate their action. The Commission may take any useful initiative to promote such coordination, in particular initiatives aiming at the establishment of guidelines and indicators, the organisation of exchange of best practice, and the preparation of the necessary elements for periodic monitoring and evaluation. The European Parliament shall be kept fully informed.
>
> 3. The Union shall contribute to the achievement of the objectives set out in paragraph 1 through the policies and activities it pursues under other

[65] European Commission, Communication of 03.03.2010, 'Europe 2020 – A strategy for smart, sustainable and inclusive growth', 20.

> provisions of the Treaties. The European Parliament and the Council, acting in accordance with the ordinary legislative procedure and after consulting the Economic and Social Committee, may decide on specific measures in support of action taken in the Member States to achieve the objectives set out in paragraph 1, excluding any harmonisation of the laws and regulations of the Member States.
>
> This Title shall not provide a basis for the introduction by the Union of any measure which could lead to a distortion of competition or contains tax provisions or provisions relating to the rights and interests of employed persons.

The afore-cited provision on industrial policy in the EU contains assumptions that are key in bringing together industrial policy and competition rules: the objective of keeping the EU's industry competitive is only achievable in a system of open and competitive markets and in an environment that favours initiative.

In essence, the EU's industrial policy is horizontal in nature, i.e. not sector-specific, and aims to secure framework conditions favourable to industrial competitiveness. It is also integrated into a number of other EU policies such as those relating to trade, the internal market, research and innovation, employment, environmental protection and public health.

Within that legal setting, the supranational legislator coordinates and provides broad guidelines. The EU's 'Europe 2020' strategy, which comprises a number of so-called 'Flagship Initiatives', most of which relate to industrial-policy objectives, is an example of the EU's attempt to create an industrial policy framework in a constitutional setting of divided powers. For example, consider the EU's strategy for better access to finance for industry, 'An Integrated Industrial Policy for the Globalisation Era'.[66] The Commission on the one hand commits to bringing forward legislation to ensure that financial markets become more resilient and efficient, to evaluate potential impacts on access to finance, especially for SMEs, to examine whether the EU's own (supranational) financial instruments can be refocused to help overcome market failures in financing small businesses and innovation. On the other hand, the Commission merely 'invites' Member States to develop and share best

[66] European Commission, Communication of 28.10.2010, An Integrated Industrial Policy for the Globalisation Era Putting Competitiveness and Sustainability at Centre Stage.

practices on governmental schemes for access to finance.[67] This illustrates the ample margin for EU Member States to pursue their own industrial policy objectives and thereby … strengthen private market power.

The EU has its supranational competition rules to control Member States' power to create market power and thereby harm competition in the internal market. The following discussion will focus on two areas where theories of harm are particularly relevant: first, the strengthening of future market power through state aid for research and development (R&D); second, the creation of market power through subsidy races in the area of state aid for regional development where ultimately the recipient of the state aid could be the only winner.

EU state aid rules in both fields provide for a number of criteria that must be met in order for state aid to be approved by the European Commission. As this is not an EU competition law textbook, the following discussion will focus only on a few quite essential and emblematic criteria.

Besides the prerogatives of state aid law set by the EU, the crucial question remains: Are EU supranational rules and their enforcement robust enough to prevent national policy makers from creating harmful market power?

4.6.1 Strengthening Future Market Power – Technology Development

State aid for research and development and innovation (R&D&I) can help to overcome market failures that prevent industry from engaging in activities in the common interest. Such aid can however also project market power into the future, as aid measures may have a built-in bias towards incumbents or inefficient companies, or may significantly change the market power of a dominant player, or may facilitate the foreclosure of emergent markets. Total state aid granted by EU Member States amounted to €93.53 billion in 2014. €10.91 billion were for R&D&I activities alone, being 0.67 per cent of the EU's GDP.[68]

In the EU, R&D&I state aid was granted to a wide variety of sectors, in particular aeronautics, microelectronics, energy, biotechnology, automotive and ICT (as shown in Figure 4.2):

---

67 Ibid., 8.

68 European Commission, state Aid Scoreboard, http://ec.europa.eu/competition/state_aid/scoreboard/index_en.html#tables, 06.07.2016.

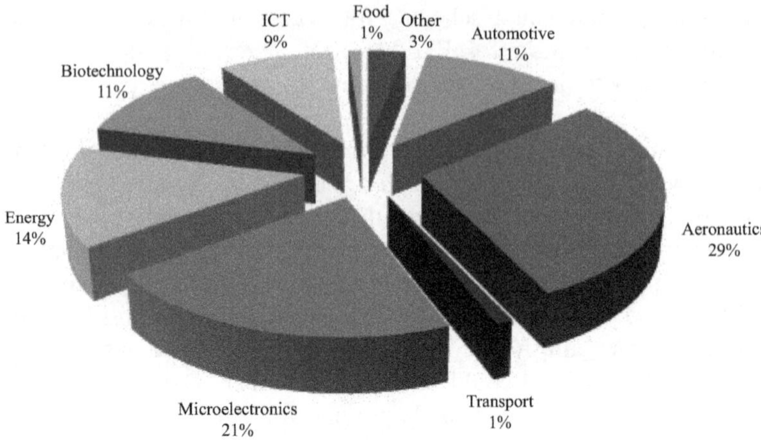

Source: European Commission, Impact Assessment accompanying the document Communication from the Commission Framework for state aid for Research, Development and Innovation, p. 26.

Figure 4.2 Sectors receiving R&D&I state aid

In the following discussion, we will see that in the area of R&D&I, the supranational regulator may content itself with a rather formal assessment of a state aid's impact on market efficiency but counterbalances this with creating rules which, albeit not being binding on Member States, have a 'structuring effect' on their interventions in favour of R&D&I.

4.6.1.1 Industrial policy and R&D&I

The promotion of R&D&I is a common policy objective of the EU: Article 179(1) TFEU stipulates that:

> The Union shall have the objective of strengthening its scientific and technological bases by achieving a European research area in which researchers, scientific knowledge and technology circulate freely, and encouraging it to become more competitive, including in its industry, while promoting all the research activities deemed necessary by virtue of other Chapters of the Treaties.

Article 173 TFEU on industrial policy, the above-cited Article 179 TFEU on research and competitiveness and, above all, the balancing test inherent to Article 107 TFEU on state aid enshrine the creed of the EU's overall economic and competition policy: only competitive pressure induces innovation; the state shall not shield industry from the risks of innovating; and neither monopolistic nor atomistic market structures are able to produce outcomes in the common EU interest. The apparently mundane middle ground is the balancing test: allowing state aid to 'moderately' strengthen market power if it comes with the added bonus of technological breakthroughs and sufficient spill-over to promote EU industry's overall competitiveness. The state can help industry to control the risk of innovation and also to generate profit large enough to leave margin to invest in future innovation. In essence, EU state aid rules have to ensure that this structure is maintained.

The EU has placed R&D&I centre stage in its strategy for sustainable growth: The EU's objective is that by 2020, 3 per cent of the EU's GDP are invested in R&D, and that the conditions for R&D investment by the private sector are improved.[69] This comprises supranational growth policy initiatives such as enhancing access to finance for innovative companies,[70] industrial innovation,[71] increased public spending on R&D in ICT[72] and public support to develop new products and services in order to increase resource efficiency.[73]

The European Commission presumes that state aid that contributes to the EU's 2020-growth strategy is 'in the common interest'.[74]

State aid rules are the necessary counteractive in this overall growth policy cocktail. Since 1986, EU state aid rules spell out conditions for R&D-aid, and later also innovation aid, to be compatible with the internal market and thus exempt from the general prohibition of state aid. In other words, these rules attempt to strike a positive balance between state aid for activities in the common interest on the one hand and distortions of competition, i.e. the creation of market power, on the other. The Commission has revised these rules regularly in order to take into

---

[69] EU-2020 Communication, COM(2010) 2020 final, 03.03.2010.

[70] 'Innovation Union', Communication from the Commission, of 06.10.2010, COM(2010) 546 final.

[71] 'An Integrated Industrial Policy for the Globalisation Era – Putting Competitiveness and Sustainability at Centre Stage', Communication from the Commission of 28.10.2010, COM(2010) 614 final.

[72] 'A Digital Agenda for Europe', Communication from the Commission of 26.08.2010, COM(2010) 245 final/2.

[73] 'A resource-efficient Europe', Communication from the Commission of 26.01.2011, COM(2011) 21 final.

[74] The EU 2020 Communication makes a general reference to the role of state aid: 'state aid policy can also actively and positively contribute to the Europe 2020 objectives by prompting and supporting initiatives for innovative, efficient and greener technologies, while facilitating access to public support for investment, risk capital and funding for research and development', 21.

account policy developments and decisional practice.[75] Since 2004, the Commission reduced bureaucratic burden and facilitated the granting of R&D-aid by empowering Member States to grant R&D-aid up to certain thresholds without prior Commission approval.[76]

4.6.1.2 EU state aid rules in the area of R&D&I. Relation to industrial policy

Today, state aid for R&D&I in the EU is subject to two legal texts: the Union Framework for state aid for Research, Development and Innovation (the Framework)[77] and the General Block Exemption Regulation (GBER).[78] The rationale behind these rules is that state aid for R&D&I activities can help to overcome market failures that prevent sustainable growth, competitiveness and employment.

> Whereas it is generally accepted that competitive markets tend to bring about efficient results in terms of prices, output and use of resources, in the presence of market failures state intervention may improve the functioning of markets and, thereby, contribute to smart, sustainable and inclusive growth. In the context of R&D&I, market failures may arise for instance because market actors do not normally take into account the (positive) externalities that ensue on other actors in the economy, and therefore engage in a level of R&D&I activities which is too low from the point of view of society. Likewise, R&D&I projects might suffer from insufficient access to finance (due to asymmetric information) or from coordination problems among firms. Therefore, state aid for R&D&I can be compatible with the internal market where it can be expected to alleviate a market failure in promoting the execution of an

---

[75] 1986: Community Framework for state Aid for Research and Development, OJ EU 1986 C 83/2; 1996: Community Framework for state Aid for Research and Development, OJ EU 1996 C 45/5; 2006: Community Framework for state aid for Research and Development and Innovation, OJ EU 2006 C 323/1; 2014: Framework for state aid for research and development and innovation (n. 23).

[76] The so-called General Block Exemption Regulations. 2004: Commission Regulation No 364/2004 of 25.02.2004 amending Regulation (EC) No 70/2001 as regards the extension of its scope to include aid for research and development, OJ EU 2004 L 63/22; 2008: Commission Regulation (EC) No 800/2008 of 09.08.2008 declaring certain categories of aid compatible with the common market in application of Articles 87 and 88 of the Treaty, OJ EU 2008 L 214/3; 2014: Commission Regulation (EU) No 651/2014 of 17.06.2014 declaring certain categories of aid compatible with the internal market in application of Articles 107 and 108 of the Treaty, OJ EU 2014 L 187/1.

[77] Framework for state aid for research and development and innovation (n. 23).

[78] Commission Regulation (EU) No 651/2014 (n. 77).

important project of common European interest or facilitating the development of certain economic activities, and where the ensuing distortion of competition and trade is not contrary to the common interest.[79]

FURTHER READING – INDUSTRIAL POLICY, KEY ENABLING TECHNOLOGIES AND STATE AID IMPLICATIONS

Under a looking glass, the tension between industrial policy goals and supranational state aid rules can be observed in one particularly important field – the promotion of key enabling technologies in the EU.[80]

The European Commission focused its industrial policy on key enabling technologies (KETs), such as micro-/nanoelectronics, nanotechnology, photonics, advanced materials, industrial biotechnology and advanced manufacturing technology. They are a 'key source of innovation' with a very high social return on public investments and with applications, e.g. in automotive, food, chemicals, electronics, textiles, energy, environment, pharmaceuticals, construction, aerospace and telecommunication. So the European Commission promotes KETs because they 'boost competitiveness and generate jobs, growth and wealth in the EU-economy'.[81]

At the supranational level: in order to promote KETs, the European Commission vowed to focus EU policies on a wide range of activities: European Investment Bank lending in favour of KETs deployment; coordinating EU and national activities; mobilising existing trade instruments to ensure fair competition and a level international playing field; allocating €6.663 billion in industrial capabilities on KETs in the EU's own R&D-funding scheme 'Horizon 2020'; implementing innovation-oriented public-private partnerships for KETs; promoting KETs-related cluster-specific actions; enhancing cooperation in the area of KETs; ensuring a favourable trade environment and a global level playing field; and many more.

At national level: Member States and regions are invited to exploit research and innovation strategies for smart specialisation to support spill-over effects of KETs-based solutions, strengthening existing and possibly developing new European industrial value chains; to encourage managing authorities responsible for the development of smart specialisation strategies to closely interact with their fellow authorities responsible for research and innovation policies.

Implications for EU state aid control: the industrial policy paper recalls the EU's supranational state aid control competences. It further recalls the European Commission's intention to modernise state aid rules, including those on R&D&I aid, to support the implementation of the above described growth strategy until 2020 and to enhance the quality of public spending. In particular, modernised

[79] Recital (46) of the GBER; in the same sense, yet more detailed, also point 4 of the Framework.

[80] European Commission, Communication of 26.06.2012, A European strategy for Key Enabling Technologies – A bridge to growth and jobs.

[81] Cf. ibid., 3 *et seq.*

rules should facilitate the treatment of state aid which is well-designed, targeted at proven market failures and has a clear incentive effect and limited impact on competition.

4.6.1.3 State aid for R&D&I. Gauging the potential to create or maintain market power

When the Commission is assessing the positive and negative effects of state aid, including aid for R&D&I, it applies common assessment principles:

- *Common interest:* State aid must aim at an objective of common interest in accordance with Article 107(3) TFEU.
- *Market failure or cohesion issue:* State aid must be targeted towards a situation where aid can bring about a material improvement that the market cannot deliver itself, for example by remedying a market failure or addressing an equity or cohesion concern;
- *Appropriateness:* state aid must be an appropriate policy instrument to address the objective of common interest;
- *Incentive effect:* state aid must change the behaviour of the undertaking(s) concerned in such a way that it engages in additional activity, which it would not carry out without the aid or would carry out in a restricted or different manner or location;
- *Proportionality:* the amount and intensity of state aid must be limited to the minimum needed to induce the additional investment or activity by the undertaking(s) concerned;
- *Limited distortive effects:* negative effects on competition and trade between Member States must be sufficiently limited, so that the overall balance of the state aid is positive;
- *Transparency:* state aid must be transparent, i.e. Member States, the European Commission, economic operators and the public must have easy access to all relevant acts and to pertinent information about the aid awarded thereunder.[82]

[82] Section 3 of the Framework for state aid for research and development and innovation, (n. 23).

FURTHER READING – STATE AID RULES IN THE AREA OF R&D&I

The General Block Exemption Regulation sets out the conditions under which state aid for R&D&I, among other types of state aid, is automatically approved by the European Commission. http://eur-lex.europa.eu/legal-content/EN/TXT/HTML/?uri=CELEX:32014R0651&from=EN.

A practical guide helps navigating in that large Regulation: http://ec.europa.eu/competition/state_aid/legislation/practical_guide_gber_en.pdf.

The Framework for state aid for research, development and innovation contains rules for the assessment of R&D&I-aid that cannot be automatically approved. http://eur-lex.europa.eu/legal-content/EN/TXT/?uri=OJ:C:2014:198:TOC.

A Commission Memorandum briefly explains the systematic and objective of both texts. http://europa.eu/rapid/press-release_MEMO-14-368_en.htm.

For the purposes of this discussion, the most relevant assessment principles are: the potential of R&D-aid to address a market failure and to have an incentive effect, and the avoidance of undue distortions of competition, in particular the strengthening of market power.

There is little controversy amongst politics, industry and scholars that certain market failures prevent firms from efficiently allocating resources to R&D: knowledge spill-overs, imperfect and asymmetric information and coordination failures. The EU allows state aid if it demonstrably addresses these market failures.

EU state aid rules are realistic enough to avoid excessive burden of proof, though: first, they do not demand *ex-ante* econometric studies to prove that a given project is facing a market failure. Rather, 'the Commission will in particular take into account any available sectoral comparisons and other studies, which should be provided by the Member State concerned'.[83] Secondly, where a project is already co-financed under a supranational EU programme (and thus the market failure had already been analysed at that level), the additional aid from the Member State is presumed to address a market failure.[84] Third, to avoid fruitless efforts to prove a market failure, the Commission warns that a rebuttable assumption of absence of market failure applies where the technological

[83] Point 52, ibid.
[84] Point 54, ibid.

content, level of risk and size of a project or activity are similar to those already delivered within the EU at market conditions – i.e. without state aid.[85]

The incentive-effect of aid must be demonstrated with a counterfactual analysis as well as with the profitability of the envisaged project. In essence, the counterfactual analysis is a quest for realistic intentions – What would the company have done if state aid was not available? This means comparing what the expected outcome and level of intended activity would be with and without aid.[86] While such approach seems absolutely reasonable, it gives rise to a number of typical questions: What actually is the realistic and credible counterfactual scenario? Is the would-be beneficiary obliged to produce, or rather 'invent', an alternative scenario even if in reality no alternative had ever been considered? That is why, after the recent revision, EU rules for R&D&I state aid make clear that the counterfactual scenario is a 'comprehensive description of what would have happened or could reasonably have been expected to happen without aid', and that it may even consist in the absence of an alternative project.[87]

Moreover, the incentive effect is an elusive concept – after all, it comes down to a process in the minds of industry executives. This is where state aid control stands at the borderline between the measurable and the cognitive. European Commission functionaries, despite their adverse reputation for intervening in everybody's affairs, cannot retrace such mental processes with absolute certainty. Consequently, the European Commission was realistic enough to provide for a long, illustrative list of documents that the Member State (and thus the beneficiary as the source of those documents) should use to demonstrate the incentive effect of aid.[88] Such information – ideally available early on in the notification process – makes the beneficiary's financial strength and business strategy more transparent and is crucial for identifying any additional activity that is induced by the aid.[89] Regarding the incentive effect of state aid for R&D&I, the core criterion is this:

> Member States must demonstrate that the aid has an incentive effect and therefore need to provide clear evidence that the aid has a positive impact on

---

[85] Point 55, ibid.
[86] Point 67 2nd indent, ibid.
[87] Point 66, ibid.
[88] Point 68, ibid.
[89] Discussion of the incentive effect analysis in von Wendland, EStAL 2015, 37, 38.

> the decision of the undertaking to pursue R&D&I activities which would otherwise not have been pursued. To enable the Commission to carry out a comprehensive assessment of the aid measure in question, the Member State concerned must provide not only information concerning the aided project but also, to the extent possible, a comprehensive description of what would have happened or could reasonably have been expected to happen without aid, that is to say the counterfactual scenario. The counterfactual scenario may consist in the absence of an alternative project or in a clearly defined and sufficiently predictable alternative project considered by the beneficiary in its internal decision making, and may relate to an alternative project that is wholly or partly carried out outside the Union.[90]

The Commission specifies measurable criteria: the specification of intended change; a counterfactual analysis, i.e. the change of behaviour has to be identified by comparing what the expected outcome and level of intended activity would be with and without aid; the level of profitability with and without aid; the amount of investment and time-frame of cash flows; the level of risk involved.[91]

The question arises: is this incentive effect check rigorous enough to prevent R&D-aid leading to socially undesirable effects or inducing the beneficiary to undertake overly risky projects or projects of a lower quality?[92] This concern is mainly about information and documentation that is available for an incentive effect check, in particular business plans. It is true that such plans can be adjusted easily to justify state aid. It is however also true, as these authors know from experience in state aid practice, that the incentive effect is an effect on individuals and their – quite subjective – decision making. The rule that R&D-aid must not exceed a certain percentage of eligible project costs, e.g. 25 per cent for close-to-market experimental development, however, provides some safeguard against excessive risk taking or accepting poor-quality R&D. Thus, even the decision to embark on a project with aid must be economically justified. 100 per cent state aid for very high-risk projects is limited to the domain of fundamental research, which is however remote from the market, and as a rule is conducted by public research organisations. Hence, the impact of such funding on the market is very small, and it is zero where the project fails. The discussion of whether aid induces projects that do not bring about the optimum result for society risks

---

90 Point 66 of the R&D&I-Framework (n 23).

91 Point 67, ibid.

92 Detailed discussion in Nicolaidis, The Incentive Effect of state Aid: Its Meaning, Measurement, Pitfalls and Application.

becoming as artificial as the discussion of how a hypothetical market operator would behave.

So far we have discussed standards for assessing the positive effects of R&D&I-aid. How does the Commission go about assessing the negative effects of aid, i.e. the distortion of competition and trade? EU rules on R&D&I state aid identify two forms of distortions – product market distortions and location effects. For this discussion, we will focus on the potential of R&D&I-aid to create or maintain market power, and this is to be seen in conjunction with the counterbalancing potential to overcome market failure and generate an incentive effect. 'Location effect' as a further distortion of competition will be discussed further below, in the context of regional development aid.

Creating or maintaining market power: The relevant core criteria under R&D&I state aid rules are these:

> Aid for R&D&I may also have distortive effects in terms of increasing or maintaining the degree of market power in product markets. Market power is the power to influence market prices, output, the variety or quality of products and services, or other parameters of competition for a significant period of time, to the detriment of consumers. Even where aid does not strengthen market power directly, it may do so indirectly, by discouraging the expansion of existing competitors or inducing their exit or discouraging the entry of new competitors.[93]
>
> The Commission is concerned mainly about those R&D&I measures which enable the aid beneficiary to strengthen market power held on existing product markets or to transfer it to future product markets. The Commission is therefore unlikely to identify competition concerns related to market power in cases where the aid beneficiary has a market share below 25% and in markets with a market concentration below 2000 on the Herfindahl-Hirschman Index (HHI).
>
> In its analysis of market power, the Commission will consider the following elements:
>
> Market power of the aid beneficiary and market structure: where the aid recipient is already dominant on a product market, the aid measure may reinforce that dominance by further weakening the competitive constraint that competitors can exert on the recipient undertaking. Similarly, state aid measures may have a significant impact in oligopolistic markets where only a few players are active;
>
> Level of entry barriers: in the field of R&D&I, there may be significant barriers to entry for new entrants. Those barriers include legal entry barriers

93 Point 101 of the R&D&I-Framework (n 23).

(in particular in respect of IPR), economies of scale and scope, access barriers to networks and infrastructure, and other strategic barriers to entry or expansion;

Buyer power: the market power of an undertaking may also be limited by the market position of the buyers. The presence of strong buyers can serve to counter a finding of a strong market position if it is likely that the buyers will seek to preserve sufficient competition in the market;

Selection process: aid measures which allow undertakings with a strong market position to influence the selection process, for example by having the right to recommend undertakings in the selection process or influencing the research path in a way which disfavours alternative paths on unjustified grounds, are liable to raise concern by the Commission.[94]

One specific aspect of market power is not explicitly included in EU state aid rules in the area of R&D: the effects of intellectual property rights (IPR) and disclosure arrangements between collaboration partners in an R&D-project. The creation or maintenance of market power, the distortion of dynamic incentives to innovation and the maintenance of inefficient market structures however can be the consequences of certain IPR-ownership models used in collaborative R&D-contracts.[95] Thus far, the European Commission has not discussed any such arrangements in its state aid decisions.

4.6.1.4 Intermediate conclusion: it is all quite difficult …

It is not the purpose of this book to discuss the details of EU case law on each and every aspect of market power assessment. The objective of this section rather was to use R&D&I aid as a platform to discuss two points: policies that have the potential to strengthen private market power; and supranational regulation to limit that potential. What one will retain from this discussion is that it is all quite difficult. What however also can be recollected is that thus far, not a single Commission decision prohibited an R&D&I state aid measure, or approved it under condition to alter it, be it after the Member State had notified the Commission of the intention to grant the aid, or after an investigation following a state aid complaint by a competitor, or be it after investigations on the Commission's own initiative.

---

94 Points 113 and 114 of the R&D&I-Framework (n 23).

95 Discussed by Cisneros, The role of EU State Aid Law in promoting a Pro-innovation Policy, 82–99.

One very obvious conclusion, certainly supported by these authors' own practical experience, is that Member States, despite the fact that applicable assessment criteria are not legally binding, already design their state aid measures in line with these assessment criteria, or present their cases in a way that correspond to these criteria, for example producing business plans that prove the necessity of aid and its incentive effect. It seems thus that EU state aid rules for R&D&I have a 'structuring effect' everybody has learned to live with. The issue of a 'democracy deficit' of such system will be discussed later in this book. We can conclude, though, that the world is not black and white in the sense that 'aid is necessary or unnecessary' or 'creates market power beyond the acceptable standard or not'. Consequently, declaring R&D&I state aid as compatible with the internal market solely on the basis of available documentation produced by Member States and aid beneficiaries is only possible under one condition: namely that the supranational regulator agrees that only innovation in the broad sense, resting on the foundations of R&D, guarantees growth and competitiveness.

4.6.2 Subsidy Races and Location Effects: Private Market Power

In this section, state aid for regional development is the platform for discussing the tension between two objectives: on the one hand, the objective to remove regional disparities within a political union of states; on the other, the objective of an efficiently functioning internal market, which implies that state aid must not merely relocate investments from one region to another. We will see that in the field of regional development, state aid regulation needs to transcend the pure market efficiency dogma.

4.6.2.1 Regional state aid and cohesion

'Cohesion' is the glue that keeps a political and economic union together. It implies political, social and economic causes and effects that cross borders. It is a concept that transcends the reach of national industrial and regional policy. It depends on dynamic, cross-border social and economic developments. The creation of a supranational regional policy in Europe in the late 1960s was not only driven by the gradual opening of frontiers that led to the vast internal market today, or by demographic, labour market and sectoral challenges that were recognised to be endemic across and within all regions of the then European Community. 'A second, and arguably the most relevant, catalyst for the creation of a Community regional policy was the deepening of the debate on Economic and Monetary Union, which had been launched in the late 1960s.'[96]

State aid for regional development addresses an equity objective: it furthers economic cohesion by reducing the development gap between the disadvantaged and the wealthier regions in the EU.

In the EU, overall regional aid expenditure over the period 2007–2011 was approximately €67.4 billion. State aid expenditure for regional development however varies considerably between Member States as not all have the same budgetary capacity to support their domestic economic activity. Five Member States accounted for approximately 77 per cent of that total amount. For example, France and Germany granted €3.3 billion and €3.6 billion of regional aid in 2011 respectively, while seven Member States[97] each granted less than €30 million of regional aid in the same year. Most of that aid was investment aid (Figure 4.3).[98]

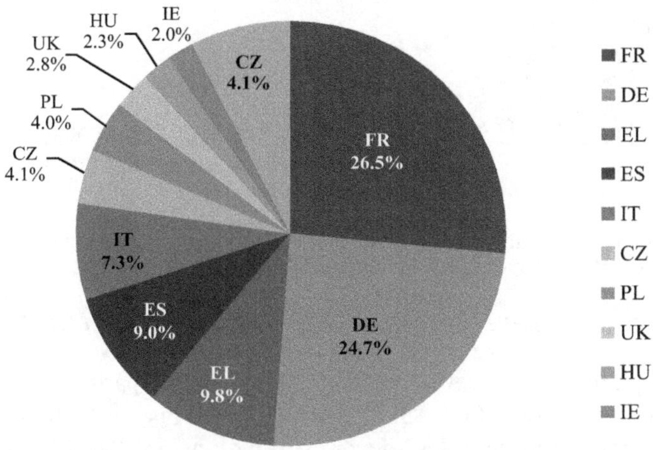

Source: European Commission, Impact Assessment accompanying the document Guidelines on Regional State Aid 2014–2020, p. 24.

Figure 4.3 Regional state aid expenditure per Member State, 2007–11

---

[96] Manzella/Mendez, Report working paper: The turning point of EU cohesion policy, 7.

[97] Bulgaria, Denmark, Estonia, Cyprus, Latvia, Malta, the Netherlands.

[98] Figures from: European Commission, Impact Assessment accompanying the document Guidelines on Regional state Aid 2014-2020, document not dated, p. 26. http://ec.europa.eu/competition/state_aid/regional_aid/impact_assessment_report_en.pdf, Date 7.7.2016.

When looking at expenditure as a percentage of GDP, the discrepancy becomes more obvious: regional development is obviously a lighter burden for rich Member States (Germany, the UK and France) than for the less rich ones, Figure 4.4.

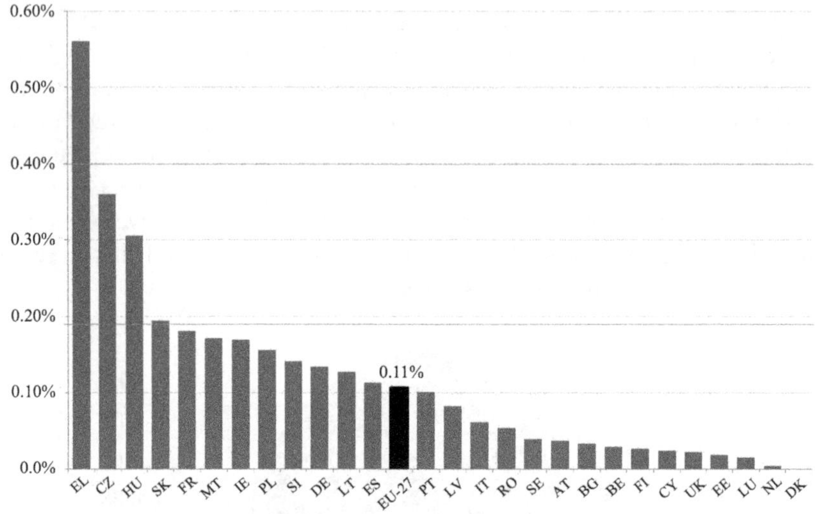

Source: European Commission, Impact Assessment accompanying the document Guidelines on Regional State Aid 2014–2020, p. 106.

Figure 4.4 Regional state aid expenditure as percentage of GDP

Massive public aid however could not wipe out disparities. On the one hand, in the period 2007–13, disparities in terms of GDP per capita between developed and less-developed regions in the EU narrowed, apparently due not to a decrease in GDP levels in the most-developed Member States but to an increase in the less-developed Member States.[99] On the other hand, though, the economic crisis continued to have a strong asymmetric impact on regional labour markets in the EU in 2011. Overall, large disparities in regional unemployment and employment rates persist between the EU's regions.[100]

---

[99] European Commission, Impact Assessment accompanying the document 'Guidelines on Regional State Aid 2014–2020', 14.

[100] Bartsch/Scirankova, Large differences in regional labour markets show asymmetric impact of the economic crisis, Eurostat, 2012.

The following discussion will focus on regional subsidy races and their potential to create or maintain market power.

Pursuant to Article 4(2)c TFEU, economic, social and territorial cohesion is an area of competences shared between the EU and its Member States. Hence, both the supranational and the national level may adopt binding legislation in that area. Cohesion, and in particular reducing disparities between the levels of development of the various regions in the EU, is the groundwork of the EU's 'overall harmonious development', Article 174 TFEU. EU state aid rules, which among others also exempt regional aid from the general prohibition of state aid if such aid is in the common interest, implies that Member States have a wide margin of autonomy in promoting less-developed regions.

In 1971, the EU – then still the 'European Economic Community (EEC)' – became aware of the issue of subsidy races: it concluded that the risk of regional subsidy races called for immediate coordination measures to limit such risk. The Community adopted, for the first time, regional aid ceilings.[101]

Cohesion policy in the EU developed at a time when the EEC started paying more attention to state intervention in the market:

> At an abstract level, the role of Cohesion policy must be seen within the context of a much broader debate concerning the relationship between the state and the market, with Cohesion policy representing an example of so-called 'regulated capitalism' through its role in redistributing resources,

---

101

> Considérant que les aides à finalité régionale, lorsqu'elles sont adéquates et judicieusement appliquées, constituent un des instruments indispensables du développement régional et permettent aux États membres de mener une politique régionale visant à une croissance plus équilibrée entre les différentes régions d'un même pays et de la Communauté; *constatant que les risques de surenchères, qui existent en matière d'aides à finalité régionale, exigent la mise au point, sans plus attendre, d'une première série de mesures de coordination destinées à limiter ces risques*; ayant pris connaissance de la communication de la Commission, du 23 juin 1971, concernant la coordination des régimes généraux d'aides à finalité regionale; prennent dès lors l'engagement de se conformer, en matière de régimes d'aides à finalité régionale, selon les modalités d'application jointes en annexe à la présente résolution, aux principes suivants: max aid intensities.

Council Conclusion of 20.10.1971, OJ EU 1971 C 11/1, emphasis provided.

pursuing social-market economy priorities and shaping partnerships among public, private and societal actors.[102]

4.6.2.2 EU state aid rules in the area of regional development – incentive effect and location effect

State aid rules for regional aid are set out in the EU's Guidelines on Regional State Aid for the period 2014–20.[103] Point 3 of these Guidelines points out the objective of EU state aid control in that area:

> The primary objective of state aid control in the field of regional aid is to allow aid for regional development while ensuring a level playing field between Member States, in particular by preventing subsidy races that may occur when they try to attract or retain businesses in disadvantaged areas of the Union, and to limit the effects of regional aid on trade and competition to the minimum necessary.

FURTHER READING – REGIONAL DEVELOPMENT POLICY IN THE EU AND STATE AID FOR REGIONAL DEVELOPMENT

A regional aid map defines the regions of a Member State eligible for national regional investment aid under EU state aid rules and establishes the maximum aid levels for companies in the eligible regions. In 2014, the European Commission adopted the maps for the period 2014–2020.

Maps 2014–2017: http://ec.europa.eu/competition/state_aid/regional_aid/regional_aid_2014_2017.pdf.

Maps 2018–2020: http://ec.europa.eu/competition/state_aid/regional_aid/regional_aid_2018_2020.pdf.

The Regional Aid Guidelines 2014–20 set out the conditions under which EU Member States can grant state aid to businesses for regional development purposes in the regions specified in the maps. http://eur-lex.europa.eu/LexUriServ/LexUriServ.do?uri=OJ:C:2013:209:0001:0045:EN:PDF.

Regional aid policy in the EU was born out of mistrust in 'the virtues of the invisible hand'. Hence, the spirit of regional aid rules is to limit the effects of a liberal approach to national public funding. The inspiration came in the late 1980s, when Jacques Delors, at that time the President of the European Commission, said:

[102] Manzella/Mendez, The turning points of EU cohesion policy, Working Paper Report to Barca Report, 2009, 24, with further references.

[103] OJ EU 2013 C 209/1.

> In the case of structural measures, there were respectable arguments for either of two concepts of what the Community should be doing. The first of these, a purely macroeconomic concept, relies on the virtues of the invisible hand operating through financial flows; as long as they are on a large enough scale, transfers of resources between Member States should bring about economic convergence. The second, both microeconomic and structural, looks to speed up the spread of innovation, eliminate bottlenecks and encourage efforts to derive the benefits of scale. In other words, it is a matter of keeping structural policies 'close to the ground'. Encouraged by the success of the integrated Mediterranean programmes, the Commission came down in favour of the latter, a less extravagant and more effective course.[104]

Despite the praiseworthy intention to not fully rely on assumed trickle-down effects, one issue remains, namely the danger of subsidy races: in the EU, it is Member States and their regions that are in control of state aid for regional development. They use EU and own funds and are at liberty to use them in the form of investment aid to achieve common EU development goals, e.g. employment, innovation or business competitiveness in a specific region. Hence, one region wins, another one loses. The dilemma of regional aid is epitomised in the Guidelines on Regional state aid:

> The geographical specificity of regional aid distinguishes it from other forms of horizontal aid. It is a particular characteristic of regional aid that it is intended to influence the choice made by investors about where to locate investment projects. When regional aid off-sets the additional costs stemming from the regional handicaps and supports additional investment in assisted areas without attracting it away from other assisted areas, it contributes not only to the development of the region, but also to cohesion and ultimately benefits the whole Union. With regard to the potential negative location effects of regional aid, these are already limited to a certain degree by regional aid maps, which define exhaustively the areas where regional aid may be granted, taking account of the equity and cohesion policy objectives, and the maximum permissible aid intensities. However, an understanding of what would have happened in the absence of the aid remains important to appraise the actual impact of the aid in the cohesion objective.[105]

For this discussion, two points are central: first, the incentive effect that is necessary to induce additional private investment in less-developed

[104] Address by Jacques Delors to the European Parliament on 18.02.1987, Bulletin of the European Communities Supplement 1/87, 18.02.1987, No 2-348, 94–102. Quoted and discussed in Manzella/Mendez, The turning points of EU cohesion policy, Working Paper Report to Barca Report, 2009, emphasis added.

[105] Point 117 of the Guidelines.

areas, i.e. the areas identified in the EU's regional aid maps; second, the location effect that must be controlled so as to avoid that the relocation of economic activities to an underdeveloped region does not entail budgetary costs and economic costs that cannot be outweighed by socio-economic benefits in terms of cohesion and welfare. In that case, the recipient of the aid is the only winner.

4.6.2.3 State aid for investments in less developed regions – focus on incentive effect and positive location effects

The common state aid assessment principles also apply to investment aid with a regional development objective, however adapted to the specific cohesion objective of such aid. The following clause of the EU's Regional Aid Guidelines highlights the particular rationale of regional development aid: 'Furthermore, where markets provide efficient outcomes but these are deemed unsatisfactory from an equity or cohesion point of view, state aid may be used to obtain a more desirable, equitable market outcome.'[106] In order to achieve '*overall harmonious development*' (Art. 174 of the TFEU) in a union of nation states, the desired outcome has to be defined at the supranational level. This is achieved, first, by a coherent EU-wide regional-development policy; secondly by 'regional aid maps' that specify the EU's regions where industry may benefit from regional-development aid, and that specify the aid levels corresponding to development levels; thirdly by rules that are applicable to regional state aid and thus prevent undue damage to the internal market.

Contrary to state aid for R&D&I, state aid for regional development is not linked to overcoming an efficiency problem. Rather, a subsidised equitable outcome, and thus the redistribution of wealth, is more desirable than efficient markets:

> Where markets provide efficient outcomes but these are deemed unsatisfactory from an equity or cohesion point of view, state aid may be used to obtain a more desirable, equitable market outcome.[107]

The European Commission however does not analyse the market's failure to produce equitable outcomes in each individual case where a Member State wants to grant regional development aid. Rather, the following non-rebuttable assumption applies: the market is not delivering the expected cohesion objectives if the aid is granted for the development of

106 Point 48 of the Regional Aid Guidelines.
107 Ibid.

areas that are included in the EU's 'Regional Aid Map' and is in accordance with the other conditions of the Regional Aid Guidelines. The transparent process of establishing regional aid maps and reviewing them for each new 'funding period' (the current one running from 2014 until 2020 inclusive), together with the legal assumption that the market fails to promote the development of the regions identified in the map, are good regulation in the sense that they prevent a fragmented and cumbersome case-by-case assessment of whether the aid is needed to address a market failure.

How do the EU's Regional Aid Guidelines go about checking if regional investment aid has an incentive effect? They link the indispensable incentive effect of the aid to its capability to either trigger an investment in an underdeveloped region or locate it there rather than in a more developed region. To this end, two alternative scenarios are considered:

In scenario 1, the investment would not be made anywhere in the EU without the aid, because it would not be profitable enough:

> (1) the aid gives an incentive to adopt a positive investment decision because an investment that would otherwise not be sufficiently profitable for the beneficiary can take place in the area concerned (35) (scenario 1, investment decision);[108] or

In scenario 2, the investment would be made in more developed regions without the aid:

> (2) the aid gives an incentive to opt to locate a planned investment in the relevant area rather than elsewhere because it compensates for the net disadvantages and costs linked to a location in the area concerned (scenario 2, location decision).[109]

The incentive effect check is based on documentation that a market operator would in all probability use for making an investment decision in each of the two scenarios.

In scenario 1:

> The Member State could prove the existence of the incentive effect of the aid by providing company documents that show that the investment would not be sufficiently profitable without the aid.[110]

---

108 Point 61 a), ibid.
109 Point 61 b), ibid.
110 Point 70, ibid.

In scenario 2:

> The Member State could prove the incentive effect of the aid by providing company documents showing that a comparison has been made between the costs and benefits of locating in the area concerned and those in alternative area(s). The Commission verifies whether such comparisons have a realistic basis.[111]

The ability of supranational supervisors to differentiate between 'realistic' and 'unrealistic' is vital: in particular, large enterprises are less exposed to market failures than small ones. At the same time, they may have significant bargaining power vis-à-vis regional administrations. Moreover, they have the resources to establish profitability forecasts and risk assessments that are tailor-made for compliance with the requirements of EU state aid rules as regards market failure, incentive effect etc. The higher the perceived value of the investment for the regional economy, e.g. in terms of jobs, the higher is the bargaining power of a large would-be aid beneficiary.

The issue lies where state aid is not necessary to promote regional development: firms may locate investments in a less-developed region even without state aid because in that region they would anyway benefit from lower production costs, skilled labour, proximity of raw materials, availability of specific infrastructure, access to new technology, pre-existing own production facilities, or easier access to new markets.

In that respect, EU state aid control seems to be not quite as effective as intended, in particular concerning regional state aid that is below the threshold beyond which the Commission carries out a more detailed case-by-case assessment: a study of 28 investment projects in seven EU Member States showed that:

> there was no evidence of cases where the incentive effects of aid on the investment or location decisions were systematically assessed as part of the ex-ante process carried out by the granting authorities. The obligation for the investors to prove that regional aid was necessary for their investments appeared largely to be dealt with as a matter of formality.[112]

The Commission itself found that in state aid case practice under regional state aid rules 2007–13:

---

111 Point 71, ibid.

112 Ramboll, Ex post evaluation of the Regional Aid Guidelines 2007-2013: final report, Report commissioned by the European Commission, 3.

> although the formal incentive-effect requirements were respected, the incentive effect of regional aid was doubtful especially in case of very small aid amounts granted on an ad-hoc basis but also when it was granted to extend an existing establishment because many of these investments were not mobile in light of higher costs to build a new establishment in a different location.[113]

Given that cohesion is a priority, damage through lacking incentive effects and negative location effects can only be limited by a rather crude instrument – the limitation of aid to projects that – more or less safely – can be presumed to bring about positive effects despite the strong bargaining power of industry: investment aid to large enterprises in less-developed areas will only be allowed for investments that bring *new* economic activity, for *initial investments for the diversification of existing establishments into new products or for new process innovation.* The assumption is that investments in new activities are more likely to be induced by the aid than investments in existing operations:

> Since regional aid to large undertakings for their investments is unlikely to have an incentive effect, it cannot be regarded to be compatible with the internal market under Article 107(3) c) of the Treaty, unless it is granted for initial investments that create new economic activities in these areas, or for the diversification of existing establishments into new products or new process innovations.[114]

Only in certain, least developed regions, state aid rules allow aid for other types of investments.

Regional aid produces specific distortive effects:

> Two main potential distortions of competition and trade may be caused by regional aid. These are product market distortions and location effects. Both types may lead to allocative inefficiencies (undermining the economic performance of the internal market) and to distributional concerns (distribution of economic activity across regions).[115]

Location effects and the incentive effect are two sides of the same coin:

> With regard to the potential negative location effects of regional aid, these are already limited to a certain degree by regional aid maps, which define exhaustively the areas where regional aid may be granted, taking account of the equity and cohesion policy objectives, and the maximum permissible aid

---

113 European Commission, Impact Assessment accompanying the document Guidelines on Regional state Aid 2014–20, 32.

114 Point 15 of the Regional Aid Guidelines.

115 Point 113, ibid.

> intensities. However, an understanding of what would have happened in the absence of the aid remains important to appraise the actual impact of the aid in the cohesion objective.[116]

Part of the location issue is thus resolved by a positive, yet crude assumption: the fact that the European Commission had already defined certain regions as underdeveloped, so that industry may receive investment aid there, and under certain conditions even operating aid, is sufficient to limit negative location effects 'to a certain degree', in particular because maximum aid intensities, i.e. the percentage of eligible costs that may be defrayed by the aid, have been fixed for those areas. However, when adopting the Regional Aid Guidelines in 2013, the Commission must have known that 'case studies that had the lowest aid intensities are also those that appeared to show the lowest overall incentive effect'.[117]

An attempt to solve the location problem is made in the last sentence of the above-cited provision: 'However, an understanding of what would have happened in the absence of the aid remains important to appraise the actual impact of the aid in the cohesion objective.' The issue is that an 'understanding of what would have happened in the absence of the aid' implicitly refers back to the issue of business plans, company-internal decision making and the bargaining power of the would-be aid beneficiary. Therefore, despite the regulator's efforts to ascertain the necessity of aid and tackle the relocation issue, industry together with the winning regions have an entry point when it comes to dividing the cake in their favour.

The credibility of the 'counterfactual scenarios', and in particular of the documents produced by Member States and industry to convince the European Commission to approve regional investment aid, is put to the test in situations where obvious negative location effects would create windfall effects and stronger market power for the aid beneficiary. This is the case where, without aid, the investment would have been located in an even less-developed region, or where the aid would induce the beneficiary to close down the same or a similar activity in another area and relocate to the target area. In those scenarios, 'regional development aid' would become mere 'relocation aid', the negative effects of which presumably do not outbalance any positive effects on the region to where the investment is relocated.

---

116 Point 117, ibid.
117 Ramboll (n. 113), 144.

Mobility is a specific facet of bargaining power: mobile investors may threaten to relocate outside the EU in the absence of aid. While EU state aid rules aim at preventing intra-EU subsidy races, the approach is quite different as regards global competition. In situations where a would-be beneficiary alleges that without aid, it would locate the investment outside the European Economic Area, no negative location effects are presumed as long as the aid is proportional, which it must be anyway.

If the counterfactual analysis suggests that without the aid the investment would have gone ahead in another location (scenario 2) which belongs to the same geographical market considering the product concerned, and if the aid is proportional, possible outcomes in terms of overcapacity or substantial market power would in principle be the same regardless of the aid. In such cases, the positive effects of the aid are likely to outweigh the limited negative effects on competition.

In essence, this clause allows aid in response to a threat to move operations outside the EU resp. the European Economic Area. Either, investors who rely on such *threat scenario* to obtain aid are indeed mobile enough to relocate, in which case they may well relocate later, soon after the mandatory period of retention of the aided investment in the region has expired. Or the counterfactual applies, namely that it may be 'proved' that the alternative to relocate outside the EU is quite hypothetical and had rather been produced for the EU's aid assessment procedure. The last case is quite likely, given the non-transparent subsidies regimes of certain non-EU countries. In either case, the region loses, the beneficiary wins.

4.6.2.4 Intermediate conclusion

Regional development depends on two critical incentives: the political incentive for the *state* to induce private investment in underdeveloped regions; the economic incentive for *industry* to move or to keep operations where the investment generates the highest return. The stronger the positive effect on the region in terms of jobs, clustering effects etc., the stronger the incentive to offer more aid. Industry, in turn, will take the aid promise into account, together with a host of other location factors, when choosing the most profitable location for its investment. Consequently, ascertaining whether the lure of aid or the region's endogenous location factors were decisive to move or maintain operations is extremely difficult. This is all the more valid in cases where large enterprises have considerable bargaining power vis-à-vis regional or local authorities.

Persistent disparities undermine the acceptance of the European ideal – peace, humanist values and the well-being of its peoples. Reducing disparities strengthens solidarity and harmonious development. State aid for regional development, amongst other policy instruments, can help reduce disparities at acceptable social cost if it has an incentive effect and does not merely relocate mobile investments to the winner of a subsidy race. State aid regulation thereby has a vocation that transcends the mission to enhance market efficiency. After all, even a very efficient internal market could produce living conditions that are intolerably unfair and unequal. If state aid effectively helps to redistribute wealth, by locating investments and jobs to less-favoured regions, it comes in as an antidote to extreme nationalism which only arises where peoples rally around leaders who promise easy national fixes to global issues.

In the EU, intelligent regulation has replaced the liberal approach to national regional investment aid and its philosophy of trickle-down effects on overall cohesion: the 'mapping' of underdeveloped regions, the setting of permitted aid levels for investment aid in those regions, the setting of assessment standards that exclude cross-border relocations and that counterbalance the bargaining power of industry can only be achieved by an honest 'supra-regional' broker.

This is the only way to effectively avoid one region winning and another one losing to the detriment of solidarity. Nevertheless, there is a price to pay: competition policy must accept that in order to promote cohesion, the conditions to limit the distortive effects of regional aid cannot be as strict as for aid that pursues an efficiency objective, e.g. R&D&I-aid. That price is not too high: after all, 'efficiency' is subordinate to the EU's fundamental social objectives. Certainly, the economic and monetary policy of EU Member States must be guided by efficiency considerations: Article 120 TFEU demands that:

> Member States shall conduct their economic policies with a view to contributing to the achievement of the objectives of the Union [...]. The Member States and the Union shall act in accordance with the principle of an open market economy with free competition, *favouring an efficient allocation of resources* (emphasis added).

Nevertheless, efficient resource allocation is a mere tool to achieve overarching social goals. These are described in Article 3 TFEU. There, one goal is 'a highly competitive social market economy, aiming at full employment and social progress'. The other goal is 'economic, social and territorial cohesion, and solidarity among Member States'.

4.7 CONCLUSION – REGULATING STATE INTERVENTION AND THE CAUSE FOR PUBLIC EXPLOITATION

In this chapter, we discussed forms of state intervention that may be politically justifiable but that may also result in unfair redistribution of resources. The public cause of exploitation can be found in multiple situations: in state investments, in state services or in state incentives to promote technologies or relocate investments.

State intervention in the market classically responds to cross-border challenges – it is a form of protectionism – but it also generates cross-border effects.

In order to establish a functioning social market economy in an internal market that is vast and is shared by a number of sovereign nation states, supranational regulation must formulate 'objectives in the common interest' and apply principles to assess the potential of state intervention to achieve those objectives. This is the only solution to solve the tension between purely national political justifications for state interventions on one hand and social welfare in the entire political union on the other hand.

Supranational regulation must be the 'honest broker' who keeps in check any abuse of the concept of the 'general economic interest' or the 'market economy investor principle' and who is in a position to foil subsidy races. It has made hidden advantages for public enterprises more transparent and is balancing particular interest against general interest in situations where the national judgement may be biased.

Still, some key concepts need adjustment: for example, the concept of 'rational public investor' should be developed in order to avoid overly hypothetic and long-winding assessment procedures. Also, the tension between the national prerogative to define 'services in the general economic interest' on the one hand and the supranational prerogative to 'check for manifest errors' on the other must be resolved.

5. The art of steering public resources towards the common interest – the supranational approach

In this chapter, we will look at EU state aid law and public procurement law and discuss what the supranational legislator can do to bring together specific – or short-term – industrial policy goals with the long-term objective of establishing an internal market that functions sustainably. Both state aid to industry and public procurement are forms of interventions that could combat market failures, which prevent sustainable and efficient solutions. Nevertheless, they could also distort competition, thereby torpedoing the internal market from within, and going against fundamental policy goals, which, as an ultimate purpose, are there to preserve wealth for future generations.

5.1 OBJECTIVES IN THE COMMON EUROPEAN INTEREST

5.1.1 Why Competition Regulation of Public Resources?

Homo politicus does not exclusively act in a political setting of power optimisation. More importantly, the political agent spends taxpayers' – not his own – money when intervening in the market. We have already discussed in Chapter 4 that government agents do not face the same behavioural restraints or substantial personal risks as private-economy operators do. They rather depend on party-backed parliamentary control and majority votes. Yet, such backing and control is not necessarily inspired by a market rationale. This allows them to make major 'investments', without considering the same return prospects as the private sector would, or to pick 'winners' and subsidise them. Even worse, political *megalomania* may sink an investment just to create a monument to the decision maker himself. This is abuse of public capital.

Of course, public market interventions may be necessary e.g. to provide infrastructures and services of general economic interest, or to create incentives where the market alone would not deliver a desired outcome. Unwise allocation of public monies, however, can do immense harm: it can crowd out private investment, distort private incentives, help foreclosing markets and, in any case, withhold scarce funds from those who need them most. The abuse of public capital thus undermines sustainability and inclusiveness, the very values the state should protect. Examples of the abuse of public funds abound, ranging from idle airports in the middle of nowhere and FIFA-standard mega stadiums where only third-league teams play, to operating aid to ailing industries that are plagued by overcapacity. Therefore, regulation of state aid and public procurement is just as essential for justice, sustainability and inclusiveness as regulation against the abuse of market dominance by private capital.

However, the supranational legislator is not entirely free to prevent the abuse of national public resources. He is limited by the principle of conferral: the Union shall act only within the limits of the competences conferred upon it by the Member States in the Treaties to attain the objectives set out therein, all other competences remaining with the Member States (Art. 5 TEU). The Member States – and they alone – confer on the Union parts of their sovereign powers with regard to public expenditure and budgets. There is only one Union objective which justifies supranational regulation to counter the abuse of public resources: the creation of an internal market. According to Article 26(1) TFEU (Treaty on the Functioning of the European Union), 'The Union shall adopt measures with the aim of establishing or ensuring the functioning of the internal market.'

What is the regulatory and economic model that makes the internal market generate sustainable welfare? Preserving wealth over generations requires a sustainable model instead of chasing short-term gain. This is true both for households and nations and also for leagues of nations that are committed to establishing an internal market without frontiers and making it function. In the grand design of economic policy, limiting the urge to seek short-term gain and promoting the responsible use of human and natural resources requires regulation.

In the EU's internal market – 'an area without internal frontiers' (Art. 26(2) TFEU) – growth is created by two complementary drivers: freedom and competition. The four fundamental freedoms – the free movement of goods, persons, services and capital – facilitate the efficient use of production factors. Effective competition drives quality, choice, innovation and global competitiveness. The Social Market Economy is the model that brings together growth factors and sustainability: It implies that, where necessary, regulation should harness competition to achieve social welfare and to prevent distortions of competition. That is why the EU is committed to the Social Market Economy to bring about internal market outcomes:

> The Union shall establish an internal market. It shall work for the sustainable development of Europe based on balanced economic growth and price stability, a highly competitive social market economy, aiming at full employment and social progress, and a high level of protection and improvement of the quality of the environment. It shall promote scientific and technological advance. (Art. 3(3) TEU)

This implies that apart from regulation to create a single market without national borders, and from competition policy that eliminates distortions of that market, another ingredient is indispensable: public intervention (i.e. regulation) in the pursuit of sustainable internal market outcomes. Such intervention, in particular state aid as its most distortive form, must be precisely targeted at social-welfare objectives. In the EU, that steering function has been conferred to the Union; the European Commission monitors EU state aid and public procurement rules.

What kind of competition is being regulated here? In particular, does the enforcement of state aid law protect fair competition between undertakings, as antitrust law does, or rather competition between Member States, the latter being the competition for investments and economic activities? The answer is: '*Both*'. However, both objectives are rather difficult to reconcile in practice.

For instance, state financing for the construction of a new airport runway is not a mere provision of infrastructure outside a market environment. Rather, it is 'state aid' and thus only permitted if in line with EU state aid rules – because operating the airport runway constitutes an 'economic activity' that is inseparable from its construction.[1] Whereas state support for the construction of an airport runway might distort upstream infrastructure competition between Member States or regions of Member States, it is more likely to enhance downstream competition between airline undertakings. The CJEU and the Commission prefer to submit such delicate assessments of state financing of airports to EU state aid control in order to strike a fair balance between infrastructure competition and competition between airlines under the compatibility test according to Article 107(3) TFEU.

---

[1] ECJ, judgment of 19.12.2012, C-288/11 P – *Mitteldeutsche Flughafen and Flughafen Leipzig-Halle GmbH*.

FURTHER READING

EU Guidelines on State aid to airports and airlines (2014/C 99/03)
http://eur-lex.europa.eu/ → Document 52014XC0404(01).

In order to cope with these delicate impact assessments of state aid effects, the Commission's regulatory tool kit has adopted specific techniques from antitrust law enforcement such as a 'refined economic approach'. At the same time the Commission has developed a pragmatic policy under the heading 'State Aid Modernisation' that introduces common assessment principles, most importantly for the assessment of the economic impact of state aid and that focuses state aid control on cases with the strongest distortive effects on competition.

5.1.2 State Aid Modernisation in the EU

Between 2012 and 2014, the EU modernised most of its state aid rules. The aim was threefold: first, to steer state aid more effectively towards the EU's growth and competitiveness priorities; secondly, to focus enforcement on aid with the biggest impact on the internal market; and thirdly, to streamline state aid rules.[2] The rationale behind that effort was that state aid control can help to improve the quality of public spending and thereby fix market failures. Overall, the EU's state aid modernisation project was proclaimed as an effective contribution to the EU's growth policy in a world that was shaken by the economic and financial crisis.

The steering and streamlining becomes visible when looking at the common assessment principles that the European Commission developed in the state aid modernisation process. We have already discussed these principles albeit briefly in Chapter 4, when looking into ways to avoid undue strengthening of market power through research and innovation aid. Since the state aid modernisation, the assessment of aid, on the basis of Article 107(3) TFEU, is following a largely uniform pattern. This can be exemplified by the EU Guidelines on state aid for environmental protection and energy 2014–20 (2014/C 200/01):

---

[2] Communication from the Commission, 'EU State Aid Modernisation (SAM)', COM (2012) 209 final, 08.05.2012.

3.1 Common assessment principles

(26) To assess whether a notified aid measure can be considered compatible with the internal market, the Commission generally analyses whether the design of the aid measure ensures that the positive impact of the aid towards an objective of common interest exceeds its potential negative effects on trade and competition.

(27) The Communication on State aid modernisation of 8 May 2012 called for the identification and definition of common principles applicable to the assessment of compatibility of all aid measures carried out by the Commission. For that purpose, the Commission will consider a State aid measure compatible with the internal market only if it satisfies each of the following criteria:

(a) contribution to a well-defined objective of common interest: a State aid measure aims at an objective of common interest in accordance with Article 107(3) of the Treaty;

(b) need for State intervention: the State aid measure is targeted towards a situation where aid can bring about a material improvement that the market alone cannot deliver, for example by remedying a well-defined market failure;

(c) appropriateness of the aid measure: the proposed aid measure is an appropriate policy instrument to address the objective of common interest;

(d) incentive effect: the aid changes the behaviour of the undertaking(s) concerned in such a way that it engages in additional activity which it would not carry out without the aid or which it would carry out in a restricted or different manner;

(e) proportionality of the aid (aid kept to the minimum): the aid amount is limited to the minimum needed to incentivise the additional investment or activity in the area concerned;

(f) avoidance of undue negative effects on competition and trade between Member States: the negative effects of aid are sufficiently limited, so that the overall balance of the measure is positive;

(g) transparency of aid: Member States, the Commission, economic operators, and the public, have easy access to all relevant acts and to pertinent information about the aid awarded thereunder.[3]

---

[3] Section 3.1 of the Guidelines on State aid for environmental protection and energy 2014–20.

> **FURTHER READING**
>
> EU Guidelines on State aid for environmental protection and energy 2014-2020 (2014/C 200/01)
>
> http://eur-lex.europa.eu/ Document 52014XC0628(01).
>
> Impact assessment: http://ec.europa.eu/smart-regulation/impact/ia_carried_out/docs/ia_2014/swd_2014_0139_en.pdf.
>
> Summary of Impact Assessment: http://ec.europa.eu/smart-regulation/impact/ia_carried_out/docs/ia_2014/swd_2014_0140_en.pdf.
>
> Public consultation and responses: http://ec.europa.eu/competition/consultations/2013_state_aid_environment/index_en.html.

In each modernised legal text, such as the above-cited Guidelines on State aid for environmental protection and energy 2014–20, those quite generic principles are then translated into specific conditions that develop the desired steering effect. In the field of environmental protection and energy, state aid is in essence being steered towards projects where:

- the objective is a higher level of environmental protection compared to the level that would be achieved in the absence of the aid;
- the aid will remedy market failures which hamper an increased level of environmental protection or a well-functioning secure, affordable and sustainable internal energy market, e.g. where part of the benefit from an investment will accrue to market participants other than the investor, which will lead undertakings to underinvest (positive externalities). This may occur for instance with investments in eco-innovation, system stability, new and innovative renewable technologies and innovative demand-response measures or in cases of energy infrastructures or generation adequacy measures that benefit many Member States (or a wider number of consumers);
- where the state aid is a more appropriate policy instrument compared to other forms of intervention, such as regulation and market-based instruments or 'soft instruments' (e.g. voluntary eco-labels, and the diffusion of environmentally friendly technologies can also improve environmental protection);
- the 'polluter-pays-principle' is not thwarted by state aid to the polluter;
- the aid is limited to the net extra cost necessary to meet the objective, economic benefits of the investment (e.g. energy saving) taken into account;

- the negative effects of aid are limited: in particular, the aid must not lead to a situation where more efficient or innovative competitors with perhaps a different, possibly even cleaner technology that would otherwise be able to enter and expand are unable to do so; this may run counter to environmental-protection objectives as interference with the competitive entry and exit process may stifle innovation and slow down industry-wide productivity improvements;
- a level of transparency is sustained: Member States must publish, amongst others, the aid schemes or the individual aid granting decisions and implementing provisions, the identity of the granting authorities and the beneficiaries, the form and amount of aid, the principal economic sector in which the beneficiary is active.[4]

The fact that the European Commission made an impact assessment and consulted stakeholders prior to revising state aid rules shows that a serious effort was made to make the steering effect real.

FURTHER READING

Impact assessment: http://ec.europa.eu/smart-regulation/impact/ia_carried_out/docs/ia_2014/swd_2014_0139_en.pdf.

Summary of Impact Assessment: http://ec.europa.eu/smart-regulation/impact/ia_carried_out/docs/ia_2014/swd_2014_0140_en.pdf.

Public consultation and responses: http://ec.europa.eu/competition/consultations/2013_state_aid_environment/index_en.html.

Despite the scope and ambition of the state aid modernisation, the EU has not yet met all challenges. In the following, we will illustrate this with the examples of aid for risk finance investments in small start-up enterprises and for the maritime transport sector.

In the core industrial policy field of risk finance investments in small- and medium-sized enterprises (SMEs), the streamlining objective was not achieved. Although access to financing for SMEs has always been close to the heart of EU industrial policy makers, 'modernised' rules on state aid to promote risk finance investments in SMEs are overly complex. Such complexity might prevent aid granting authorities from providing financing where it is legal and desirable, simply because they shy away

[4] The detailed conditions set out in Section 3.2 ibid.

from inadvertently granting illegal aid or lengthy assessment procedures. Indeed, since the entry into force of the current state aid rules on SME risk finance aid, the Commission has only approved one single measure.[5] The absence of any negative decisions in that area indicates that apart from that single case, there were no other risk finance measures which the Member States had planned, but were not allowed to implement. Hence, risk-finance aid seems to be relegated to cases that do not need prior Commission approval and which are capped at € 15 million per firm.

FURTHER READING

Guidelines on State aid to promote risk finance investments, OJ 2014 C 19/4, http:.eur-lex.europa.eu/legal-content/EN/TXT/HTML/?uri=CELEX:52014XC0122(04)&from=EN.

Up to certain limits, SME risk financing aid may also be granted without prior Commission approval, in accordance with the General Block Exemption Regulation, OJ 2014 L 187/1, http://eur-lex.europa.eu/legal-content/EN/TXT/?uri=uriserv:OJ.L_.2014.187.01.0001.01.ENG&toc=OJ:L:2014:187:FULL.

In the state aid modernisation process, both substance and structure of risk finance aid rules have undergone profound changes. For example, the new rules in that field allow much higher aid amounts than the previous rules. Applicable assessment principles have however become more restrictive, and assessment criteria are far more complex and enter in far greater technical detail than the previous rules.

With the objective of keeping the EU's shipping industry competitive on the global market, the Maritime Aid Guidelines[6] allow, under certain conditions, the favourable taxation of income from *maritime transport* of passengers or freight. These Guidelines date back to 2004 and thus far have been spared a revision. Today, these rules do not any longer ensure that aid is effectively targeted at an objective in the common interest.

---

[5] Commission decision of 05.11.2015, State aid SA.41265 – France, Dispositif ISF PME pour les investissements dans des FCPI et FIP, http://ec.europa.eu/competition/elojade/isef/case_details.cfm?proc_code=3_SA_41265, 06.07.2016.

[6] Commission communication, Community guidelines on State aid to maritime transport, OJ EU 2004 C 13/03, 3.

FURTHER READING

The Community guidelines on State aid to maritime transport, OJ 2004 C 013/3, http://eur-lex.europa.eu/legal-content/EN/TXT/HTML/?uri=CELEX:52004XC0117(01)&from=EN.

The current guidelines are in force since 17 January 2004 and have not been amended since.

They allow aid that counters the trend to use 'flags of convenience', that is the flags of certain third countries where taxes are friendlier, crews are cheaper, safety is laxer, and where the environment is less of a concern. Among the aid instruments permitted by the Guidelines, the one with the greatest impact is 'tonnage taxation': that fiscal aid measure allows shipowners to pay tax for a notional profit that is based on ship tonnage operated, as an alternative to standard corporate taxation that is based on actual profits. Tonnage tax is usually more favourable than standard corporate tax. The beneficiaries are ship-owning companies, but only to the extent their ships carry out *'maritime transport'*, that is the transport of goods and persons by sea.

The current Guidelines are vague, do not at all correspond to the above-mentioned common assessment principles (see above 5.1.2.) and do not contain definitions of some key legal terms. For example, the Guidelines stipulate that only '*maritime transport*' activities, i.e. the 'transport of goods and persons by sea', are eligible for aid. As an overall eligibility criterion, this is certainly adequate, but alas, reality is more complex than that. Certain shipping activities other than classic cargo or passenger services are of a dual nature, for instance off-shore service, cable-laying, pipeline laying, research or exploration vessels. They certainly comprise a 'transport' element, but the main activity is not 'transport' in the strict sense. On the one hand, the promotion of such shipping should be in the interest of the EU as such vessels are exposed to global competition. On the other hand, there is legal uncertainty about whether these activities fit under the rather vague legal definition of '*maritime transport*'. Therefore, the eligibility of an entire shipping sector for state aid is not regulated by the Guidelines. Thus far, the Commission applied the Guidelines by analogy on a case-by-case basis where a Member State intended to include such vessels.

This has two principal consequences: first, partially inconsistent and even contradictory decision practice and thus legal uncertainty; and second, the award of aid that is not in line with common EU objectives.

The cases of favourable tax treatment of the shipping sector in two seafaring EU Member States exemplify this problem: Malta's system does not only apply to income from maritime transport, which is the legitimate state aid objective, but also to fishing vessels, yachts, oil rigs, shipowners without any shipping activity of their own, i.e. pure lessors and financial institutions providing loans and guarantees to shipowners, operators or managers. In 2012, the EU found that 'this seems neither justified from a competition perspective, nor appropriate in times of high budgetary constraints.'[7] When this book was written, the European Commission had still not decided in the matter. The impact of unclear rules on competition becomes particularly evident in the case of Greece. After all, the fleet registered in that country is the fifth largest in the world, being 5.3 per cent of world 'dead-weight tonnage'. In December 2015, the Commission found that Greece's favourable shipping taxation, which had been in place since 1975, was not 'well targeted' at maritime transport and benefited insurance intermediaries, maritime brokers, other maritime intermediaries (including shareholders of shipping companies) and also operators not conducting genuine maritime transport activities, e.g. fishing vessels, port tugboats and charter yachts, none of whom needed state aid to be globally competitive.

There are no political or economic reasons that prevent the EU supranational regulator from establishing legal certainty, transparency and, most importantly, effective regulation that targets aid for the shipping sector at objectives in the common interest.

5.1.3 The Steering Effect of EU State Aid Rules – Industrial Policy in Disguise?

Is EU enforcement of state aid law still confined to protecting competition between undertakings or between Member States or is it rather pursuing industrial policy goals? The clear answer is yes to the latter. However, the Commission has to observe the above-cited principle of conferral ('the Union shall act only within the limits of the competences conferred upon it by the Member States in the Treaties', Art. 5 TEU). The correct legal basis for EU industrial policies is provided for by Article 173 TFEU.

---

[7] The European Competition Commissioner in a press statement of 25.07.2012.

FURTHER READING

European Commission (DG Internal Market, Industry, Entrepreneurship and SMEs): EU Industrial Policy
http://ec.europa.eu/growth/industry/policy/eu/index_en.htm.

According to Article 173(1) TFEU, 'the Union and the Member States shall ensure that the conditions necessary for the competitiveness of the Union's industry exist'. For that purpose, both, the Union and the Member States, interact by

- speeding up the adjustment of industry to structural changes,
- encouraging an environment favourable to initiative and to the development of undertakings throughout the Union, particularly small and medium-sized undertakings,
- encouraging an environment favourable to cooperation between undertakings,
- fostering better exploitation of the industrial potential of policies of innovation, research and technological development.

EU state aid control may, within the limits of Article 173(3) TFEU, 'contribute to the achievement of the [industrial policy] objectives [...] through the policies and activities it pursues under other provisions of the Treaties'. Hence, the Commission is neither allowed to define the objectives nor the formats of industrial policies unilaterally under the terms of state aid law enforcement. Therefore, the Commission pursues as much as possible a pragmatic, consensual approach with the Member States while drafting state aid guidelines and frameworks with reference to objectives and formats of industrial policies.

The Commission's reticent approach to formulating industrial policy objectives towards which state aid may be steered is exemplified by 'technological neutrality' in the field of 'key enabling technologies' (KETs), namely: photonics, industrial biotechnology, nanotechnology, advanced materials, micro-/nanoelectronics and advanced manufacturing systems. These technologies are knowledge- and capital-intensive and associated with high R&D-intensity, rapid and integrated innovation cycles, high capital expenditure and highly-skilled employment. On the one hand, the European Commission strongly favours supporting KETs. On the other hand, it did not commit to directing state aid at these specific technologies, e.g. by adopting more liberal and permissive favourable state aid rules for public KETs-support. Rather, state aid rules are limited to creating a KET-friendly yet neutral environment. The following text passage from state aid rules in the field of R&D&I illustrates the technologically neutral approach to state aid, as it makes clear that aid for research infrastructure – for which specific aid conditions exist – will automatically help KET-development:

> The Commission has identified a series of R&D&I measures for which State aid may, under specific conditions, be compatible with the internal market: […] Aid for the construction and upgrade of research infrastructures, which mainly addresses the market failure stemming from coordination difficulties. High-quality research infrastructures are increasingly necessary for ground-breaking research, as they attract global talent and are essential for example for information and communication technologies and key enabling technologies.[8]

The Commission's KET-strategy complements the 'neutral' state aid approach: It is not proposing an increase of KET-specific public financing. Rather, its overarching aim is to create synergies between EU policies and instruments and ensure coordination of EU and national activities.[9]

FURTHER READING

The European Commission outlines its KET-strategy in the Communication from the Commission of 26.6.2012 COM(2012) 341 final, A European strategy for Key Enabling Technologies – A bridge to growth and jobs, point 2, http://eur-lex.europa.eu/LexUriServ/LexUriServ.do?uri=COM:2012:0341:FIN:EN:PDF.

State aid rules in the area of R&D&I: http://eur-lex.europa.eu/legal-content/EN/TXT/HTML/?uri=CELEX:52014XC0627(01)&from=EN. See also Chapter 4.6.1.

---

[8] Point 12 c) of the Framework for State aid for research and development and innovation, OJ EU 2014 C 198/1.

[9] European Commission, Communication of 26.06.2012, A European strategy for Key Enabling Technologies – A bridge to growth and jobs', 6.

5.2 PUBLIC PROCUREMENT RULES AND COMPETITION

Where the state procures goods or services, it intervenes in the market. Since public bodies, as a rule, are not comparable to normal market operators, i.e. do not aim to make a profit and do not face the economic consequences of losses, such intervention has a great potential to distort competition. Apart from the primary objective to procure goods and services the state needs to pursue its mission, public procurement is an ambiguous tool: on the one hand, it can be used to overcome market failures and thereby create tremendous innovative potential; on the other hand, it can be used as an invisible border that protects national industries from competitive pressure, at the expense of the taxpayer. Both purposes show that these secondary objectives of public procurement are akin to state aid and have the potential to distort competition.

5.2.1 The Mantras of Transparency, Openness and Non-discrimination

The EU's supranational public procurement rules regulate the purchase of goods and services by the Member States and their various bodies. It is true that the EU Treaties do not contain any specific provisions on public procurement. The free movement of goods (Arts 28 subs. TFEU) and services (Arts 56 subs. TFEU) however requires that Member States keep their public procurement markets open for suppliers from other Member States. From these fundamental freedoms flow the principles of equal treatment, non-discrimination, mutual recognition, proportionality and transparency – the 'internal market mantras'. Consequently, the European Commission as a supranational competition authority construes public procurement as an issue of competition policy within the internal market.

Those mantras alone however were not be powerful enough to convince, for instance, the French government to purchase police cars from Volkswagen instead from the national champion Renault. The same holds true for all Member States' governments and all kinds of 'essential' goods and services supplied by national champions. National employment prerogatives or simply old boys' networks between industries and governments have traditionally foreclosed providers from other Member States to enter national public procurement markets. Removing such barriers to the internal market required the European lawmaker to take regulatory action to establish transparency, openness and non-discrimination in public procurement. Hence, government procurement in the EU has been standardised and harmonised by virtue of supranational directives since the 1970s. European public procurement directives ensure that the purchase of goods and services by the Member States and their various bodies not only adhere to common principles, but also to standardised and harmonised public procurement procedures preventing Member States from discriminating against any economic actor by ensuring a non-discriminatory, transparent and open bidding process.

5.2.2 The Tool Kit of EU Public Procurement in a Nutshell

Public procurement under the terms of transparency, openness and non-discrimination enhances innovative business opportunities and thereby economic growth, but only if the competitive procedural formats are designed well enough to combat fraud and corruption effectively, including in their hidden and soft forms. Positively speaking, well-designed public procurement procedures simulate private-market mechanisms, while embedding these mechanisms within a regulatory framework to pursue public objectives. Moreover, digital procurement tools – 'e-procurement' – in real time do not only technically improve public buyers governance by cutting red tape, but also discipline both, suppliers and public buyers, to focus on modern market economy behaviour.

EU supranational public procurement directives provide for competitive procedural formats for the purchase of services, works and supplies by public authorities. Those directives are transposed into Member States' laws and apply to tenders whose monetary value exceeds certain threshold amounts. If public tenders do not reach these threshold values, national rules of Member States' budgetary laws will apply, though still subject to the mantras of transparency, openness and non-discrimination as general principles of EU law.

EU public procurement law applies if the following cumulative conditions are met:

(1) the appointing contracting partner acts in a public capacity (is a 'contracting authority');
(2) the contract is a public works, services or supplies contract;
(3) the estimated value of the contract reaches or exceeds specific thresholds – e.g. € 5 186 000 for all public works contracts, € 134 000 for supplies and service contracts with central government authorities, € 207 000 for supplies and services contracts with other, e.g. sub-central, authorities, and € 750 000 for certain social

and other service contracts; specific thresholds apply in the fields of water, energy, transport and postal services;

(4) no exception to the applicability of public procurement rules applies.

In essence, these conditions and thresholds pursue an objective comparable to competition rules: they only apply where the 'state' and the bodies under state control intervene and where a certain minimum threshold is exceeded, below which no significant distortion of competition can be presumed. Just as standardised state aid procedures ensure that aid granting states – and thereby aid beneficiaries – are treated on an equal footing, standardised public procurement procedures should ensure that interested tenderers have a fair chance to enter a national bidding procedure.

EU public procurement rules basically prescribe four types of procedures through which public contracts may be awarded.

5.2.2.1 Open procedure

Any supplier may submit a tender in response to a published call for competition, within a minimum time limit. This is the most commonly used procedure which is mainly used for contracts of smaller value.[10]

5.2.2.2 Restricted procedure

Any supplier may ask, within a minimum time limit, to participate in a first stage *but* only those who are *pre-selected* will be invited to *submit a tender* in a second stage. The restricted procedure is the second most popular procedure, but it is used for contracts with higher values: the average contract size is €8.2 million, compared to €2.1 million for the open procedure.[11]

5.2.2.3 Negotiated procedure

In sectors other than water, energy, transport or postal services, the negotiated procedure may be used in exceptional cases only, e.g. where a previous open or restricted procedure or competitive dialogue (below) have not brought about useful tenders or where the nature or risk profile of the goods or services make it impossible to establish certain technical criteria or contract value with sufficient precision. That situation may arise in large contracts for complex/innovative infrastructure projects

---

[10] European Commission, Evaluation Report – Impact and Effectiveness of EU Public Procurement Legislation, x.

[11] Ibid.

where bidders would have to develop solutions to engineering issues. Consequently, contracting authorities in the utilities sectors water, energy, transport or postal services may use the negotiated procedure as a standard procedure. The negotiated procedure is by nature the least transparent contract award procedure. It is also the least frequently used but the total values involved are significantly higher – up to 8.6 per cent of total value of contracts awarded in 2010, with a mean contract value of €40 million.[12] Moreover, contracts awarded by negotiated procedure with prior publication have a particularly high success rate of cross-border tenders.[13] The negotiated procedure thus has a major impact on competition in the internal market, both due to the contract values involved and its cross-border effect. This, combined with the lack of transparency highlights the need for good governance at national level and good regulation at the supranational level.

5.2.2.4 Competitive dialogue

If the public authority cannot define appropriate technical specifications at the beginning (e.g. in cases of *complex* large infrastructure projects), a competitive dialogue may be used as an exceptional procedure. After the publication of the contract notice, interested providers have to request participation within a time limit. Then, the public authority defines the final technical, legal and economic aspects in a dialogue with selected candidates. After the dialogue, the candidates submit their final tenders. Competitive dialogue appears to be mainly used for services (67 per cent by value), and to a lesser extent for works (29 per cent by value of all contracts awarded on the basis of competitive dialogue).[14] That procedure is of use where contracting authorities are unable to define the means of satisfying their needs or of assessing what the market can offer in terms of technical, financial or legal solutions. This situation may arise in particular with innovative projects, the implementation of major integrated transport infrastructure projects, large computer networks or projects involving complex and structured financing.[15] The competitive dialogue seems to be less relevant for public work contracts in the utilities sector where the negotiated procedure with a prior publication of a contract notice is the standard procedure anyway.

---

[12] Ibid.
[13] Directive 2014/24/EU of 26.02.2014 on public procurement, recital (42).
[14] European Commission, Evaluation Report (n. 10), xi.
[15] Directive 2014/24/EU (n. 13), recital (42).

FURTHER READING – EU SUPRANATIONAL PUBLIC PROCUREMENT RULES

At the supranational level, public procurement in the EU is regulated by 'directives' which Member States must transpose into national law. Although obligatory to implement, directives normally leave Member States some leeway as to the exact rules to be adopted. In 2014, the EU adopted a new generation of directives in that field:

Award of concession contracts*:* In contrast to a more straightforward type of contract where an economic actor agrees to provide certain goods or services in exchange for payment (a simple *quid pro quo*), a 'concession' is a type of contract based on an economic actor's right to benefit from the work it has undertaken. Put simply, instead of an economic actor receiving payment in e.g. money for carrying out certain works, it is granted a right to exploit the work it has undertaken, or to exploit that work and also charge fees to users in downstream markets. For instance, the concessionaire for the operation of a multifunctional arena may charge fees to commercial users (e.g. concert promoters) to perform their economic activities in the arena. A concession exists when a contracting authority grants to a concessionaire the special or exclusive right to operate a particular service, and the latter enjoys a certain economic freedom to determine the conditions under which that right is exercised. Inherent in such a situation is that a concessionaire is, to a large extent, exposed to the risks involved in financing the operation of the service by prices for the service products being related to the demand from final consumers (and often subject to retail price (cap) regulation (e.g. in the public transportation sector)). Contracts concluded with a concessionaire during a given period must comply with the conditions laid down in the concession agreement. Directive 2014/23/EU on the award of concession contracts, OJ 2014 L 94/1, http://eur-lex.europa.eu/legal-content/EN/TXT/HTML/?uri=CELEX:32014L0023&from=EN.

The 'classic' case – procurement of public supply, works and service contracts: Directive 2014/24/EU on public procurement, OJ 2014 L 94/65, http://eur-lex.europa.eu/legal-content/EN/TXT/HTML/?uri=CELEX:32014L0024&from=EN.

Procurement in the utilities sectors – water, energy, transport and postal services: The key factor under the Utilities Procurement Directive is not the (public or private) nature of the body awarding the contract but instead the nature of the activity to be performed (e.g. water supply, energy supply, transportation and postal services). Procurement in the telecommunications sector is no longer regulated since the sector has been liberalised in the EU (see Chapter 6.1.2). The Utilities Directive applies to the state and its related bodies, but also to private undertakings to whom special or exclusive rights have been granted in sectors where limited or no competition exists due to the granting of the special or exclusive rights. In essence, public procurement rules in the utilities sector are another tool for opening those markets up to competition. OJ 2014 L 94/243, http://eur-lex.europa.eu/legal-content/EN/TXT/HTML/?uri=CELEX:32014L0025&from=EN.

Grosse modo, the abovementioned Directives aim to

- simplify the procurement procedures and make them more flexible;

- increase the use of *e-procurement*;
- reduce administrative burden on suppliers;
- move away from the price criterion alone and take into account social and environmental criteria such as sustainable procurement, life cycle costs of a tender or the integration of vulnerable and disadvantaged persons;
- be more effective in combating corruption and improving integrity, e.g. by introducing further obligations to investigate abnormally low tenders and further conditions for amendments to concluded contracts.

Further Reading

The European Commission's website on public procurement: http://ec.europa.eu/growth/single-market/public-procurement/index_en.htm.

Evaluation Report – Impact and Effectiveness of EU Public Procurement Legislation: Part 1 http://ec.europa.eu/internal_market/publicprocurement/docs/modernising_rules/er853_1_en.pdf; Part 2 http://ec.europa.eu/internal_market/publicprocurement/docs/modernising_rules/er853_2_en.pdf.

In summary, EU public procurement rules strive to replicate market conditions. A public purchase that is in line with these procedures, as transposed in national law, can be considered to be at market terms. Consequently, the state can be presumed to behave as a 'market economy operator' (see Chapter 4.4).

EU public procurement rules however do not explain under which circumstances public procurement constitutes state aid. State aid rules, in turn, apply a universal market-condition presumption: state aid is excluded if an '*open tender procedure*' is carried out in accordance with the applicable Public Procurement Directives.[16] Those directives are however not applicable to all public contracts. Rather, only one-fifth of total public expenditure on goods and services is covered by the EU directives.[17] Consequently, the bulk of total public expenditure on goods,

[16] Point 32 of the Framework with reference to Article 27 of Directive 2014/24/EU on public procurement, OJ EU 2014 L 94/65 and Article 45 of Directive 2014/25/EU on procurement by entities operating in the water, energy, transport and postal services sectors OJ EU 2014 L 94/243. Likewise, in the case of a restricted procedure within the meaning of respectively Arts 28 of Directive 2014/24/EU and 46 of Directive 2014/25/EU, the Commission will also consider that no state aid is awarded to undertakings, unless interested providers are prevented from tendering without valid reasons.

[17] Evaluation Report – Impact and Effectiveness of EU Public Procurement Legislation: Part 1, 27; according to that report, over 150 000 invitations to tender were published by 35 000 authorities in conformity with EU directives in 2009. The estimated value for these contracts was €420 billion. This represents

services, and works is not organised in accordance with EU procurement legislation. Most prominently, military procurement (especially armament, i.e. arms and equipment with which the Member States' military apparatus is supplied) is largely excluded from the Public Procurement Directives. From the perspective of state aid control, this has two essential implications: first, also in areas where public procurement law is not applicable, distortions of competition can only be safely excluded if the procurement was nevertheless in line with the conditions of public procurement law; second, and most importantly, there is a large grey zone of legal uncertainty as regards competition distortions through public procurement.

5.2.3 Pre-commercial Procurement and Innovation Partnerships: Testing the Limits of Transparency, Openness and Non-discrimination – Case Study

Public procurement is a legitimate tool for achieving certain socio-economic goals. 'Innovation' is at the centre of such goals, as it enables growth, jobs and competitiveness. It is a priority in the EU's common economic growth strategy.[18] Fair competition and public procurement are two prominent elements of that strategy. On the one hand, the European Commission seems to give priority to the competition element: 'The potential of the single market should also be activated through policies that stimulate the demand for innovation, starting with an effective competition policy.'[19] On the other hand, the Commission states that 'commercial and pre-commercial public procurement are needed to create a vibrant Single Market for innovative goods and services'.[20] Moreover, the innovation-policy initiative demands the 'strategic use of our massive procurement budgets'.[21]

Hence, there is potential conflict between, on one side, massive public budgets and national industrial policy, even with protectionist goals, and

---

approximately 20 per cent of total public expenditure on goods, works and services. Public contracts below the EU thresholds fall outside the scope of the EU public procurement directives but they are of significant importance. Below-threshold procurement was estimated at around €250 billion in 2008 or around 2 per cent of EU GDP.

[18] Communication from the Commission of 03.03.2010, COM(2010) 2020, EUROPE 2020, a strategy for smart, sustainable and inclusive growth, 5.

[19] Europe 2020 Flagship Initiative Innovation Union, 15.

[20] An Integrated Industrial Policy for the Globalisation Era, 13.

[21] Europe 2020 Flagship (n. 19), 3.

on the other side the overarching common goal of a functioning internal market. Short-term gains versus sustainability in a league that is larger than the nation state. In concrete terms, this means that where, despite political lip service, policy goals are given priority over the public procurement mantras, conflicts with fair competition and the responsible use of public resources may arise.

This potential conflict can be illustrated in the area of R&D&I: in that field, certain forms of procurement may comprise massive advantages to industry as the public purchaser might enter into long-term supply contracts already in the phase where the product or service have to be developed.

In the following, we use that example to discuss how the EU supranational legislator attempted to resolve the 'national policy vs competition' conflict in two specific procurement models: 'pre-commercial procurement' of R&D-services and public-private 'innovation partnerships'. On the one hand, those models could speed up innovation and the results could improve the efficiency and quality of public services. On the other hand, those models come with the risk of foreclosure of future technology markets, crowding out of other R&D investments, and suboptimal price/quality solutions.

EXPLANATORY NOTE

In the area of R&D-services, EU public-procurement rules only apply to *exclusive* procurement, i.e. if the benefits accrue exclusively to the contracting authority for its use in the conduct of its own affairs, and the service provided is wholly remunerated by the contracting authority.[22]

Exclusive R&D-procurement leaves the least room for competition distortions since the risks and benefits are borne by the purchaser and the supplier is remunerated on market terms. This option would however only be effective if there is a large enough market for the specific innovative solution that is sought by the public procurer, so that a sufficient number of bidders would be interested in developing that solution.

'**Pre-commercial procurement**' implies a *non-exclusive* arrangement: the contracting public entity does *not* reserve all the benefits of the R&D-service contract exclusively for itself but shares them with the providers under market conditions. R&D can cover activities such as solution exploration and design, prototyping, up to the original development of a limited volume of first products or services in the form of a test series. Sharing risks and benefits with the supplier could result in better value for money for the public procurer e.g. in situations where leaving IPR ownership with economic operators makes sense because of the concrete market value of IPRs for the economic operators.

[22] Article 14 of Directive 2014/24/EU resp. 32 of Directive 2014/25/EU.

Further reading: European Commission, Communication of 14.12.2007, COM(2007) 799 final, 'Pre-commercial Procurement: Driving innovation to ensure sustainable high quality public services in Europe'. That Communication is supplemented with a Commission 'staff-working paper' of 14.12.2007, SEC(2007) 1668. The aim of these papers was to draw attention to pre-commercial procurement that at that time was underutilised.

Innovation partnership is an exclusive arrangement that implies the purchase of both the R&D *and* resulting end products in one and the same procedure. Such a procurement model can be justified in cases where the public purchaser needs unique or specialised products or services, e.g. IT solutions for e-government, where a separate procurement procedure for the final end-product after the R&D-result was procured could be counterproductive: it may not trigger more competition or better procurement outcomes, but could dissuade industry to participate even in the first, risky phase and thus prevent the entire development. Combining R&D and the supply of the end product could generate the necessary 'market-pull'. The innovation partnership model is thus a means to combat market failures that prevent innovation. In the EU regulator's terms, such procedure may be useful:

> where a need for the development of an innovative product or service or innovative works and the subsequent purchase of the resulting supplies, services or works cannot be met by solutions already available on the market [...]. This specific procedure should allow contracting authorities to establish a long-term innovation partnership for the development and subsequent purchase of a new, innovative product, service or works provided that such innovative product or service or innovative works can be delivered to agreed performance levels and costs, without the need for a separate procurement procedure for the purchase.[23]

There is only one EU supranational legal text where state aid rules and public procurement in the field of R&D&I are brought together – the Union Framework for state aid for Research, Development and Innovation (the Framework; see also Chapter 4.6.1).[24] This is the principal legal text to look at when seeking legal certainty about whether public R&D-procurement distorts competition.

Independently of the underlying contract's nature (exclusive or non-exclusive) the Framework provides for the above mentioned universal market-condition presumption: state aid is excluded if an '*open tender procedure*' is carried out in accordance with the applicable public procurement directives.[25] In the area of R&D, this situation first and

[23] Recital (49) of Directive 2014/24/EU resp. (59) of Directive 2014/25/EU.

[24] Communication from the Commission. Framework for state aid for research and development and innovation, OJ EU 2014 C 198/1.

[25] Point 32 of the Framework with reference to Article 27 of Directive 2014/24/EU on public procurement, OJ EU L 2014 94/65 and Article 45 of

foremost occurs when a public purchaser procures 'exclusive' development in a separate procedure.[26] The Framework further clarifies that the public procurement of innovative solutions resulting from a '*preceding R&D procurement*' is included in this general presumption, as well as the procurement of non-R&D products and services that are to be delivered to a performance level requiring a product, process or organisational innovation.[27]

The Framework however, despite being the product of the above-described state aid modernisation with its 'simpler and clearer rules' objective, is not so simple and clear when it comes to explaining the state aid relevance of the various procurement procedures. While the Framework's main text makes explicit reference only to '*open tender procedures*', a footnote extends the market-condition presumption to 'restricted procedures', under the provision that interested providers are not prevented from tendering without valid reasons.[28] Other procurement procedures – competitive procedures with prior call for negotiations, competitive dialogues and innovation partnerships – are thus not included in the general assumption that exclusive procurement according to the rules does not distort competition through state aid to the supplier. This highly important explanation could have been more obvious.

The Framework also explains how state aid to the supplier can be avoided in cases other than 'classic' exclusive procurement: those explanations explicitly comprise pre-commercial procurement.[29] Implicitly, they also apply to procurement procedures that are not caught by the previously discussed 'market-condition presumption', namely negotiated procedures and dialogue procedures, as well as innovation partnerships. In essence, the Framework explains that state aid to the supplier in those other cases is excluded if the following conditions are met:

Directive 2014/25/EU on procurement by entities operating in the water, energy, transport and postal services sectors OJ EU 2014 L 94/243. Likewise, in the case of a restricted procedure within the meaning of respectively Articles 28 of Directive 2014/24/EU and 46 of Directive 2014/25/EU, the Commission will also consider that no state aid is awarded to undertakings, unless interested providers are prevented from tendering without valid reasons.

[26] Point 15 i) of the Framework.

[27] Point 32, footnote.

[28] Footnote 24 last sentence.

[29] Points 33, 34 of the Framework.

- the public procurement mantras – openness, transparency, non-discrimination – are observed, regardless of their actual applicability strictly under public procurement standards (e.g. the threshold values);
- the supplier is not automatically put in the position of preferred supplier of the final product or service and the foreclosure of future technology markets is prevented, in particular through adequate knowledge dissemination: Most importantly, third parties must have access to R&D-results under market conditions;
- moreover, the Framework's legal definition of 'pre-commercial procurement' stipulates that 'the contract, the object of which falls within one or several categories of research and development defined in this Framework, must be of limited duration and may include the development of prototypes or limited volumes of first products or services in the form of a test series. The purchase of commercial volumes of products or services must not be an object of the same contract.[30]

Obviously, EU state aid rules are being used as a line of defence against a push to promote more innovation that, despite its good intention, could have harmful effects in the internal market. Another battleground is public-private 'innovation partnership', which we will discuss in the following.

Innovation partnership is procurement that spans both the development of an innovative solution *and* the subsequent purchase of the resulting products or services; it is subject to the public procurement directives.[31] In a nutshell, the idea is that reopening the procurement of final end-products after the development is complete may not trigger more competition or better procurement outcomes, but at the same time, such reopening clause could put off market operators from entering into a risky development in the first place. The presumption is that the state is the only potential buyer, and that it is able to identify all economic operators that can both perform the development and then supply the final product/service.

Innovation partnerships must be regulated by state aid law: otherwise, EU Member States might use them to give some suppliers selective, preferential treatment that distorts competition. A public contract that combines both the development and the supply of commercial volumes

---

30 Point 15 aa) of the Framework.

31 Articles 31 of Directive 2014/24/EU resp. 49 of Directive 2014/25/EU.

could be such preferential treatment. Maintaining a margin to use the innovation partnership model while at the same time avoiding anti-competitive results is possible if the supplier does not receive any advantages outside market terms.

Although the Framework unfortunately does not explicitly refer to innovation partnerships, it implies specific limitations to that model's anti-competitive potential.

EU public procurement directives provide for some generic requirements to introduce some degree of competition and openness: The public 'partner' (i.e. purchaser) must publish the procedure so that all interested market operators have a chance to participate in the initial selection procedure. The recitals of the directives also state that public purchasers should not use innovation partnerships to prevent, restrict or distort competition.[32] However, the directives do not define in which situations this can be ensured. In essence, the innovation partnership model must be based on the above described negotiated procedure and consists of two phases:

- Tendering phase: the public 'partner' (contracting authority) selects the most suitable industry 'partner(s)' to develop an innovative solution; the public partner awards the contract on the basis of the best price-quality ratio.
- R&D and commercialisation phase: industry partner(s) develop the new solution, manufactures the products/provides the services/ completes the works. Industry partners must attain specific intermediate targets. Depending on the industry partners' performance, the public partner may decide to terminate the innovation partnership or reduce the number of partners.

With such generic rules in place, public procurement directives alone neither effectively prevent market foreclosure, crowding out and price/ quality issues, nor do they guarantee the necessary 'market-pull' to spur development efforts in cases where otherwise no such incentive would exist.

EU state aid rules for R&D&I attempt to fill that regulatory gap, by interpreting the objective notion of state aid in the area of innovation procurement: procurement must not give any provider preferential treatment in the supply of commercial volumes of the final products or

---

32 Recital (49) 2014/24/EU resp. (59) of Directive 2014/25/EU.

services 'without prejudice to procedures that cover both the development and the subsequent purchase of unique or specialised products or services'.[33] In essence, this implies that innovation partnerships can only be considered to be at market terms, and thus not to distort competition, if:

- the public 'partner' procures products or services that are demonstrably unique or so specialised that the public partner is the only potential buyer;
- the public partner must be able to identify in advance of the selection procedure all potential suppliers that can both perform, if necessary collaboratively, the development and then supply the final products or services;
- all potentially capable suppliers must have a possibility of becoming a 'partner'.

Otherwise, such partnership involves state aid which is in principle prohibited and can only be permitted if in line with state aid rules.

The case of innovation partnership illustrates how difficult it is to bring together a specific yet important socio-economic policy objective – resolving innovation market failures by public demand side measures – with a fundamental objective – an internal market where competition is free and undistorted. Both objectives, albeit so closely related, seem to coexist with only one intermediary – state aid rules in the area of R&D&I where a few explanations attempt to prevent anti-competitive behaviour by both public and private 'innovation partners'. Unfortunately, these explanations are not as clear and simple as they could be. Nevertheless, the supranational regulator obviously withstood the temptation to loosen state aid control in order to enable Member States to shackle themselves to industry in the name of innovation, and thereby jeopardise the innovative power of competition.

5.3 CONCLUSION

National legislators should not over-prioritise innovation goals, but keep them subordinate to state aid principles and public procurement mantras. Those principles and mantras were discussed above. The supranational legislator in the EU made a valiant effort to bring together legitimate national industrial policy goals with overarching supranational objectives

[33] Point 33 c) of the Framework.

that require a sustainable approach. Nevertheless, the entire set of applicable supranational competition rules should be adapted to pressing competition challenges. Otherwise, the sectors spared by such revision could lose out. Competition law should also take a clear, comprehensive and comprehensible stance on the anticompetitive potential of public procurement. This is particularly important in the field of innovation where deep public pockets could help foreclosing markets and binding public purchasers to suppliers in the long term.

6. The art of sector-specific regulation in the internal market

The modern no less than the ancient government unhesitatingly takes a hand in administering the conveniences of society.[1]

In this chapter, we will discover the basic elements of good market regulation and how the supranational level 'unhesitatingly took a hand in administering the conveniences of society': by stimulating competition; by unilateral action in situations where the national level lacks political resolve; by drafting legislation that structurally adapts to the pace of market development; by accompanying regulatory cross-border impact with adequate standardisation and harmonisation; by respecting the principle of 'subsidiarity'; by providing support and coordination in the implementing phase; and by appointing independent supervisory bodies.

We will start on the premise that intelligent economic policy and rule of law are the guarantors of inclusive welfare.

6.1 PRINCIPLES AND METHODOLOGY AS EXEMPLIFIED BY THE FRAMEWORK OF TELECOMMUNICATION REGULATION

6.1.1 Why Regulation?

How swiftly times have changed. Only 30 years ago, when bold pioneers in the European Commission conceived the liberalisation of telecommunication markets, it was up to them to justify the abolition of state monopolies against fierce political opposition in most Member States.

In the early 1990s, communication networks were still operated by state entities in most Member States. In the late 1980s, terminal equipment (i.e. the standard telephone, available only in limited colour variations) was mandatorily provided for end-users by said state institutions. Early attempts by long-haired computer scientists to 'abuse' the

[1] Wilson, 'The State – Elements of Historical and Practical Politics', 1260.

sacred voice telephony network for the purpose of electronic data transmission (using computers and modems) were suspiciously observed by the eye of the law. Good old days? Most certainly for Member States' monopolies – but not so much for end-users. Besides poor quality of service and obsolete terminal equipment, consumers' bondage within state monopolies used to entail much higher prices for voice telephony services compared to liberalised markets, e.g. in the US or more than a decade later in liberalised Europe itself.

Today, reflections on telecom liberalisation and regulation depart from the opposite springboard: we have found consensus that, fundamentally, the rules on market access applying to strawberries should apply to telecommunication, postal, and railway services, or energy supply likewise. What differs is the degree and substance of regulation, adjusted to competitive obstacles that newcomers face, and the needs or safety of consumers exercising their freedom of choice.

Whenever we discuss regulation, i.e. *state intervention in market allocations of resources in order to direct market behaviour towards the public interest,* the knee-jerk reaction is to ask for justification. Most network industries are still regulated on several levels, but we have inverted the relationship between rule and exception. The dynamics of the telecom markets allow us to extrapolate observations that apply to regulation as a broader concept. Electronic communications have been catapulted more than any other industry by radical technological changes, such as convergence, in the digital time lapse of just a few years.

EXPLANATORY NOTE

Convergence: the migration of multiple logical communication services into a single physical network or device. Convergence of previously distinct media such as telephony, TV, the web, or data communications via common interfaces on single devices, e.g. smart phones, laptops, or tablets, has made it possible for network, service, and content providers to deliver voice, text, audio, and video services and content over the same fixed or mobile broadband connection within bundled products.

Notwithstanding the substantial differences between industries as regards market allocation mechanisms and the input of resources, the challenge of fast-learning regulation in the telecommunications sector serves as a structural pattern for adequate regulatory adjustments in other industries. The digital time lapse in electronic communications illustrates that good regulation is not an accumulated trend of past normative decisions.

Rather, it is an economically and policy driven public enforcement in order to distribute inclusive welfare under the rule of law. In order to avoid this chapter's size getting out of hand, we will focus on the regulatory basics in the electronic communications sector, highlighting cross-sectoral regulatory lessons.

Before we delve into said regulatory principles, some reflections on the rationale behind regulation should decondition us from the political *communis opinio*.

Why regulation? – Market failure is the bread-and-butter justification for both market regulation and direct state intervention, and the seemingly straightforward logic is quite tempting: where the free market fails to allocate resources in a welfare-maximising manner, governments should intervene. On closer inspection, not every discrepancy between political goals and market reality constitutes market failure. An undersupply of broadband networks, post offices or railway stations in rural regions is usually caused by consumers' lack of willingness to pay charges that would compensate necessary investments. When companies react reasonably to negative investment incentives, we cannot say that the market has failed. To the contrary, the market is indicating precisely the bitter, but necessary truth for investors: stay away from the middle of nowhere!

Again: Why market regulation? – A more honest paradigm of regulation justification will revolve around a socio-economic perspective, no matter how unorthodox that notion might appear to scholars in the fields of law and economics. The social implications of unadulterated market dynamics are not always politically bearable. We cannot afford to cut off underdeveloped regions from modern infrastructure, even if a cost-efficient operation of adequate infrastructure is impossible. The consequential costs of a deepening divide between those who can benefit from modern infrastructure and those who cannot would constitute an even greater burden on society.

European law safeguards the provision of a 'minimum set of good-quality' postal, railway, energy, and telecommunication services across regions 'accessible to all users at an affordable price, while minimising market distortion'[2] through the instrument of *universal service*. The specific scope of 'good-quality' service is subject to an ongoing debate. Should the availability of broadband internet to all interested consumers be mandatory or is a traditional land line sufficient? While the former

---

2 http://eur-lex.europa.eu/legal-content/EN/TXT/?uri=URISERV:l24108h, 06.07.2016.

would help overcome what some call a 'digital divide' of society, it might also result in an excessive market distortion.

Regulation, because – Before the mechanisms of universal service are activated, less invasive regulatory instruments, notably *access regulation* and *access price regulation*, need to be exhausted in upstream markets. These access instruments can enable fruitful service-based competition, leading to the supply of sufficient services across all regions and accessible to all users at affordable prices, especially if facility-based (infrastructural) competition is not a viable option. This multi-layered approach, well-tried in telecom markets, has the potential to refuel limping liberalisation progress on railway and postal service markets.

6.1.2 Triggering Liberalisation and Regulation

The litmus test for European liberalisation flanked by open market regulation was submitted in the electronic communications sector. No other network industry has been driven by such radical changes in technology. Therefore, this chapter will focus on the electronic communications sector, which stands, despite all sector-specific idiosyncrasies, as a regulatory prototype for other network industries, such as postal services, energy, and railways. Telecommunications have illustrated that European liberalisation and regulation are capable of taking the fast lane in order to adapt to global industrial challenges. Another example of Europe's regulatory fast lane is the emergence of renewable energies.

Until the early 1990s, European telecommunications markets were closed state-run monopolies vested with exclusive and special rights[3] for the provision of telecommunications networks and services. These telecommunications monopolies proved a hindrance to technological progress and the ability to compete with the rest of the world, especially with regard to the widely liberalised markets in the US and Japan, whose telecommunications industries were much more innovative due to competition. European telecommunications equipment (network as well as terminal) and services markets were deprived of innovation incentives within self-complacent state monopolies.

It is above all the objective lack of competitive pressure which erodes self-discipline, self-control, innovation incentives, and hence quality of service. The absence of 'competition on the merits' deprives consumers at least of choice and, much worse, of adequate supply at affordable prices. Still in the 1980s, consumers in Germany, France, Italy and other

---

[3] Article 106(1) TFEU.

European countries who could not afford an expensive land line at home would buy voice telephony services at the public callbox for a multiple of the prices consumers paid for equivalent services delivered in liberalised markets, e.g. in the US or more than a decade later in liberalised Europe itself. Another prominent example of excessive exploitation of consumers is the still existing municipal monopoly on grid-based water supply in Germany. In one of the rainiest countries worldwide, water supply is among the most expensive in the world, even when taking high quality and environmental standards into account. Here, the lessons from telecommunications liberalisation still have to be learnt.

Despite the lack of any explicit EC Treaty competence with regard to telecommunications, the European Commission pursued a rather distinctive telecommunications policy towards liberalisation flanked by secondary law (directives) regulation by virtue of existing EC Treaty competition rules and the Community's general powers with regard to the establishment of the Internal Market.[4]

The Commission adopted a dualistic approach: On the one hand, the Commission cracked the Member States' telecommunications monopolies by virtue of a series of 'liberalisation' directives under Article 90 (now Art. 106 of the Treaty on the Functioning of the European Union (TFEU)) para. 1 in conjunction with para. 3 EC Treaty providing:

> 1. In the case of public undertakings and undertakings to which Member States grant special or exclusive rights, Member States shall neither enact nor maintain in force any measure contrary to the rules contained in the Treaties, in particular to those rules provided for in Article 18 and Articles 101–109.
>
> (...)
>
> 3. The Commission shall ensure the application of the provisions of this Article and shall, where necessary, address appropriate directives or decisions to Member States.

On the other hand, these 'liberalisation' directives were flanked by 'harmonisation' directives adopted under Article 95 EC Treaty (now Art. 114 TFEU) in order to safeguard the liberalisation process with efficient open market regulation.

The process started in 1988 with the opening of the terminal equipment market for competition under 'liberalisation' Directive 88/301/EEC. The Directive obliged Member States to withdraw special or exclusive

[4] Koenig/Bartosch/Braun/Romes, EC Competition and Telecommunications Law, 41 *et seq.*

rights for the importation, marketing and connection of telecommunications terminal equipment combined with full mutual recognition of type approval for telecommunications terminal equipment. The 'liberalisation' power under Article 90(3) EC Treaty (now Art. 106(3) TFEU) proved to be very straightforward: it empowered the Commission to unilaterally (neither the European Parliament nor the Council are involved) address directives and decisions to Member States in order to safeguard the application of Internal Market rules, in particular competition rules, or to address decisions to (public) undertakings which had been granted exclusive (monopolistic) or special rights by Member States. Due to the exclusion of the European Parliament and the Council from 'liberalisation' legislation, political interference from Member States was effectively bypassed. Notwithstanding issues of democratic legitimacy with regard to the exclusion of national political agents from the supranational legislative process,[5] the unilateral lawmaking by the Commission turned out to be the most efficient kick-off in European liberalisation history. Traditionally, national politics tend to abuse state monopolies as hidden pension schemes for politicians (appointed to the board of directors) and as public shadow budgets for cross-subsidisation options. While these motives are never publicly articulated, they are a very strong impetus to defend and protect state-run monopolies. Through unilateral lawmaking by the Commission, the inherent resistance of national political agents against liberalisation has effectively been paralysed. The liberalisation of telecommunications markets acted as an ice-breaker for the modernisation of other politically embattled network industries, such as energy, postal services, and railways. Only grid-based water supplies, still incarcerated in municipal monopolies in some Member States, is yet to be released.

Inevitably, the competence of the Commission to issue directives unilaterally under Article 90(3) EC Treaty (now Art. 106(3) TFEU) was challenged before the Court of Justice: France pled to annul Directive 88/301/EEC on telecommunications terminal equipment.[6] The Court held that 'even though that Article 90(3) EC Treaty [now Article 106(3) TFEU] presupposes the existence of undertakings which have certain special or exclusive rights, it does not follow that all the special or exclusive rights are necessarily compatible with the Treaty'.[7] The Court thus emphasised that the Commission's supervisory function under

---

[5] And also considering that stakeholder lobbyism is part of the democratic process.

[6] ECJ, judgment of 19.03.1991, C-202/88 – *France v Commission.*

[7] Ibid., para. 20.

Article 86(3) EC (now Art. 106(3) TFEU) is vested with the competence to specify the obligations of the Member States under the EC Treaty with regard to the exercise of exclusive rights. The Court decided that the Commission had not exceeded these powers at the expense of those of the Council and European Parliament with regard to 'harmonisation' directives adopted under Article 95 EC Treaty (now Art. 114 TFEU). That terminal equipment judgment greatly encouraged the Commission to carry on with its mission to abolish monopoly rights. The Telecommunications Services Directive 90/388/EEC, providing for a step-by-step liberalisation of telecommunications services markets (except for voice telephony), had already been adopted before this crucial judgment. Challenging it before the Court[8] failed for the same reasons as with regard to Terminal Equipment Directive 88/301/EEC. The Telecommunications Services Directive 90/388/EEC went even further, obliging Member States to separate regulatory and entrepreneurial functions, and to establish a transparent and non-discriminatory procedure in the admission of new telecommunications services.

Clearing away the fundamental objections raised by Member States against liberalisation, the European judiciary paved the way for abolishing special and exclusive rights for the provision of satellite services, of cable TV, and of mobile communications. The Full Competition Directive led to the abolition of special and exclusive rights regarding voice telephony as of 1 January 1998. The process was flanked by the creation of an institutional regulatory framework for the liberalised markets.

More importantly from a wider perspective, the ECJ judgments on the Terminal Equipment Directive and the Telecommunications Services Directive supplied the Commission with powerful ammunition in the stand-off with Member States towards the liberalisation of other network industries, such as energy, postal services, and railways. The Commission's mere implicit threat of unilateral lawmaking has proved to be rather intimidating towards Member States, especially after the positive judgments. The Commission has thus never had to use this unilateral power in the energy, postal, and railway sectors. Instead, Member States have preferred to cooperate with the Commission in the liberalisation process under the terms of 'harmonisation' legislation[9] and its co-decision procedures between the Council and European Parliament.

---

[8] ECJ, judgment of 17.11.1992, joined cases C-271/90, C-281/90, C-289/90 – *Spain and others v Commission.*

[9] Art. 95 EC Treaty, now Art. 114 TFEU.

That wider perspective however gives rise to a surprising and encouraging insight: ask which level – national or supranational – in that process acted in the interest of the citizen? Further ask: what was the level that had full democratic legitimacy? You will find that both the national and the supranational level had the obligation, each within its competence, to pursue the general economic interest of the citizen to have access to quality telecommunication services. Both had the powers to enact corresponding regulation in the interest of the citizen. Only the supranational level though, which in the EU, despite constitutional reform, is still blemished by a lack of democratic legitimacy, effectively pursued that citizen's interest.

6.1.3 Liberalisation Requires More Regulation!

A rather common misconception in the political arena is that liberalisation equates to deregulation. The opposite is true: liberalisation requires more regulation.

Following liberalisation, a former monopolist telecommunications, railway or postal services provider, called the incumbent, may refuse a newcomer access to its upstream network infrastructure. As a consequence, the newcomer would not be in a viable economic position to offer competing services to end-users in the relevant downstream markets. In the case of the incumbent's refusal to grant upstream network access to an infrastructure built in times of the monopoly, newcomers would be compelled to duplicate the infrastructure required to produce competing downstream services. In network industries, especially in telecommunications, gas, electricity, and transportation networks, it is not economically viable for new competitors in downstream service or supply markets to establish (i.e. duplicate) the necessary network facilities ('essential facilities') upstream and to maintain the necessary domestic and off-shore physical infrastructure. Imagine you were trying to build your own railway network, in addition to the existing one. The construction of competing infrastructures such as the 'last mile' (local loop) in telecommunications or electricity/gas distribution grids/pipelines would be nearly impossible to finance given the high sunk costs, i.e. expenses which a company cannot recoup at market prices upon exiting the market. Hence, any newcomer to the market, or at least the financing of such an undertaking, would be deterred in the absence of a special regulatory regime supporting market entry via access to the incumbent's physical networks under non-discriminatory and fair terms defined by an independent regulator.

General (non-sector specific) competition law fails to ensure sustainable competitive access to liberalised markets. Even if an incumbent's refusal to grant upstream network access constitutes an abuse of dominant market power (prohibited under Art. 102 TFEU), mere *ex-post* competition control will not prevent irrecoverable harm to a newcomer in time. In order to provide timely remedies, EU sector-specific directives and regulations in the fields of telecommunications, gas, electricity, postal services, and railway network infrastructure have established a harmonised *ex-ante* access regime regulated by National Regulatory Authorities (NRAs) in Member States under the supervision of the European Commission. NRAs are entrusted under this *ex-ante* EU regime to monitor contractual network access conditions and to approve beforehand access fees for the use of the incumbent's network facilities.

Most prominent, also from a cross-sectoral point of view, is the Open Network Provision (ONP) access regime established in the telecommunications sector under Article 95 EC (now Art. 114 TFEU), in a first step by ONP Directive 90/387/EEC adopted on the same day as the Services Directive 90/388/EEC. ONP has served as a convincing regulatory prototype for other network industries.

Since the 1990s, ONP has provided for the harmonisation of technological interfaces and the crucial conditions of network access, use, interconnection, and tariffs. Parallel to the liberalisation process, the Community introduced ONP principles step-by-step to more and more telecommunications markets by virtue of harmonisation directives (1992: leased lines, 1995: voice telephony, 1997: fully liberalised telecommunications environment and interconnection). The point of no return was passed with the Interconnection Directive 97/33/EC, codifying a comprehensive regulatory framework to ensure interconnection of all kinds of telecommunications networks (mobile, fixed, satellite) as an instrument to enhance competition. However, ONP is applied to both vertical market levels, i.e. to downstream telecommunications services provided to end-users as well as to upstream access to hardware and software facilities necessary to provide these services to end-users.

In addition to ONP, the Community introduced a harmonised Universal Services regime to ensure that the liberalised markets will not exclude end-users living in underdeveloped or remote areas from affordable basic telecommunications service.

6.1.4 More Regulation Requires Close Scrutiny with Regard to New Market Impacts

Again, the telecommunications example illustrates that regulation must not rely on its past or even present liberalisation success if rapid technological developments demand instant regulatory adjustments of innovation and investment incentives. Great appetite for broadband capacity in conjunction with the convergence of network technologies demanded a very close scrutiny regarding new market impacts of the then existing regulatory design which had been conditioned by 'old' liberalisation policies. If competition in telecommunication service markets heats up, fuelled by sharply falling prices and a growing number of service providers, reducing sector-specific regulation within an adaptive regulatory framework becomes a priority.

By contrast to rather short innovation cycles in digital communications, more traditional hardware or labour-driven network industries such as postal services, gas and electricity or railways are considerably less exposed to technological revolutions and can therefore rely much more heavily on longer-lasting normative settings within the regulatory framework.

A new adaptive regulatory framework has been introduced in telecommunications – now defined as 'electronic communications' – with the 2002 regulatory package shifting the regulatory approach from static normative settings to wide discretionary powers exercised by the national regulators and supervised by the Commission within an EU network of regulators. The new approach has been introduced with the following co-decision directives of the European Parliament and the Council under Article 95 EC (now Art. 114 TFEU):

(1) Directive 2002/21/EC on a common regulatory framework for electronic communications networks and services (Framework Directive),
(2) Directive 2002/19/EC on access to, and interconnection of, electronic communications networks and associated facilities (Access Directive),
(3) Directive 2002/20/EC on the authorisation of electronic communications networks and services (Authorisation Directive),
(4) Directive 2002/22/EC on universal service and users' rights relating to electronic communications networks and services (Universal Service Directive),
(5) Directive 2002/58/EC concerning the processing of personal data and the protection of privacy in the electronic communications sector (Privacy Directive).

The new regulatory framework has been revised in its details, but not in its fundamental structure, through the Reviews of 2012 and 2015. It pursues the promotion of service and network competition as an allocative mechanism to optimise consumer benefits and the establishment of a harmonised regulatory enforcement within the EU, as well as the guarantee of universal services, consumer and data protection.

According to the new regulatory framework, any access regulation under the Access Directive has to pass the following three-step procedure which is embedded into a sophisticated regulatory mechanism ('consolidation procedure') between the national regulators (the NRAs) and the Commission as an EU network of regulators:

(1) Market definition
(2) Market analysis
(3) Choice and imposition of proportional access remedies.

6.1.5 First Step: Market Definition

Article 15 – Framework Directive

Market definition procedure

1. After public consultation and consultation with national regulatory authorities the Commission shall adopt a recommendation on relevant product and service markets (hereinafter 'the recommendation'). The recommendation shall identify in accordance with Annex I hereto those product and service markets within the electronic communications sector, the characteristics of which may be such as to justify the imposition of regulatory obligations set out in the Specific Directives, without prejudice to markets that may be defined in specific cases under competition law. The Commission shall define markets in accordance with the principles of competition law.

The Commission shall regularly review the recommendation.

2. The Commission shall publish, at the latest on the date of entry into force of this Directive, guidelines for market analysis and the assessment of significant market power (hereinafter 'the guidelines') which shall be in accordance with the principles of competition law.

3. National regulatory authorities shall, taking the utmost account of the recommendation and the guidelines, define relevant markets appropriate to national circumstances, in particular relevant geographic markets within their territory, in accordance with the principles of competition law. National regulatory authorities shall follow the procedures referred to in Articles 6 and 7 before defining the markets that differ from those defined in the recommendation.

4. After consultation with national regulatory authorities the Commission may, acting in accordance with the procedure referred to in Article 22(3), adopt a decision identifying transnational markets.

Any access regulation, being a public intervention in the freedom of undertakings, requires a lack of effective competition on the relevant market due to dominance of an actor. The (product and geographic) market definition forms the very basis for identifying any dominance, i.e. *significant market power* (SMP), and for choosing appropriate regulatory remedies. SMP can only be measured within a precisely defined relevant market space. Market definition, both in terms of products and of geographical scope, follows general competition law principles of demand and supply substitution as discussed in Chapter 3.5. In contrast to general competition law, specific electronic communications access markets are pre-defined under the Framework Directive by a Commission Recommendation on relevant product and service markets which national regulators have to consider for *ex-ante* regulation. This Recommendation 2014/710/EU defines the following product and service markets within the electronic communications sector susceptible to *ex-ante* regulation:

(1) Wholesale call termination on individual public telephone networks provided at a fixed location;

> EXPLANATORY NOTE
>
> **Call termination:** the routing of phone calls from a point of interconnection to the end user connected to the *terminating* provider. The opposite of call termination is **call origination:** the routing of phone calls from the end user connected to the originating provider towards a point of interconnection.

(2) wholesale voice call termination on individual mobile networks;
(3) wholesale local and central access provided at a fixed location;
(4) wholesale high-quality access provided at a fixed location.

When identifying markets other than those aforementioned four wholesale markets (predefined by Recommendation 2014/710/EU), NRAs should demonstrate, and the Commission will verify, that the following three criteria are cumulatively met with regard to the market:

(1) the presence of high and non-transitory structural, legal or regulatory barriers to entry;
(2) a market structure which does not tend towards effective competition within the relevant time horizon, having regard to the state of infrastructure-based and other competition behind the barriers to entry;
(3) competition law alone is insufficient to adequately address the identified market failure(s).

This *three-criteria test* qualifies as a fundamental indicator for any *ex-ante* access regulation in network industries within and beyond the electronic communications sector. Even if the three-criteria test is not explicitly referred to in gas, electricity, postal services, and railway network market regulation, in substance, it justifies public intervention in the freedom of contract and business on the basis of a sophisticated and well-structured proportionality test. By contrast to the more advanced state of regulatory art in the electronic communications sector (wide discretionary powers exercised by regulators), gas, electricity, postal services, and railway regulation still rely on static normative settings in EU directives and regulations and the respective national implementation laws.

6.1.6 Second Step: Market Analysis

> Article 16 Framework Directive
>
> Market analysis procedure
>
> 1. As soon as possible after the adoption of the recommendation or any updating thereof, national regulatory authorities shall carry out an analysis of the relevant markets, taking the utmost account of the guidelines. Member States shall ensure that this analysis is carried out, where appropriate, in collaboration with the national competition authorities.
>
> 2. Where a national regulatory authority is required under Articles 16, 17, 18 or 19 of Directive 2002/22/EC (Universal Service Directive), or Articles 7 or 8 of Directive 2002/19/EC (Access Directive) to determine whether to impose, maintain, amend or withdraw obligations on undertakings, it shall determine on the basis of its market analysis referred to in paragraph 1 of this Article whether a relevant market is effectively competitive.
>
> (…)

Within market analysis, NRAs have to check whether effective competition exists on a relevant market.[10] Except for the four wholesale access markets, for which Recommendation 2014/710/EU assumes that they are susceptible to *ex-ante* regulation, effective competition is deemed existent if no operator holds significant market power on the relevant market in the electronic communications sector.

The identification of significant market power follows the same criteria as *dominance* according to Article 102 TFEU.

> Article 14(2) Framework Directive
>
> An undertaking shall be deemed to have significant market power if, either individually or jointly with others, it enjoys a position equivalent to dominance, that is to say a position of economic strength affording it the power to behave to an appreciable extent independently of competitors, customers and ultimately consumers.
>
> In particular, national regulatory authorities shall, when assessing whether two or more undertakings are in a joint dominant position in a market, act in accordance with Community law and take into the utmost account the guidelines on market analysis and the assessment of significant market power published by the Commission pursuant to Article 15. Criteria to be used in making such an assessment are set out in Annex II.

Thereby, the intervention threshold for *ex-ante* regulation in the electronic communications sector is subject to a discretionary and well-structured proportionality test. Following general competition law principles explained in Chapter 3, only operators holding a strong economic position that enables them to behave in the market to a large extent independently of competitors, wholesale customers, and ultimately consumers are subject to *ex-ante* regulation.

It may be that the incumbent operator holds significant market power only in particular geographic (metropolitan or rural) areas of a Member State. In such a case, the respective NRA may decide to regulate only those regional or even local SMP areas. Vice versa, geographic markets with effective competition (e.g. some wholesale broadband access markets within attractive metropolitan areas) have to be deregulated.

However, the presence of effective competition on a given market must not be assessed in isolation but with regard to its neighbouring markets. An operator with SMP on market A may be able to leverage its SMP to the neighbouring market B where no SMP exists under isolated terms.

---

[10] Article 16(1) Framework Directive.

Article 14(3) Framework Directive

> Where an undertaking has significant market power on a specific market, it may also be deemed to have significant market power on a closely related market, where the links between the two markets are such as to allow the market power held in one market to be leveraged into the other market, thereby strengthening the market power of the undertaking.

Article 14(3) Framework Directive empowers NRAs to impose *ex-ante* obligations in neighbouring, upstream, and downstream markets where vertically and/or horizontally integrated operators leverage their SMP from one market to another.

However, the imposition of regulatory obligations in retail markets is only considered as a last resort. Access regulation and access price regulation need to be exhausted on upstream (infrastructure) markets before NRAs are entitled to:

> impose appropriate regulatory obligations on undertakings identified as having significant market power on a given retail market in accordance with Article 14 of Directive 2002/21/EC (Framework Directive) where:
>
> as a result of a market analysis carried out in accordance with Article 16 of Directive 2002/21/EC (Framework Directive), a national regulatory authority determines that a given retail market identified in accordance with Article 15 of that Directive is not effectively competitive. (Article 17(1) Universal Service Directive)

Supremacy of access over retail regulation is based on the experience in the electronic communications sector that well-targeted access regulation on upstream markets (e.g. wholesale voice call termination on fixed and mobile networks) serves as an efficient driver for service-based competition in downstream retail markets, leading to the supply of sufficient good-quality services across all regions accessible to all users at affordable prices.

For instance, in its review (NRA's market analysis) of the wholesale mobile call termination markets for the period 1 April 2015–31 March 2018, UK regulator *Ofcom* focuses in detail on distributional effects on vulnerable consumers caused by specific (upstream) regulatory settings of mobile termination rates charged by terminating mobile communications providers:

> However, we believe it is important to maintain this competition, and that we should regulate the key wholesale market of access to termination on other networks in such a way as to facilitate effective retail competition. Given the importance of competition in producing efficient outcomes, we put significant

weight on this. In identifying the appropriate cost standard for the charge control, our key focus is to address consumer harm associated with the market failure arising from SMP.

FURTHER READING

Ofcom (UK) review of the wholesale 'mobile call termination' (MCT) markets for the period 1 April 2015 – 31 March 2018 at points 6.163 subs.

Click http://stakeholders.ofcom.org.uk/consultations/mobile-call-termination-14/statement/.

6.1.7 Third Step: Choice and Imposition of Proportional Access Remedies

Article 16 Framework Directive

(…)

3. Where a national regulatory authority concludes that the market is effectively competitive, it shall not impose or maintain any of the specific regulatory obligations referred to in paragraph 2 of this Article. In cases where sector specific regulatory obligations already exist, it shall withdraw such obligations placed on undertakings in that relevant market. An appropriate period of notice shall be given to parties affected by such a withdrawal of obligations.

4. Where a national regulatory authority determines that a relevant market is not effectively competitive, it shall identify undertakings with significant market power on that market in accordance with Article 14 and the national regulatory authority shall on such undertakings impose appropriate specific regulatory obligations referred to in paragraph 2 of this Article or maintain or amend such obligations where they already exist.

(…)

Choice and imposition of access remedies are strictly based, under proportional terms, on the results of the market analysis.

Article 8 Access Directive

Imposition, amendment or withdrawal of obligations

1. Member States shall ensure that national regulatory authorities are empowered to impose the obligations identified in Articles 9-13.

(…)

> 4. Obligations imposed in accordance with this Article shall be based on the nature of the problem identified, proportionate and justified in the light of the objectives laid down in Article 8 of Directive 2002/21/EC (Framework Directive). Such obligations shall only be imposed following consultation in accordance with Articles 6 and 7 of that Directive.
>
> (…)

With due regard to the particular circumstances on relevant markets, *ex-ante* regulation is, as a matter of principle, only proportionate on wholesale markets. There, competitors are to a large extent still dependent on access and access price regulation of infrastructure services to be provided by the incumbents. Otherwise, competitors, especially newcomers, would not be able to compete with the incumbents on the downstream retail markets.

The Access Directive provides for the following regulatory remedies to be imposed on an operator holding SMP:

OBLIGATION OF TRANSPARENCY (ART. 9)

In relation to interconnection and/or access, requiring operators to make public specified information, such as accounting information, technical specifications, network characteristics, terms and conditions for supply and use

OBLIGATION OF NON-DISCRIMINATION (ART. 10)

In relation to interconnection and/or access to ensure that the operator applies equivalent conditions in equivalent circumstances to other undertakings providing equivalent services, and provides services and information to others under the same conditions and of the same quality as it provides for its own services, or those of it subsidiaries or partners

OBLIGATION OF ACCOUNTING SEPARATION (ART. 11)

In relation to specified activities related to interconnection and/or access in order to make transparent the operator's wholesale prices and its internal transfer prices inter alia to ensure compliance where there is a requirement for non-discrimination

OBLIGATIONS OF ACCESS (ART. 12)

To, and use of, specific network facilities to meet reasonable requests for access to, and use of, specific network elements and associated facilities, inter alia in situations where the NRA considers that denial of access or unreasonable terms and conditions having a similar effect would hinder the emergence of a sustainable competitive market at the retail level, or would not be in the end-user's interest.

Operators may be required inter alia:

(a) to give third parties access to specified network elements and/or facilities, including access to network elements which are not active and/or unbundled access to the local loop, to inter alia allow carrier selection and/or pre-selection and/or subscriber line resale offers;
(b) to negotiate in good faith with undertakings requesting access;
(c) not to withdraw access to facilities already granted;
(d) to provide specified services on a wholesale basis for resale by third parties;
(e) to grant open access to technical interfaces, protocols or other key technologies that are indispensable for the interoperability of services or virtual network services;
(f) to provide co-location or other forms of associated facilities sharing;
(g) to provide specified services needed to ensure interoperability of end-to-end services to users, including facilities for intelligent network services or roaming on mobile networks;
(h) to provide access to operational support systems or similar software systems necessary to ensure fair competition in the provision of services;
(i) to interconnect networks or network facilities;
(j) to provide access to associated services such as identity, location and presence service.

NRAs may attach to those obligations conditions covering fairness, reasonableness and timeliness.

PRICE CONTROL AND COST ACCOUNTING OBLIGATIONS (ART. 13)

Relating to cost recovery and price controls, including obligations for cost orientation of prices and obligations concerning cost accounting systems for the provision of specific types of interconnection and/or access in situations where a market analysis indicates that a lack of effective competition means that the operator concerned might sustain prices at an excessively high level, or apply a price squeeze, to the detriment of end-users.

To encourage investments by the operator, including in next generation networks, NRAs shall take into account the investment made by the operator, and allow him a reasonable rate of return on adequate capital employed, taking into account any risks specific to a particular new investment network project. NRAs shall ensure that any cost recovery mechanism or pricing methodology that is mandated serves to promote efficiency and sustainable competition and to maximise consumer benefits.

FUNCTIONAL SEPARATION (ART. 13A)

Where the NRA concludes that the appropriate obligations imposed under Articles 9–13 have failed to achieve effective competition, it may, as an exceptional measure, impose an obligation on vertically integrated undertakings to place activities related to the wholesale provision of relevant access products in an independently operating business entity. That business entity shall supply access products and services to all undertakings, including to other business entities within the parent company, on the same timescales, terms and conditions, including those relating to price and service levels, and by means of the same systems and processes.

6.1.8 Cooperation among NRAs and the Commission

To enhance cooperation among NRAs and the Commission, the *Body of European Regulators for Electronic Communications (BEREC)* was established by Regulation (EC) No 1211/2009. BEREC's mission is to expedite *independent, consistent, high-quality regulation of electronic communications markets* by ensuring a consistent application of the EU regulatory framework, thus aiming to promote an effective internal market in the electronic communications sector. BEREC supports the NRAs and the Commission in implementing the EU regulatory framework for electronic communications by supplying advice on request and on its own initiative to the NRAs, the Commission, and the European legislator, i.e. the Parliament and Council. BEREC thereby complements on the European level the regulatory tasks performed at national level by the NRAs. In particular, BEREC is empowered to develop and disseminate among NRAs regulatory best practices, methodologies or guidelines on the implementation of the EU regulatory framework. According to Regulation (EC) No 1211/2009, NRAs and the Commission have to take utmost account of any opinion, recommendation, guidelines, advice or regulatory best practice adopted by BEREC.

> **FURTHER READING**
>
> http://berec.europa.eu/.

Article 7 of the Framework Directive integrates BEREC into a rather intricate and tedious cooperation mechanism among NRAs and the Commission to supervise national regulatory measures through supra-national consultation and consolidation.

> Article 7(2) Framework Directive
>
> Consolidating the internal market for electronic communications
>
> National regulatory authorities shall contribute to the development of the internal market by working with each other and with the Commission and BEREC in a transparent manner so as to ensure the consistent application, in all Member States, of the provisions of this Directive and the Specific Directives. To this end, they shall, in particular, work with the Commission and BEREC to identify the types of instruments and remedies best suited to address particular types of situations in the marketplace.

Before NRAs adopt decisions with potential effects on cross-border trade, including market definitions, market analysis or regulatory (access) remedies, they have to consult each other (within the BEREC framework) and the Commission on draft decisions. According to Articles 7 and 7a of the Framework Directive, NRAs' findings of market definition, market analysis (SMP assessment) and the proposed regulatory remedies have to be notified to the Commission and other NRAs. These draft measures are assessed by the Commission within one month ('Consolidation Phase I').[11] If the NRA's intended decision deviates from a market definition contained in Recommendation 2014/710/EU on relevant product and service markets within the electronic communications sector susceptible to *ex-ante* regulation and this deviation provokes an obstacle for the internal market, the Commission can block the NRA's planned market definition. The same applies to draft decisions regarding market analysis and, thus, the ascertainment of SMP of operators.

After this initial one-month period, and provided that the notified measure does not raise serious doubts as to its compatibility with EU law, the Commission may submit comments to the respective NRA.

---

[11] Art. 7(3) Framework Directive.

If the Commission however has serious doubts about NRAs' notified draft measures, its investigation period will be extended for two more months in cases of NRAs' market definition and market analysis ('Consolidation Phase II').[12] By contrast, the investigation period of Phase II for the consistent application of regulatory remedies is extended for three months.[13]

Consolidation Phase II entitles the Commission to request the NRA not to adopt the planned decision (i.e. a veto). In doing so, the Commission takes utmost account of BEREC's regulatory best practices, methodologies and guidelines on the implementation of the EU regulatory framework. Therefore, BEREC issues an opinion on whether these serious doubts raised by the Commission are justified. If BEREC shares the Commission's serious doubts over the planned regulatory remedies notified by the NRA, BEREC's task force (the 'Expert Working Group') will cooperate closely with concerned NRA in order to identify the most suitable and effective remedies.

On 14 September 2016, the Commission submitted a proposal for a new consolidated Directive of the European Parliament and of the Council (the "Draft on the European Electronic Communications Code"). Although, the scrutiny based approach on market definition, market analysis, and remedies is maintained under this Draft Code, significant changes, inter alia with regard to the modernisation of universal services, the broadband rollout, and an enhanced role of BEREC, are to be discussed now between the Commission, the European Parliament and the Member States.

FURTHER READING

Article 7(1)–(9) Framework Directive on the consolidation procedure in the internal market for electronic communications

Article 7a(1)–(8)Framework Directive on the procedure for the consistent application of remedies

https://ec.europa.eu/digital-agenda/en/telecoms-rules – regulatory framework for electronic communications.

---

12 Art. 7(4) ibid.

13 Art. 7a(1) ibid.

6.2 SNAPSHOTS OF OTHER REGULATED INDUSTRIES

6.2.1 Gas and Electricity

Energy networks, which comprise gas and electric power distribution as well as transmission systems, have historically been constructed and operated on a national basis by vertically integrated monopolies. In most EU Member States, these distribution and transmission grid operators were held in full or partial state ownership, with the state's control exercised either via central, regional, or local governments.

> EXPLANATORY NOTE
>
> The **transmission system** is the bulk high-voltage/high-pressure transfer of electricity and gas from generating power plants to electrical substations or, in the case of gas, from cross-border importation. This is distinct from the local wiring between high-voltage/high-pressure substations and customers, i.e. the *distribution system.*
>
> The **distribution system** is the final network level in the delivery of gas and electricity. Distribution grids carry gas and electricity from the transmission grid to individual consumers. In case of electricity distribution, substations connect to the transmission grid, lowering the transmission voltage to medium voltage ranging between 2 kV and 35 kV with the use of transformers. While natural gas traveling through long-range transmission pipelines may be compressed to as much as 1 500 pounds per square inch (psi), natural gas traveling through the distribution network requires as little as 3 psi of pressurisation and arrives with ¼ psi at the customer's meter.
>
> Big industrial customers demanding a much larger amount of power may be connected directly on the transmission level.

After EU energy policy had initially focused on ***liberalisation*** and grid access regulation of transmission and distribution systems enhancing cross-border trading, cooperation and integration of EU-wide energy networks has become the next policy target in the development of an ***efficient internal energy market***. Integrated networks are now considered crucial for the connection of renewable energies to the grids. Not only in the context of renewable energies, ***security of supply*** remains a challenge, but also with regard to the transfer of electricity and gas within the EU and between EU and neighbouring states.

FURTHER READING

Julia Black: European Union energy regulation, in: International Regulatory Co-operation: Case Studies, Vol. 2: Canada-US Co-operation, EU Energy Regulation, Risk Assessment and Banking Supervision, OECD (ed.)

http://www.oecd.org/gov/regulatory-policy/euenergyregulation.htm → case study on EU energy regulation.

European Union electricity and gas legislation actually comprises the following instruments, collectively known as the *Third EU Energy Package:*

(1) Directive 2009/72/EC (the Electricity Directive);
(2) Directive 2009/73/EC (the Gas Directive) of the European Parliament and of the Council, concerning common rules for the internal market in electricity and gas, respectively;
(3) Regulation (EC) No 714/2009 on conditions for access to the network for cross-border exchanges in electricity (the Electricity Regulation);
(4) Regulation (EC) No 715/2009 on conditions for access to the natural gas transmission networks (as amended) (the Gas Regulation);
(5) Regulation (EC) No 713/2009 establishing an Agency for the Cooperation of Energy Regulators (the Agency Regulation).

The directives and regulations of No (1)–(4) of the Third EU Energy Package establish measures aimed at further opening up the internal energy market to competition, especially concerning network access (price) regulation and unbundling. While access and access price regulation are not as rigidly imposed compared with the telecommunications sector, the Third EU Energy Package relies more heavily on a rather sector-specific unbundling regime. Cooperation between NRAs is established under Regulation (EC) No 713/2009 by the *Agency for the Cooperation of Energy Regulators (ACER).*

FURTHER READING

http://www.acer.europa.eu/.

Within the Third EU Energy Package, ownership unbundling is a core instrument under both the Electricity and the Gas Directive, which stipulate a separation between generation/importation/supply of electricity/gas on the one hand from transmission and on the other hand distribution networks.

Unbundling is intended to remedy the risk of vertically integrated operators abusing their dominant market power. However, under the Electricity and Gas Directives, Member States are allowed to substitute ownership unbundling with the concepts of an *independent system operator (ISO) or an independent transmission operator (ITO).*

> EXPLANATORY NOTE
>
> Under the concept of **independent system operators (ISO)**, Member States retain the option to allow transmission networks to remain under the ownership of vertically integrated operators. However, ISOs are required to transfer operation and control of their day-to-day transmission business to an independent *transmission system operator* (TSO). Investments in the network are funded by the owner, but managed by the ISO. The ISO therefore provides for functional ownership unbundling under the terms of an independent trusteeship of TSO operations in order to avoid conflicts of interest and to remove incentives for the abuse of dominant market power within a vertically integrated group.
>
> The concept of *independent transmission operators* (*ITO*) implies vertically integrated operators retaining ownership of their transmission networks, but the TSO subsidiaries must be established as legally independent joint stock companies operating under their own brand name and under a strictly autonomous management subject to stringent regulatory control. According to the ITO concept, investment decisions are made jointly by the owner (parent company) and the NRA. To exclude discrimination against competitors, a compliance officer must be deployed with the independent task of monitoring a specific programme of well-defined measures against market abuse supervised by the NRA.

Last but not least, the EU 2020 climate and energy package, which is based on four instruments and a directive, namely:

- emissions trading;
- national targets for other emissions;
- national targets for renewables;
- carbon capture and storage;
- the Energy Efficiency Directive

aims at:

- 20 per cent (respectively 30 per cent) reduction in EU greenhouse gas emissions from 1990 levels;
- 20 per cent of EU energy consumption produced from renewable resources;
- 20 per cent improvement in energy efficiency.

FURTHER READING

http://ec.europa.eu/clima/policies/strategies/2020/documentation_en.htm.

6.2.2 Postal Services and Logistics

Full market opening (liberalisation) for all postal services, in particular on letter markets, had to be implemented by 1 January 2011 in the old EU Member States. Both postal services and logistics markets are interrelated, and both are vitally affected by digitalisation and e-commerce trends. Even under the umbrella of the European harmonisation framework, mainly under Postal Directive 2008/6/EC, traditional postal markets (in particular the letter markets) are still regulated under national and rather (dysfunctional) sector-encapsulated terms. Although e-commerce tremendously increases the share of cross-border trade on all value chain levels, in particular of upstream postal services, e-commerce driven, integrated cross-border trade is not yet properly addressed under the EU regulatory framework for postal services. Still, the EU regulatory framework and its implementation by Member States' laws rely on traditional approaches of access regulation, encapsulated in hardware patterns of 'good old' postal practices. Moreover, adjustments of the Universal Service are required in order to cope with letter markets declining due to the rise of electronic communications.

In 2015, the EU Competition Commissioner opened a sector enquiry to investigate barriers to cross-border e-commerce from both the sector-specific (regulatory frameworks for postal and electronic communications services) as well as the general competition law perspective.[14]

[14] Cf. Press release of the European Commission 'Competition: Commissioner Vestager announces proposal for e-commerce sector inquiry', 26.03.2015, http://europa.eu/rapid/press-release_IP-15-4701_en.htm, 06.07.2016.

To boost growth and jobs in Europe, the promising EU *Digital Single Market (DSM)* flagship initiative[15] is consequently much wider than the 'Telecoms Single Market' and, in particular, embraces *e-commerce*, thus linking electronic communications with postal services. The DSM Strategy pursues three main objectives:

(1) ***better access*** for consumers and businesses to digital goods and services to facilitate cross-border e-commerce under harmonised consumer and contract rules for online shopping, thereby ensuring efficient and affordable cross-border parcel delivery;
(2) shaping the cross-sector environment for digital networks and e-commerce services by virtue of a ***(cross-sector) Review of the 2009 regulatory framework for electronic communications and services***, taking into account the tremendous growth of data traffic and the emergence of new services and applications, changing rapidly the traditional postal, logistics and telecommunications markets and business models;
(3) Developing an ***adequate regulatory framework for interoperable e-services (including e-government)*** to connect the 'old' and the 'new', digital economy, taking into account emerging services such as *big data* or *cloud computing*.

FURTHER READING

http://ec.europa.eu/priorities/digital-single-market/index_en.htm.

These and other regulatory challenges, i.e. those with regard to the substitution of traditional postal services with digital communication, will also be dealt with by the *European Regulators Group for Postal Services (ERGP)* through regulatory cooperation to ensure a consistent application of the (future) European framework for postal markets within the Digital Single Market.

[15] Cf. Press release of the European Commission: Digital Single Market Strategy: European Commission agrees areas for action, 25.03.2015, http://europa.eu/rapid/press-release_IP-15-4653_en.htm, 06.07.2016.

FURTHER READING

http://ec.europa.eu/growth/sectors/postal-services/ergp/index_en.htm → Mission of the ERGP.

6.2.3 Railways

Railways infrastructures and services are key factors to the completion of the internal market for transportation and (sustainable) mobility. Cross-border passenger service markets have been liberalised since 2010, subject to a harmonised licensing procedure ensuring specified professional and financial standards. Since 2007, national and international rail freight transportation services have been liberalised for licensed EU railway companies with the necessary safety certification upon application for capacity.

Railways Directive 2012/34/EU and its amendments by Regulation 2015/10 (Railways Framework) proclaim a single European railways area. However, both railways service providers, who depend on efficient upstream access to railway infrastructure to produce domestic and international rail services in cross-border competition, and stressed passengers waiting downstream for their trains on the platform experience every day that the European railways reality is still far from the single market ideal.

The EU Railways Framework provides:

(1) rules applicable to the management of railway infrastructure and to rail transport activities of the railway undertakings established or to be established in a Member State;
(2) criteria applicable to the issuance, renewal or amendment of licences by a Member State intended for railway undertakings which are or will be established in the Union; and
(3) principles and procedures applicable to the setting and collecting of railway infrastructure charges and the allocation of railway infrastructure capacity.

As in other network industries, NRAs have to ensure effective and non-discriminatory access to the rail network and services according to the harmonised rules under Directive 2001/14/EC. The NRA's regulatory task is in particular to supervise that the setting of charges and the allocation of railway infrastructure capacity by the infrastructure manager to competitors comply with the principles set out in Directive 2001/14 providing for an effective and competitive use of available infrastructure capacity.

A Trans-European Conventional Rail System is established under Directive 2008/57 (amended by Directive 2014/106) and Regulations 1299/2014 to 1305/2014 in order to harmonise technical specifications to safeguard interoperability and to prevent interruptions in the movement of high-speed trains throughout the European Union.

Regulation 1371/2007 establishes rights of passengers, i.e. such with regard to information requirements, ticketing, liability of railway operators and their insurance obligations with respect to passengers and their luggage, compensation in cases of delay, assistance to disabled, and the handling of complaints.

As in other network industries, a European regulatory body, namely the *European Railway Agency* established under Regulation 881/2004, is entrusted with the task of harmonising the railway systems to ensure interoperability and safety.

FURTHER READING

http://ec.europa.eu/transport/modes/rail/market/regulatory_bodies_en.htm → Mission of the ERGP.

6.3 THE FINANCIAL CRISIS: A FIRE TEST TO EU REGULATION

6.3.1 It all Started – with a Market-made Financial Earthquake

While network regulation focuses on access to bottlenecks operated by dominant undertakings, access pricing, network interoperability, and the availability and affordability of universal services, financial regulation was established in order to safeguard systemic functions such as the supply of financial markets with liquidity and, in particular, lending. Fundamentally, any regulatory toolkit follows the path of market functions and the Achilles' heels of the respective sector.

As in any sector, regulation cannot substitute market performance of financial service providers, but it may prevent or, at least, remedy market-made perturbations, which are often caused by folly and greed. Regulation primarily supervises (and coaches) systemic financial institutions, which, on the one hand, are market players (and as such to be kept competitive), while, on the other hand, are too big or too important to fail due to their systemic functions in the relevant financial markets and the economy as a whole. In cases of perturbations, such as breakdowns of financial institutions or accidental shortage of liquidity, in particular with respect to lending, regulation has to balance the safeguarding of systemic functions and competitiveness of financial market players on the merits.

The global financial crisis has served as a perfect laboratory to refine the art of regulation to adapt to the function of institutions as market players and, at the same time, as systemic pillars in the relevant financial markets and the economy as a whole.

When the financial crisis accelerated in the aftermath of Lehman Brothers' collapse in 2008 and the subprime (mortgage) crisis extended into a sovereign debt crisis, the EU had to rely heavily on state aid law remedies (see below Chapter 6.3.11.). In the absence of a seismic regulatory and supervisory (*ex-ante*) system which could have prevented systemic financial institutions from failing, partly due to non-prudential investment practices, EU state aid law (see Chapters 4 and 5) had to step in as the only available last resort.

The universal lack of adequate *ex-ante* supervisory powers, regulatory rules and institutions enabled reckless voracity, in particular for derivatives which are widely decoupled from the performance of the 'real' economy, to prevail over prudential traditional long-term investments in stocks, real estate or bonds. Derivatives, such as in subprimes, turned out, amongst others, to be banana skins on which the financial system slipped into the worldwide crisis.

EXPLANATORY NOTE

In order to make high-risk ('**subprime**') mortgages available, lenders funded these subprime mortgages by bundling and repackaging them into pools that were sold to investors. New financial products, i.e. derivatives, were developed to apportion the implied high default risks, e.g. 'private-label mortgage-backed securities' (PMBS). After PMBS and PMBS-backed securities were downgraded to 'high-risk', several leading subprime lenders filed for bankruptcy due to the collapsing bond funding of subprime mortgages since 2007. Thus, lenders stopped engaging in subprime mortgages, thereby lowering the demand for real estate, leading to sliding real estate prices that fuelled fears of a crash in the relevant real estate markets. Among the lenders 'too big to fail' were US government-sponsored Fannie Mae and Freddie Mac, to be seized by the Federal Government while collapsing in 2008.

Derivatives are securities with prices 'derived' from underlying assets (stocks, bonds, currencies, mortgages, commodities, interest rates or market indexes). The price of derivatives is determined by fluctuations in the underlying assets. Derivatives regularly use a high degree of leverage effects and are rather complex (abstract) in nature. Their 'mathematics of leverage effects', limited regulations and relative lack of liquidity may widely decouple them from the prudential performance of the 'real' economy. Derivatives can be used either for hedging, i.e. insuring against risks on assets and exchange rates, or for speculating in betting on future prices of assets. Most derivatives are traded over-the-counter (OTC) and, due to their lack of regulation, imply greater risks for the counterparty than (more regulated) derivatives traded on exchanges.

Since the outbreak of the financial crisis, EU legislation and regulation have been enacted with breathtaking speed in order to establish a seismic system to detect and react on an early *ex-ante* basis. The following snapshots of EU financial markets regulation are neither intended to be exhaustive nor presented in any historical order. They rather illustrate the regulatory and institutional impact within the early warning system.

6.3.2 Single Supervisory Mechanism (SSM), European Banking Authority (EBA) and Single Resolution Mechanism (SRM)

Council Regulation (EU) No 1024/2013 of 15 October 2013 established the ***Single Supervisory Mechanism*** **(SSM),** conferring substantial supervisory powers on the European Central Bank (ECB) to ensure the prudential conduct of credit institutions. Under the SSM regulatory framework, the ECB conducts asset quality reviews and solvency stress tests of large European banks. A few days later, on 22 October 2013, Regulation (EU) No 1022/2013 of the European Parliament and of the Council specified the supervisory powers of ECB pursuant to the SSM Regulation (EU) No 1024/2013.

On 26 October 2014, the results of ECB's asset quality reviews and stress tests of 130 European banks were published.

FURTHER READING

https://www.bankingsupervision.europa.eu/banking/comprehensive/html/index.en.html.

The institutional SSM setting provides for a cooperation network between ECB and the competent national authorities. Under SSM, the ECB retains direct supervisory powers over the 'most systemically important Euro area banks'. Below this threshold of 'most systemically important Euro area banks', credit institutions are supervised by competent national authorities which also retain supervisory powers with regard to branches of third-country banks and consumer protection.

SSM complements the mission of the *European Banking Authority* (EBA) established on 1 January 2011 on the basis of Regulation (EU) No 1093/2010 of the European Parliament and of the Council. EBA was established as an independent EU authority as part of the European System of Financial Supervision (ESFS) and is entrusted with an effective and consistent supervision to ensure the integrity and systemic operation of the European banking sector and to assess risks and vulnerabilities within the sector. EBA is constantly working on a European Single Rulebook in banking to codify a single set of harmonised prudential rules for financial institutions and of convergent supervisory best practices in the EU. Furthermore, EBA ensures the implementation of the Basel III framework in the EU by issuing Binding Technical Standards (BTS), Guidelines and reports for the implementation of the EU Capital Requirements Regulation No 575/2013 (CRR) and Directive 2013/36/EU (CRD IV).

EXPLANATORY NOTE

The **Basel international minimum standards for banks' capital** are defined by the Basel Committee on Banking Supervision (BCBS), represented by expert members from, inter alia, Australia, Argentina, Belgium, Canada, China, Germany, Hong Kong, India, the Netherlands, Switzerland, Turkey, Japan, the UK and the US. The ECB and the European Commission enjoy, among other institutions, observer status.

The Basel standards have been improved substantially since the outbreak of the financial crisis. The EU CRD IV and CRR legislation adapted the Basel III standards for more and better capital in banks, balanced liquidity, supervised leverage and capital buffers.

The ***Single Resolution Mechanism*** (SRM) Regulation (EU) No 806/2014 of the European Parliament and of the Council with regard to *ex-ante* contributions to the Single Resolution Fund (SRF) within the Banking Union provides that SRF will be capitalised over a period of eight years by virtue of *ex-ante* contributions from the banking industry (see also Council Implementing Regulation (EU) No 2015/81). The rules on the transfer of contributions from the National Resolution Authorities to the SRF as well as those on the terms and conditions of their use have been agreed upon by the participating Member States in an inter-governmental agreement. The Single Resolution Board established under the SRM regulations obtains broad powers in cases of bank resolutions if it is informed by the ECB that a bank is failing or likely to fail. The Single Resolution Board is empowered to adopt a scheme on its own initiative subjecting failing banks to resolution and to determine appropriate resolution tools which imply the use of the SRF.

> FURTHER READING
>
> European Court of Auditors, European banking supervision taking shape – EBA and its changing context, Special Report No 05/2014
>
> http://www.eca.europa.eu/Lists/ECADocuments/SR14_05/SR14_05_EN.pdf.
>
> http://www.eba.europa.eu/.

6.3.3 European Securities and Markets Authority (ESMA)

The ***European Securities and Markets Authority (ESMA)*** was established by Regulation (EU) No 1095/2010 as an independent EU regulatory authority within the European System of Financial Supervision (ESFS), comprising three supervisory authorities: the European Banking Authority (EBA), ESMA and the European Insurance and Occupational Pensions Authority (EIOPA).

ESMA's task is to safeguard the stability of the EU's financial system and to protect investors. It supervises risks to investors, markets and financial stability. Step by step, ESMA is completing a single rulebook for EU financial markets, thereby enhancing supervisory convergence between itself, other European supervisory authorities (EBA, EIOPA), and competent national authorities. ESMA directly *supervises* credit rating agencies and trade repositories and is accountable towards the Economic and Monetary Affairs Committee (ECON) of the European Parliament, towards the Council of the European Union, and towards the European Commission.

> FURTHER READING
>
> https://www.esma.europa.eu/.

6.3.4 European Market Infrastructure Regulation (EMIR)

The ***European Market Infrastructure Regulation*** (EU) No 648/2012 (EMIR) establishes a supervisory mechanism for derivatives, central counterparties (CCPs) and trade repositories in order to enhance transparency and reduce the risks associated with the derivatives market. EMIR has created a regulatory framework based on common organisational, conduct of business, and prudential standards for CCPs and trade repositories (i.e. obligations of clearing and reporting for over-the-counter (OTC) derivatives, measures to reduce counterparty credit risks and operational risks for bilaterally cleared OTC derivatives, interoperability between CCPs).

FURTHER READING

http://www.fca.org.uk/firms/markets/international-markets/emir.

6.3.5 Short Selling Regulation (SSR)

The ***Short Selling Regulation*** (EU) No 236/2012 of the European Parliament and of the Council (SSR) submits holders of net short positions in shares or sovereign debt to notification requirements upon certain thresholds. The SSR imposes contracting restrictions on investors with regard to uncovered short positions. ESMA regularly publishes consultation papers on guidelines in order to facilitate the coherent and convergent application of the SSR by competent national authorities. National authorities are empowered under the SSR to suspend or limit short selling transactions if the respective share, sovereign or corporate bond prices sink by defined percentage rates compared to previous day's closing price. The SSR mechanisms apply likewise to short selling transactions of (sovereign) credit default swaps (CDS) and related instruments admitted to trading within the EU/EEA unless they are primarily traded on a third country (non EU/EEA) market.

FURTHER READING

http://www.fca.org.uk/firms/markets/international-markets/eu/short-selling-regulations.

6.3.6 Market Abuse Regulation (MAR)

The ***Market Abuse Regulation*** (EU) No 596/2014 (MAR) strengthens market integrity and investor protection across the EU, providing a single rulebook on prohibitions of insider dealing and unlawful disclosure of inside information, and on prohibitions of market manipulation. All financial instruments admitted to trading on a regulated market or for which a request for admission to trading on a regulated market has been made are subject to the prohibitions of insider dealing and unlawful disclosure of inside information, as well as to the prohibitions of market manipulation. The prohibitions apply likewise to financial instruments to be traded on a multilateral trading facility (MTF) or on an organised trading facility (OTF) and to emission allowances. Issuers of financial instruments as defined by the MAR are required to notify to and obtain consent from the competent national authorities prior to delaying disclosure of inside information due to financial stability concerns. The MAR codifies with direct effect in all EU Member States' jurisdictions that inducing or recommending to another person to transact on the basis of inside information amounts to unlawful disclosure of inside information. Manipulation offences embrace, for instance, acting in collaboration to gain a dominant position over the supply or demand of a financial instrument, or abusive algorithmic trading strategies which disrupt the functioning of a trading venue. Attempted manipulations are covered as well. The MAR allows competent national authorities to define accepted market practices subject to specific terms and conditions. The MAR imposes an obligation on issuers of financial instruments to provide a list of all persons working for them who have access to inside information. Managers' transactions and suspicious transactions of third parties must be reported to the competent authorities. The issuer is obliged to publicise information on managers' transactions within three business days. Conflicts of interest have to be disclosed by persons providing investment recommendations. Whistleblowing has to be accepted as an efficient warning tool.

FURTHER READING

http://www.fca.org.uk/firms/markets/market-abuse/mar.

6.3.7 Credit Rating Agencies (CRA)

The regulatory framework on ***Credit Rating Agencies*** (CRA) is built upon the following pillars under Regulation No 462/2013 and Directive 2013/14/EU, in particular upon rules:

- to reduce overreliance on credit ratings;
- to improve the quality of ratings of sovereign debt of EU Member States;

- on liability and accountability of credit rating agencies for their actions;
- to reduce conflicts of interest as a result of the issuer-pays-remuneration model;
- to publish all available ratings on a European Rating Platform improving comparability and helping investors to make their own credit risk assessment.

ESMA directly *supervises and, in case of misconduct, sanctions* CRAs.

FURTHER READING

European Commission, MEMO on new rules on credit rating agencies (CRAs) enter into force – frequently asked questions, 18 June 2013

http://europa.eu/rapid/press-release_MEMO-13-571_de.htm.

6.3.8 Undertakings for Collective Investment in Transferable Securities (UCITS)

Directive 2014/91/EU and its predecessor directives of the European Parliament and the Council on the coordination of laws, regulations and administrative provisions relating to ***Undertakings for Collective Investment in Transferable Securities*** (UCITS) target the crucial sites of a risk-adequate regulation of investment funds available to the general public throughout the EU. UCITS V (Directive 2014/91/EU) improves common standards of investors' protection and confidence in UCITS (already provided under its predecessor directives) by tightening the rules on the responsibilities of depositaries and by introducing remuneration policy requirements for UCITS fund managers. UCITS V also paves the legal ground of common powers of regulators for the supervision of UCITS funds and their managers to investigate and sanction any breaches of the rules implemented by Member States under the UCITS Directives.

FURTHER READING

https://www.the-fca.org.uk/authorised-and-recognised-funds/ucits-v.

6.3.9 Revised Markets in Financial Instruments Directive (MiFID II) and Markets in Financial Instruments Regulation (MiFIR)

The ***Revised Markets in Financial Instruments Directive*** 2014/65/EU (MiFID II) of the European Parliament and the Council succeeded the MiFID I Directive applicable in the EU since 2007. MiFID I provided for regulatory harmonisation of authorisation and supervision of investment firms and trading venues, as well as harmonisation of the requirements for the provision of investment services, which, however, failed during the financial crisis. In the aftermath of the financial crisis, MiFID I has been revised (with part of the revisions being included in the ***Markets in Financial Instruments Regulation*** (EU) No 600/2014 (MiFIR)). MiFID II and MiFIR facilitate integration, competitiveness, and efficiency of EU financial markets. They enhance the protection for retail investors through:

- limits on the use of commissions;
- conditions for the provision of independent investment advice;
- stricter organisational requirements for product design and distribution;
- regulatory product intervention powers;
- the disclosure of costs and charges;
- tighter transparency requirements for a broader range of asset classes;
- the obligation to trade derivatives on-exchange;
- requirements on algorithmic and high frequency trading;
- refined supervisory tools for commodity derivatives.

> FURTHER READING
>
> https://www.the-fca.org.uk/about-mifid.

6.3.10 Alternative Investment Fund Managers Directive (AIFMD)

The ***Alternative Investment Fund Managers Directive*** 2011/61/EU (AIFMD) of the European Parliament and the Council has drawn a lesson from the subprime crisis by establishing remedies against systemic risks from alternative investment products inherent in hedge and private equity funds (i.e. investments outside the three traditional asset types (stocks, bonds and cash) with a rather complex (abstract) nature, limited regulations and relative lack of liquidity such as derivatives which are widely decoupled from performance of the 'real' economy). All alternative investment fund managers (AIFM) have to apply and qualify *ex ante* for authorisation under the AIFMD and, thereby, have to submit to regulation before operating in the EU. The Commission has issued numerous implementing regulations establishing refined rules and procedures, i.e. for determining the Member State of regulatory reference of a non-EU AIFM pursuant to Directive 2011/61/EU. The supervision of hedge funds and managers of other alternative investments under the AIFMD enables the EU to meet commitments made within G-20.

FURTHER READING

http://ec.europa.eu/finance/investment/alternative_investments/index_en.htm.

6.3.11 EU State Aid Law as a Last Resort Safety Net

If the seismic system enacted under EU legislation and regulation fails despite its refined *ex-ante* mechanisms, in particular if endangered financial institutions are 'too big or too important to fail' due to their systemic function in relevant financial markets and the economy as a whole, EU state aid law will step in as a safety net of last resort.

The last resort function of EU state aid law has been exercised and refined during the financial crisis. In the absence of good governance under public supervisory and regulatory powers (subsequently enacted as described above), the European Commission effectively filled the gap through its decision-making on state aid for financial institutions since the beginning of the financial and, later, the sovereign debt crisis. EU Member States have granted huge aids for the rescue and restructuring of financial institutions: between 2007 and 2014, the European Commission approved, by virtue of more than 450 state aid decisions on the restructuring or orderly resolution of 112 European banking institutions, state aid amounting to €671 billion in capital or in repayable loans, and €1 288 billion in guarantees to financial institutions in distress.

Like any other state aid, rescue and restructuring aids for financial institutions need to comply with the EU state aid regime (see Chapters 4 and 5): state aid is, as a matter of principle, prohibited (Art. 107(1) TFEU) and permitted only if it is considered compatible with the internal market (Art. 107(3) TFEU) subject to the Commission's approval (Art.

108(3) TFEU). While general rescue and restructuring aid has been traditionally approved under Article 107(3) c) TFEU and the EU Rescue and Restructuring Guidelines, the financial and sovereign debt crisis has triggered the application of Article 107(3)b) TFEU, i.e. aid to remedy a serious disturbance in the economy of a Member State. It is worthwhile recalling that even state aid with that emergency 'objective' is subject to approval of the European Commission. The Commission has a wide margin of discretion when balancing the positive and negative effects of such measures. Approved state aid measures in favour of financial institutions during the financial and sovereign debt crisis comprise state guarantees as well as granting of credit, the purchase of voting or non-voting shares of ailing banks for the purpose of recapitalisation or hybrid capital, the acquisition of risk positions by a Member State, especially impaired assets, and the installation of bad banks. Faced with such different instruments of state aid for the rescue and restructuring of financial institutions during the crisis, the Commission has developed a distinct set of crisis rules since 2008.

In the aftermath of the collapse of Lehman Brothers in September 2008, the Commission qualified the crisis as a serious disturbance in the economy of the Member States within the meaning of Article 107(3)b) TFEU, thereby acknowledging that state aid for financial institutions suffering from the crisis is not primarily a means to help the ailing financial institution itself, but also serves to combat systemic risks and to prevent a severe disruption of the financial system and the economy as a whole. The Commission has issued a number of specific communications on the application of Article 107(3)b) TFEU to state aid granted to financial institutions during the crisis:

- the Communication on the application of state aid rules to measures taken in relation to financial institutions in the context of the current global financial crisis (the *2008 Banking Communication*);[16]
- the Communication on the recapitalisation of financial institutions in the current financial crisis: limitation of aid to the minimum necessary and safeguards against undue distortions of competition (the *2009 Recapitalisation Communication*);[17]

16 OJ EU 2008 C 270/8.
17 OJ EU 2009 C 10/2.

- the Communication on the treatment of impaired assets in the Community banking sector (the *2009 Impaired Assets Communication*);[18]
- the Communication on the return to viability and the assessment of restructuring measures in the financial sector in the current crisis under the state aid rules (the *2009 Restructuring Communication*)[19] setting out the particular features for restructuring and viability plans in the specific context of crisis-related state aid granted to financial institutions under Article 107(3)b) TFEU;
- the Communication on the application, from 1 January 2011, of state aid rules to support measures in favour of banks in the context of the financial crisis (the *First 2011 Prolongation Communication*)[20] extending the Restructuring Communication on amended terms; and
- the Communication on the application, from 1 January 2012, of state aid rules to support measures in favour of banks in the context of the financial crisis (the *Second 2012 Prolongation Communication*),[21] extending the Restructuring Communication beyond 31 December 2011 and supplementing the Recapitalisation Communication with detailed guidance on adequate remuneration for capital instruments that do not bear a fixed return on the basis of a revised methodology on compensation for guarantees.

With regard to the compatibility assessment under Article 107(3)b) TFEU, all rescue and restructuring aid measures have to comply with three key principles, which are based on the general Rescue and Restructuring Guidelines of the Commission, but have been modified with regard to the particularities of the financial sector during the crisis:

1. The beneficiary can achieve *long-term viability* without state aid within a reasonable period of time according to a detailed rescue and restructuring plan. Recital 13 of the 2009 Restructuring Communication defines this goal as follows: 'Long-term viability is achieved when a bank is able to cover all its costs including depreciation and financial charges and provide an appropriate return on equity, taking into account the risk profile of the bank.' At the

18 OJ EU 2009 C 72/1.
19 OJ EU 2009 C 195/9.
20 OJ EU 2010 C 329/7.
21 OJ EU 2011 C 356/7.

beginning of the financial crisis, the primary objective was to rescue banks by providing liquidity and reinforcing the capital base, whereas later state aid measures approved by the Commission aim at the recovery of the long-term viability of the aid recipient or its liquidation if long-term viability without state aid cannot be achieved within a reasonable period of time. Restoring viability is the key element of state aid policy. Keeping unviable banks on the market longer than (systemically) necessary would risk crowding out viable banks capable of lending capital to the economy. Unviable banks may receive liquidation aid only to wind down business in an orderly manner.

2. Shareholders and hybrid capital holders need to contribute through bans on dividends or coupon payments and limitations on the repurchase of capital instruments; additionally, the aid needs to be adequately remunerated by the beneficiary as a mean to limit state aid to the minimum necessary and to minimise the Member State's, i.e. the taxpayers', burdens. This concept of *'burden sharing'* has been designed to supersede the strict '50 per cent own contribution' rule under the Rescue and Restructuring Guidelines in order to avoid contagious fire sales of assets by the beneficiary.
3. Beneficiaries need to provide measures like capacity reductions and divestments going beyond those required to ensure the beneficiary's viability to *limit the distortions of competition* caused by the aid to the minimum necessary while maintaining an adequate flow of credit to the real economy.

The Commission's review of the restructuring plan comprises checks, in particular, of the following elements of the new or improved business model defined in legally binding commitments made by the respective Member State and the bank:

- the bank's return to sustainable profitability within five years;
- monitoring of the implementation of the restructuring plan and commitments by trustees;
- identification of and remedies on the root causes of the bank's problems;
- technical feasibility assessment and a stress scenario to ensure that the bank can withstand shocks;
- the quality of the bank's risk and credit management;
- the bank's funding strategy and the development of its solvency position;

- the governance structure and the appropriateness of manager remunerations; and
- incentive structures.

The success story of the Commission's crisis-related state aid policy is confirmed by the Single Supervisory Mechanism (SSM) established in 2014 (see above Chapter 6.3.2). Under SSM, the ECB also has to approve the capital-generating actions implemented according to the state aid regime within the SSM regulatory framework of asset quality reviews and solvency stress tests of the large European banks. The majority of banks under EU state aid control has successfully passed the ECB's stress test. Banks that failed the stress test still get a chance to improve their asset quality and solvency basis. After all, most of them have just commenced restructuring as required by the EU state aid regime.

To sum up: in spite of the exceptional circumstances of the financial and sovereign debt crisis and the vast volume of approved state aids, the Commission has succeeded in integrating the crisis-related state aid measures into the 'classical' *de lege lata* schemes under Article 107(1) and (3) sanctioned by the pre-approval implementation ban *(stand still)* under Article 108(3) TFEU. This success story is due to the Commission's flexible and pragmatic crisis policies pursued according to the aforementioned 'soft law' communications combined with a sophisticated consensual regulatory approach, in particular by virtue of binding commitments relating to new or improved business models under the respective restructuring plans.

Under the severe conditions of crisis, the thin line between *instant* emergency lawmaking and interpretation has vanished. Under these exceptional conditions, the Commission has exercised good regulation in the absence of good governance.

FURTHER READING

Adamczyk/Windisch, State aid to European banks: returning to viability, in: European Commission, Competition State aid brief, issue 2015-01 (February 2015), pp. 1–7

http://ec.europa.eu/competition/publications/csb/csb2015_001_en.pdf.

6.4 OUTLOOK: PREVENTING SECTOR-SPECIFIC REGULATION FROM GOING ASTRAY

The guiding principle behind the internal market is that the interplay of supply and demand in an environment of open competition will bring forth an efficient allocation of resources (Art. 26(2) TFEU: 'The internal market shall comprise an area without internal frontiers in which the free movement of goods, persons, services and capital is ensured ...'). The prohibition of 'internal frontiers' should be seen as a means to remove barriers to welfare-producing innovation. Regulation may be justified if the market alone fails to allocate resources in a welfare-bringing manner while keeping the window wide open for innovation incentives.

We have looked at certain markets, in particular network industries, where states intervene in the allocation of resources, and we have examined how regulatory intervention is justified. The monopolistic legacy of network industries may still, at least in part, be structurally distortive to competition. That is why good regulation must aim to protect new market entrants and enable service-based competition where bottlenecks impede facility-based competition. In this respect, regulation facilitates market dynamics in the first place. Financial market regulation, by contrast, safeguards economic stability and effectiveness of supervision through a seismic system to detect systemic dangers and to react on an early *ex-ante* basis.

In the context of unprofitable airports located in remote areas, we have cautioned against the slippery slope of mischaracterising political discontent with raw market reality as market failure, supposedly justifying regulatory intervention, while the market is indicating precisely the bitter, but necessary truth for investors ('stay away from the middle of nowhere').

Actually, the threat of failure is how markets bring forth innovation. Embracing the market implies accepting the fact that businesses can fail.

Where previously incontestable incumbents struggled to keep pace with consumers' changing needs, innovative newcomers get a chance to fill the vacuum. The ongoing digitalisation of all areas of life and economy facilitates that process at dizzying speed. In particular, consumers have become used to convenient access to digital content. When digital music technology became available, widespread piracy threatened the entire music industry. Incumbents reacted by developing inconvenient Digital Rights Management (DRM) technology; lawmakers attempted to regulate human behaviour by tightening the enforcement of copyright. It was not until Apple's iTunes Store started offering DRM-free music files and catering to consumers' preference for simplicity, that music revenues started to recover. Streaming services like Pandora and Spotify have since made music consumption even more straightforward, in turn forcing Apple to offer a similar service.

Lesson learned: consumers expect vendors to exploit technological progress in order to simplify everyday life. Tightening intellectual property laws while right holders fail to adjust to market transitions has only made it socially acceptable to break the law, thus eroding its authority. Lawmakers are well advised to map, not shape social norms.

When news publishers cannibalise their very own revenues by making their intellectual property available on the web for free, failing to develop sustainable business models for the digital economy beyond advertising, should states intervene in the market by introducing an ancillary copyright that effectively forces search engine providers to subsidise the news industry? Publishers would no longer feel the necessity to develop a sustainable business model that encourages competition. Responding to supposed market failure by dismissing the market in its entirety is not the purpose of regulation.

Companies participating in an open market expose themselves to global innovation competition. But competition does not constitute market failure and it does not justify regulation. Shielding European companies from the need to innovate means rewarding entrepreneurial indolence and violating the principles of the internal market. In the long run, keeping obsolete business models on life support by virtue of regulation while the rest of the world is adjusting to new technological parameters not only hurts the competitive edge, but also Europe's welfare.

7. The dilemma of regulation – global competitiveness vs integrity of the internal market

> As the medieval states emerge into modern times, we find trade and commerce handled by statesmen as freely as ever, but according to the reasoned policy of mercantilist thinkers; and in our own days according to still other conceptions of national advantage.[1]

> Trade is not an end in itself. It is a tool to benefit people. The aim of EU trade policy is to make the most of those benefits. That means making sure that trade and investment policy is effective. It must tackle real issues based on an up-to-date understanding of the fact that the world economy is tightly linked by global value chains. [...] Trade and investment policy must equally take responsibility for supporting and promoting EU values and standards.
> (European Commission, Trade for All, p. 35)

These two quotes were written more than 125 years apart. Their common object – trade restrictions – is as ancient as trade between nations itself. Nevertheless, these quotes epitomise that trade policy objectives have changed over time: from mercantilism to a trade policy that responds to the complexities of a globalised economy and that promotes values nobler than the maximisation of economic welfare.

In this chapter, we will discuss the relations between the EU's internal market objectives and the World Trade Organization's global trade objectives. We will also discuss the EU's ambivalent position in the pursuit of both a functioning internal market and competitiveness on the global market. How to minimise distortions of the internal market and at the same time respond to distortions of the global market? The discussion will focus on state intervention in favour of industry – 'state aid' in EU legal terms and 'subsidies' in WTO legal terms. For this chapter, we use both terms interchangeably, despite some differences that we will briefly explain below. This chapter is not about explaining the functioning of the global trade order, which is regulated by WTO-rules and multiple bilateral trade agreements. It is about explaining the difficult position of

[1] Wilson, 'The State', 1256.

the EU supranational regulator: on the one hand, he has to fight off attempts to soften internal-market rules and thereby keep up with subsidy levels abroad. This is because he is bound by a policy that combines competitiveness with values such as sustainability and equity, and with competition principles such as the proportionality and necessity of state aid and, not least, transparency; on the other hand, representing EU Member States in the WTO, he cannot turn a blind eye to the fact that industries abroad are indeed subsidised in many, and often non-transparent, ways.

Global trade flows are gigantic: in 2014, countries exported merchandise worth USD 18 422 billion and imports were worth USD 18 569 billion. The EU's economy is integrated in that flow: its exports to the rest of the world were worth USD 2 262 billion and the import value was USD 2 232 billion.[2] Integration of the EU into the global economy is highlighted by domestic value added content of EU exports, which in 2009 was 86 per cent, falling from 90 per cent in 1995. The relatively high proportion of domestic value added indicates strong regional economic integration among EU Member States, while its decrease indicates that integration of the EU into the global economy has not slowed down.[3]

Competitiveness – i.e. the ability to sell to the rest of the world – is vital. Some 31 million jobs in the EU – over 14 per cent of total employment – depend on sales to the rest of the world; on average, each additional €1 billion of exports supports 14 000 additional jobs across the EU.[4] It is true that intra-EU trade is about twice the value of extra-EU trade. With value chains in the EU's internal market becoming increasingly complex and cross-border, the benefits of trade are spread much more deeply and widely than is often realised.[5]

Although the EU still is the world's largest exporter, with a 15.3 per cent market share, its position has deteriorated since the crisis, much more so than the US's, and its comparative advantage in knowledge-intensive goods and services has been partly eroded (despite its EU Framework for State aid for Research, Development and Innovation

---

[2] Trade flow figures from WTO, International Trade Statistics 2015.

[3] European Commission, ECFIN Economic Brief – Has the EU's leading position in global trade changed since the crisis?, 6.

[4] European Commission, How Trade Policy and Regional Trade Agreements Support and Strengthen EU Economic Performance, 2.

[5] Ibid., 4.

discussed in Chapter 4).[6] This is also partly due to too-late perceptions of 'new resources', such as big data, by European incumbents.

It is not only exports, though, that matter: two-thirds of EU imports are raw materials, intermediary goods and components needed for production processes. This, in turn, feeds into exports, as the share of foreign imports in the EU's exports has increased by more than half since 1995, to reach 13 per cent in 2015.[7] Moreover, trade with the rest of the world helps productivity, as long-term evidence from EU countries shows that a 1 per cent increase in the openness of the economy is associated with an increase of 0.6 per cent in labour productivity.[8]

The above figures show that the EU cannot rely on its domestic market alone, in particular in times when domestic demand remains weak. In a multipolar world where large trading blocks are competing, where new centres of growth are emerging and where value chains are global, that dependency on trade is likely to grow. This is the scenery in which the EU supranational regulator must strike a balance between global competitiveness and the integrity of the internal market.

Why are we looking at this scenery? Because these authors think that nations which in today's multipolar world join forces should do so to achieve sustainable competitiveness. This, in turn requires market and policy integration that goes beyond mere trade regulation. This objective eventually leads to tension between 'narrow' global trade objectives and 'broad' regional integration objectives. The purpose is to make aware of that tension, in particular as regards 'global' and 'internal' subsidisation rules, and to propose an approach to resolve them.

7.1 SUBSIDIES REGULATION IN THE GLOBAL MARKET

7.1.1 The World Trade Organization

Trade is the exchange of goods and services against an economic remuneration between individual economic operators. Globally, however, trade is across borders and nations have the prerogative to influence trade, by restricting market access or granting subsidies. Global trade is thus to be seen as an exchange between countries. The WTO is the

[6] Discussion in European Commission, ECFIN Economic Brief (n. 3).

[7] European Commission (n. 4), 4; with reference to the World Input Output Database (WIOD).

[8] European Commission, ibid., 3.

multilateral organisation that regulates trade between its 162 Member States. The EU's 28 Member States constitute a large trading bloc within that global order.

This book is not intended to explain the functioning of the WTO and its regulatory framework, so only a very brief outline of the WTO will be given hereunder. A more detailed description of some relevant WTO institutions and rules will be given further below in the text, where necessary.

FURTHER READING – THE WTO

Main elements of WTO rules

- General Agreement on Tariffs and Trade (GATT) 1994: the goal is to reduce tariffs and other trade restriction in the international merchandise trade. The GATT established the principles of most-favoured nation (any trade or tariff advantage granted to one contracting country needs to be granted to all), national treatment (principally no discrimination between national and foreign companies) and prohibition of quantitative restrictions of import or export.
- Agreement on Subsidies and Countervailing Measures (SCM Agreement): prohibits any subsidies that are contingent upon export performance or upon using domestic goods over imported goods.
- Other agreements include: the General Agreement on Trade in Services (GATS) which is the GATT's counterpart for the Service Sector, Agreement on Trade-Related Aspects of Intellectual Property Rights (TRIPS), or the Agreement on Agriculture (AoA).

Dispute settlement under WTO rules

Dispute settlement understanding (DSU): the preferred objective of the DSU is for the Members concerned to settle the dispute between themselves in a manner that is consistent with the WTO Agreement (Art. 3.7 of the DSU). Accordingly, bilateral consultations between the parties are the first stage of formal dispute settlement (Art. 4 of the DSU). They give the parties an opportunity to discuss the matter and to find a satisfactory solution without resorting to litigation (Art. 4.5 of the DSU). Only after such mandatory consultations have failed to produce a satisfactory solution within 60 days may the complainant request adjudication by a panel (Art. 4.7 of the DSU). Even when consultations have failed to resolve the dispute, it always remains possible for the parties to find a mutually agreed solution at any later stage of the proceedings.

So far, a majority of disputes in the (WTO) have not proceeded beyond consultations, either because a satisfactory settlement was found, or because the complainant decided for other reasons not to pursue the matter further. This shows that consultations are often an effective means of dispute resolution in the WTO and that the instruments of adjudication and enforcement in the dispute settlement system are by no means always necessary.

7.1.2 The EU as a Member of the World Trade Organization

The EU supranational executive – i.e. the European Commission – represents its Member States in the WTO. As EU Member States are also WTO Members in their own right, the Commission, when negotiating on behalf of the EU, coordinates with the EU Member States and needs the formal authorisation of the EU legislative bodies – the Council and the European Parliament – to sign WTO agreements on behalf of the EU. In other words, EU Member States speak with one voice in global trade matters.

> **FURTHER READING**
>
> How the EU works with the WTO: http://trade.ec.europa.eu/doclib/docs/2013/april/tradoc_150988.pdf.
>
> The EU and WTO: http://ec.europa.eu/trade/policy/eu-and-wto/.
>
> Trade and its effects on employment and income: European Commission, Directorate General Trade, Chief Economist Note – EU Exports to the World: Overview of Effects on Employment and Income, Issue 1, February 2016, http://trade.ec.europa.eu/doclib/docs/2016/february/tradoc_154244.pdf.
>
> EU trade strategy: http://ec.europa.eu/trade/policy/in-focus/new-trade-strategy/.

In the WTO, the EU is pursuing a two-tier strategy that projects both the EU's interests and values. 'Interests' includes public procurement, competition and subsidies issues, and also public services where the EU vowed to not prevent governments from providing, supporting or regulating services in areas such as water, education, health, and social services. 'Values' that the EU strives to promote through trade agreements are sustainable development, human rights, fair and ethical trade and the fight against corruption.

> **FURTHER READING**
>
> The European Commission explains its trade strategy in a paper 'Trade for all – Towards a more responsible trade and investment policy', October 2015, http://trade.ec.europa.eu/doclib/docs/2015/october/tradoc_153846.pdf.

The EU's trade strategy does not entirely focus on promoting trade interests in a multilateral forum. Rather, the EU also plays the bilateral card: it has concluded or is negotiating bilateral free trade agreements (FTAs) with other trading partners. While FTAs covered less than one-quarter of EU-trade in 2005, they covered more than one-third of EU trade in 2015. FTA-coverage could reach two-thirds if all negotiations ongoing in 2015 were concluded.[9]

The EU has not always followed the same strategy; rather, its trade strategy has undergone substantive shifts. When the WTO was born in 1995, the EU was mostly concerned with 'classical' trade issues (tariffs, agricultural subsidies, levies, trade facilitation) but then gradually developed a broader strategy that prioritised multilateralism over bilateral or regional trade agreements and thus advocated a stronger WTO. Then, from 2006, the EU resumed bilateral and regional trade negotiations while still prioritising the WTO as a regulatory forum. That change was in essence due to the emergence of new powerful economies, notably China, India and Brazil, which brought about a change in the balance of global trade interests. Then, from 2010, the EU put competitiveness at the top of its trade agenda and placed even more emphasis on bilateral trade negotiations.[10] The European Commission's current trade strategy makes an effort to reconcile its WTO-vocation with its bilateral approach, by declaring the latter as a sort of supplement to the former: it declares that 'the EU should do everything possible to restore the centrality of the WTO as a trade negotiation forum' and that it needs 'to pursue bilateral and regional agreements in a manner that supports returning the WTO to the centre of global trade negotiating activity'.[11]

7.1.3 'State Aid' and 'Subsidies' – the Relation Between EU and WTO Law

WTO law is not directly applicable in the EU: the last recital of the Council decision on the conclusion of the Uruguay Round multilateral negotiations, where most of the WTO's rules including the SCM Agreement (SCMA) were adopted, is clear:

---

[9] Figures according to European Commission, Trade for all – Towards a more responsible trade and investment policy, October 2015, 9.

[10] Discussion of EU trade strategies in Dee, The European Union in a Multipolar World, 48–62.

[11] European Commission, Trade for all (n. 11), 27, 29.

> Whereas, by its nature, the Agreement establishing the World Trade Organization, including the Annexes thereto, is not susceptible to being directly invoked in Community or Member State courts.[12]

Nevertheless, with respect to the application of the Agreement on Trade-Related Aspects of Intellectual Property Rights (TRIPs), the ECJ has ruled that EU national rules should be applied 'as far as possible, in the light of the wording and purpose of Article 50 of the TRIPs Agreement'.[13]

As regards subsidies, the situation is different: Article 32.5 of the SCMA stipulates that:

> Each Member shall take all necessary steps, of a general or particular character, to ensure, not later than the date of entry into force of the WTO Agreement for it, the conformity of its laws, regulations and administrative procedures with the provisions of this Agreement as they may apply to the Member in question.

Hence, in the absence of any more specific rule, it is for WTO Member States to either give direct effect to the SCMA or to adopt national laws that correspond to it. As EU state aid law however was not adopted to give effect to the SCMA but rather serves a fundamentally different purpose, namely the compatibility of state aid with the internal market, there is no need to interpret it in conformity with the SCMA.[14] Consequently, WTO Member States may complain about or even take countervailing measures against 'internal-market compatible' state aid that an EU Member State has legally granted in accordance with EU state aid rules.

Subsidies control standards, however, differ significantly. WTO Members are obliged once a year to notify subsidies granted or maintained within their territories to the WTO. Hence, this is an ex-post notification obligation (Art. 25.1, 25.2 SCMA). The WTO provides for a central authority, the Dispute Settlement Body. When a Member complains about harmful subsidies granted by another Member, that authority establishes

---

[12] Last recital of Council decision No 94/800/EC of 22.12.1994, concerning the conclusion on behalf of the European Community, as regards matters within its competence, of the agreements reached in the Uruguay Round multilateral negotiations (1986–1994), OJ EU 1994 L 336/1.

[13] ECJ, judgment of 16.06.1998, C-53/96 – *Hermès International v FHT Marketing Choice*, para. 28, with reference to other case law.

[14] Discussion in Flett *et al.*, The Relationship between WTO Subsidies Law and EC State Aid Law, in EC State Aid Law, 454–6.

'Panels' and accepts or rejects the Panels' findings or the results of an appeal. It monitors the implementation of the rulings and recommendations. It can also allow the complaining side to retaliate if no satisfactory compensation is agreed in the dispute settlement procedure. Such a 'countervailing measure' could, for example, take the form of blocking imports by raising import duties on products from the other country above agreed limits to levels so high that the imports are too expensive to sell – within certain limits.[15] In essence, there is no WTO authority controlling the implementation of the SCMA. Moreover, the WTO Secretariat has no authority to take any action against the subsidies.

FURTHER READING – DISPUTE SETTLEMENT IN THE WTO

https://www.wto.org/english/thewto_e/whatis_e/tif_e/disp1_e.htm.

EU Member States are obliged to notify state aid measures to the Commission and to not put them into effect before the Commission has approved them (Art. 108(3) of the Treaty on the Functioning of the European Union (TFEU)). The EU supranational executive controls the compatibility of national subsidies with EU state aid law and has authority to prohibit state aid *ex ante* or, if unlawful aid has already been granted, to order the aid-awarding Member State to recover the aid. Here, a fundamental difference between WTO law and EU law becomes obvious: while the SCMA only allows for a complaint–settlement–retaliation process without aiming at a stable level playing field, EU state aid law is more ambitious as it vests the supranational executive with the power to prevent market distortions in the first place and, if necessary, to re-establish the *status quo ante*. There is no retaliation between EU Member States but common objectives that go beyond removing trade barriers.

Outside the remit of Article 107 TFEU, the EU has adopted law that implements the countervailing measures rules set out in the SCMA; Article 1 of the Regulation on protection against subsidised imports from countries not members of the European Community[16] stipulates that:

---

[15] WTO, https://www.wto.org/english/thewto_e/whatis_e/tif_e/disp1_e.htm, 06.07.2016.

[16] Council Regulation (EC) No 597/2009 of 11.06.2009 on protection against subsidised imports from countries not members of the European Community, OJ EU 2009 L 188/93.

> A countervailing duty may be imposed for the purpose of offsetting any subsidy granted, directly or indirectly, for the manufacture, production, export or transport of any product whose release for free circulation in the Community causes injury.

That Regulation's definition of 'subsidy' is identical to the one set out in the SCMA. So in essence, the EU does not prescribe its Member States a WTO-conform state aid 'subsidies' regime, but only specifies the application of countervailing measures. Rather, it is up to EU Member States to ensure the conformity of their subsidies and the legal basis on which subsidies are granted with the SCMA.

As regards the competence of supranational judicial or executive bodies to interpret the SCMA respectively EU state aid law, the following differences can be noted: Under WTO law, the 'recommendations and rulings of DSB cannot add to or diminish the rights and obligations in the covered agreements' (Article 3.2 DSU). In the EU, 'Member States shall provide remedies sufficient to ensure effective legal protection in the fields covered by Union law' (Article 19(1) TEU) and the ECJ has the following competences to review EU law that implements the EU Treaties:

Article 267 TFEU:

> The Court of Justice of the European Union shall have jurisdiction to give preliminary rulings concerning:
>
> (a) the interpretation of the Treaties;
> (b) the validity and interpretation of acts of the institutions, bodies, offices or agencies of the Union;
>
> Where such a question is raised before any court or tribunal of a Member State, that court or tribunal may, if it considers that a decision on the question is necessary to enable it to give judgment, request the Court to give a ruling thereon.
>
> Where any such question is raised in a case pending before a court or tribunal of a Member State against whose decisions there is no judicial remedy under national law, that court or tribunal shall bring the matter before the Court.

What about the EU as a subsidies awarding WTO Member? One of the elements of the 'subsidies' concept (Art. 1 SCMA) is that a financial contribution is granted, 'by a government or any public body within the territory of a Member'. Hence, funding directly provided by the EU and not under Member State control, such as research and innovation funding under the EU's large 'Horizon 2020' programme, could be subject to the SCMA's definition of subsidy. Such direct EU funding, however, is not subject to EU state aid law which only applies to Member States ('state resources'; 'state aid'). EU law does not provide for any clarification on whether such funding is in compliance with WTO rules. We will dwell on the EU's 'Horizon 2020' programme to illustrate the peculiar situation of the EU as a 'subsidy' granting 'public body'. That programme refers to WTO rules only in the context of EU support for public tender preparation and/or the call for tender implementation, where it refers to the WTO Agreement on Government Procurement and delineates its applicability to eligible procurement procedures.[17] Nevertheless, the EU seems to acknowledge that despite being beyond the EU Treaty's concept of state aid, the 'Horizon 2020' programme, with nearly € 80 billion of funding available over seven years (2014–20), could do harm to competition. In an effort obviously inspired by the principle of *tu patere legem ipsi fecisti*, the EU Regulation establishing Horizon 2020 in its recitals states that:

> in order to maintain a level playing field for all undertakings active in the internal market, funding from Horizon 2020 should be designed in accordance with State aid rules so as to ensure the effectiveness of public spending and to prevent market distortions, such as crowding-out of private funding, creating ineffective market structures or preserving inefficient businesses.[18]

Hence, EU-funding is rather brought in line with EU state aid rules 'by analogy', rather than with WTO-rules.

The legal definition of '*subsidy*' is set out in Articles 1.1 and 1.2 of the SCMA. That definition is broadly comparable to the concept of state aid under Article 107(1) TFEU. *Grosso modo*, the SCMA stipulates that a subsidy is a financial contribution by a government or public body within the territory of a WTO Member, which gives a benefit to one or more recipients and that is specific. This excludes general measures that benefit all enterprises that are in the same legal and factual situation vis-à-vis the granting body, or public investments that do not provide any advantage that could not be obtained under market conditions. Recall that support given directly by the EU does not qualify as 'state aid' under EU state aid rules but may be a subsidy according to the SCMA. Interestingly, the

---

[17] Specific requirements for innovation procurement (PCP/PPI) supported by Horizon 2020 grants, http://ec.europa.eu/research/participants/data/ref/h2020/wp/2014_2015/annexes/h2020-wp1415-annex-e-inproc_en.pdf, 06.07.2016.

[18] Recital (42) of Regulation No 1291/2013 of 11.12.2013 establishing Horizon 2020 – the Framework Programme for Research and Innovation (2014-2020), OJ EU 2013 L 347/104; the European Commission's 'Horizon 2020' website: https://ec.europa.eu/programmes/horizon2020/en, 06.07.2016.

SCMA's subsidy concept does not require 'cost' to the government, contrary to the EU's state aid concept, which requires a transfer of resources that is imputable to the state, in other words, a cost to the state.

The definition of subsidy according to the SCMA is:

Article 1 – Definition of a Subsidy

1.1 For the purpose of this Agreement, a subsidy shall be deemed to exist if:

(a)(1) there is a financial contribution by a government or any public body within the territory of a Member (referred to in this Agreement as 'government'), i.e. where:

(i) a government practice involves a direct transfer of funds (e.g. grants, loans, and equity infusion), potential direct transfers of funds or liabilities (e.g. loan guarantees);
(ii) government revenue that is otherwise due is foregone or not collected (e.g. fiscal incentives such as tax credits);[19]
(iii) a government provides goods or services other than general infrastructure, or purchases goods;
(iv) a government makes payments to a funding mechanism, or entrusts or directs a private body to carry out one or more of the type of functions illustrated in (i) to (iii) above which would normally be vested in the government and the practice, in no real sense, differs from practices normally followed by governments;

or

(a)(2) there is any form of income or price support in the sense of Article XVI of GATT 1994;

and

(b) a benefit is thereby conferred.

Article 2 – Specificity

2.1 In order to determine whether a subsidy, as defined in paragraph 1 of Article 1, is specific to an enterprise or industry or group of enterprises or industries (referred to in this Agreement as 'certain enterprises') within the jurisdiction of the granting authority, the following principles shall apply:

---

[19] In accordance with the provisions of Art. XVI of GATT 1994 (Note to Art. XVI) and the provisions of Annexes I through III of this Agreement, the exemption of an exported product from duties or taxes borne by the like product when destined for domestic consumption, or the remission of such duties or taxes in amounts not in excess of those which have accrued, shall not be deemed to be a subsidy.

(a) Where the granting authority, or the legislation pursuant to which the granting authority operates, explicitly limits access to a subsidy to certain enterprises, such subsidy shall be specific.

(b) Where the granting authority, or the legislation pursuant to which the granting authority operates, establishes objective criteria or conditions[20] governing the eligibility for, and the amount of, a subsidy, specificity shall not exist, provided that the eligibility is automatic and that such criteria and conditions are strictly adhered to. The criteria or conditions must be clearly spelled out in law, regulation, or other official document, so as to be capable of verification.

(c) If, notwithstanding any appearance of non-specificity resulting from the application of the principles laid down in subparagraphs (a) and (b), there are reasons to believe that the subsidy may in fact be specific, other factors may be considered. Such factors are: use of a subsidy programme by a limited number of certain enterprises, predominant use by certain enterprises, the granting of disproportionately large amounts of subsidy to certain enterprises, and the manner in which discretion has been exercised by the granting authority in the decision to grant a subsidy.[21] In applying this subparagraph, account shall be taken of the extent of diversification of economic activities within the jurisdiction of the granting authority, as well as of the length of time during which the subsidy programme has been in operation.

2.2 A subsidy which is limited to certain enterprises located within a designated geographical region within the jurisdiction of the granting authority shall be specific. It is understood that the setting or change of generally applicable tax rates by all levels of government entitled to do so shall not be deemed to be a specific subsidy for the purposes of this Agreement.

2.3 Any subsidy falling under the provisions of Article 3 shall be deemed to be specific.

2.4 Any determination of specificity under the provisions of this Article shall be clearly substantiated on the basis of positive evidence.

When comparing this to Article 107(1) TFEU and case law interpreting the concept of state aid, discussed above in Chapter 3.2.4. and Chapter 4,

---

[20] Objective criteria or conditions, as used herein, mean criteria or conditions which are neutral, which do not favour certain enterprises over others, and which are economic in nature and horizontal in application, such as number of employees or size of enterprise.

[21] In this regard, in particular, information on the frequency with which applications for a subsidy are refused or approved and the reasons for such decisions shall be considered.

it becomes obvious that a 'subsidy' in the sense of Article 1 SCMA would qualify as state aid.

Article 1.2 SCMA – the 'commercial reasonableness test' is akin to the EU's 'market economy investor principle', that is the concept that a state intervention does not confer any advantage, and thus does not fall under the prohibition of state aid, if it is comparable to a commercial investment (see the 'Market Economy Operator Principle' in Chapter 4.4).

7.1.4 Available Data and the Transparency Issue

WTO Trade Policy Reviews – The WTO conducts regular reviews of individual countries' trade policies, so-called trade policy reviews which contain information, amongst other things, on the subsidy policy of the Member under review. For instance, the review of the trade policies and practices of China finds that 'updated notifications appear to be necessary in the area of subsidies'[22] and that China provides industry-specific subsidies for inputs, land and technology.[23]

> FURTHER READING
>
> WTO Trade Policy Reviews by country: https://www.wto.org/english/tratop_e/tpr_e/tp_rep_e.htm#bycountry.
>
> Trade Policy Review China 2015: https://www.wto.org/english/tratop_e/tpr_e/s300_e.pdf.

World Trade Report 2006 – In 2006, the WTO published its fourth World Trade Report 'Exploring the links between subsidies, trade and the WTO'. This report compares countries' subsidy levels by using data from various sources. Between 1998 and 2002, the share of subsidies in GDP was 1.5 per cent in the EU, the highest among the five comparator countries, see Table 7.1 below. According to the report, only Belarus, the Russian Federation and India had a higher percentage of subsidies compared to GDP than the EU (5.7 per cent, 2.5 per cent and 2.6 per cent respectively). In general, the report indicates that subsidy levels are generally lower in developing countries.

[22] Point 25 of the China Trade Policy Review.
[23] Point 27, ibid.

Table 7.1 WTO subsidy numbers

	Subsidies	
	as % of government expenditures	as % of GDP
	(1998-2002)	(1998-2002)
EU (25, average)	6.8	1.5
US	3.1	0.5
Japan	4.9	0.8
Korea	1.7	0.2
China	5.7	1.1

FURTHER READING – WTO WORLD TRADE REPORTS

The WTO publishes annual World Trade Reports about trends in trade, trade policy issues and the multilateral trading system: https://www.wto.org/english/res_e/reser_e/wtr_e.htm.

The World Trade Report 2006 on the links between subsidies, trade and the WTO: https://www.wto.org/english/res_e/publications_e/wtr06_e.htm.

According to the World Trade Report 2006, the EU is the most generous granter of subsidies. This should be taken with a grain of salt, though, as the notion of 'subsidy' is broader than the notion of 'state aid', and as the lack of transparency in other jurisdictions may lead to distorted statistics. Notifying the WTO of a subsidy before it is granted is not required. No effective sanction exists for non-compliance with the WTO *ex-post* notification rules, meaning the required notification is not submitted or is incomplete. The notifications are reviewed in the WTO Subsidies Committee. Up to now, the compliance record has been poor. Thus, illegal subsidies are difficult to identify. A report from 2007, commissioned by the American steel industry, claims that over the preceding 15 years, Chinese steel producers had received over USD 52 billion in subsidies. The report claims that its findings are conservative estimates and that the actual amount of subsidisation is '*undoubtedly many times larger*'.[24] That

[24] Price *et al.*, Money for Metal, 3.

could be the main reason of the present steel markets being close to a collapse due to overcapacity.

FURTHER READING – SUBSIDY TRANSPARENCY AND REPORTING:

The annual Report of the Committee on subsidies and countervailing measures lists the notification practice of all WTO Members:

https://goo.gl/Jr06gh.

For the year 2015, 21 WTO Members (the EU being counted as one Member) have notified subsidies, six Members have indicated that they maintain no notifiable subsidies; 115 Members did not submit a notification. China notified subsidies for that year; India, Brazil and the Russian Federation did not. Even if the report indicates that a country has notified, it does not evaluate the completeness and quality of the notifications. Note that Notifications pursuant to Art. 25 SCMA are only obligatory for subsidies to goods but the EU notification does not differentiate between goods and services.

EU state aid:

State aid reporting and transparency: the EU's 'State Aid Scoreboard' comprises state aid expenditure made by Member States, based on annual reporting by Member States; this comprises expenditure under all existing aid measures to manufacturing industries, services, agriculture and fisheries, approved by the European Commission: http://ec.europa.eu/competition/state_aid/scoreboard/index_en.html.

EU state aid decisions are published in the Official Journal of the EU and on the website of the European Commission: http://ec.europa.eu/competition/state_aid/register/.

EU notifications to the WTO of subsidies and countervailing measures:

https://goo.gl/5MNawJ.

7.1.5 Subsidies in the Global Trade Order and the Internal Market – Different Regulatory Objectives

Trade is a main driver of social welfare and there is global agreement on that point at least. Nevertheless, as was described above, the EU and the WTO in trade matters pursue different regulatory objectives: while the EU views trade and competition as mere tools to achieve broader objectives, the WTO is content with removing trade barriers and harmful subsidies.

Where a supranational legislator seeks both market and political integration within its constituency, it allows subsidies to reach common political objectives. Thereby, it necessarily allows distortions of competition and trade in the internal market. In the EU, this does not mean a clash of principles, though, as the internal market and trade and competition within that market are mere tools to achieve prosperity as an overall political goal. The EU even uses trade as a vehicle to project its internal values globally: 'Trade policy will become more responsible, meaning it will be more effective, more transparent and will not only project our interests, but also our values.'[25] Obviously, the EU has a common vision that justifies public market intervention. Is there any such vision at the global level?

The lacklustre performance of the international community in the seemingly endless 'Doha Round' is symptomatic of the lack of a common global vision. Since 2001, WTO Members in that negotiations round have been discussing issues such as reforming agricultural subsidies, bringing trade liberalisation in line with sustainable growth in developing countries, and improving those countries' access to global export markets. In contrast, despite intra-EU day-to-day political wrangling, EU Member States share a common vision that precisely enables them to create a functioning internal market where weaker economies can develop sustainably, where there is a common agricultural policy, and where trade barriers do not exist.

As was explained above, EU law does not transpose the SCMA in that it would define subsidies that cause 'adverse effects to the interests of another Member' (Art. 5 SCMA). EU state aid law, in turn, allows subsidies for multiple activities in the common EU interest but is not relevant for clearing a subsidy under the SCMA. When discussing the EU's industrial policy strategy until 2020, the potential conflict between 'compatible' state aid and 'actionable' subsidies is the elephant in the room:

> In the last decade the global business environment has changed radically. This results in both challenges and opportunities for European industry: industrial policy should help industry seize these opportunities. EU industry competes with China, Brazil, India and other emerging economies also on high-value products. Technology, ICT and skills are becoming increasingly important for international competitiveness. International value chains are becoming increasingly interlinked and there is increasingly strong competition for scarce energy and raw materials.[26] [...] State Aid control is essential to avoid

[25] EU Trade Commissioner Malmstrom in her foreword to the Commission paper 'Trade for all' (n. 9).

[26] European Commission, An Integrated Industrial Policy for the Globalisation Era – Putting Competitiveness and Sustainability at Centre Stage, 3.

> distortion in the Single Market; moreover, the design of State Aid rules contributes to promote the competitiveness of industry in Europe. State Aid rules provide a framework that directs Member States' investments to address identified market failures.[27]

The EU seems to be aware of the issue of bringing state aid and WTO-rules in line: 'New areas including competition policy, state aid and foreign direct investment should be addressed.'[28]

Alas, the world's nations cannot bring themselves to discuss the interaction between trade and domestic competition policy. Precisely that – the so-called 'new issues' – were taken off the Doha agenda already in July 2004.[29]

7.1.6 Comparing Subsidies Regulation (WTO) and State Aid Regulation (EU) – Conclusion

WTO Members seem to agree that subsidy races are harmful. However, there is no global vision and thus no common global objective that could justify certain subsidies. As long as a global vision of inclusiveness and equity is lacking, the WTO's system of subsidy prohibition, *ex-post* monitoring, dispute settlement, and retaliation will continue.

EU state aid rules are regulation that precisely defines the general prohibition of state aid and that provides for exemptions from that principle. That system is based on common objectives and defines 'negative effects' which, if outbalancing the positive effects in the common interest, would disqualify a state aid measure. As regards 'subsidies' in the sense of the WTO's SCMA, such regulation however is lacking. This is due to the following facts: first, there is no motivation to vest a supranational 'world trade' authority with powers to control subsidies upon notification *ex ante*, to prohibit subsidies, and to enforce that prohibition; secondly, there is no motivation to define common objectives that go beyond facilitating trade flows and a number of opportunities for developing countries to make gains. In particular, as

---

[27] Ibid., 10.

[28] Ibid., 18.

[29] In July 2005, the General Council of the WTO decided that the issues of the interaction between trade and competition policy (in addition to investment, and transparency in government procurement) would no longer form part of the Work Programme set out in the Doha Ministerial Declaration and therefore that no work towards negotiations on any of these issues will take place within the WTO during the Doha Round, https://www.wto.org/english/tratop_e/comp_e/comp_e.htm, 06.07.2016.

regards subsidies, there is no understanding that would define categories of 'non-actionable' subsidies that are in the common 'global' interest. Obviously, the world's nations are caught in a prisoner's dilemma. Overcoming that prisoner's dilemma does not seem feasible: the WTO is driven – or blocked – by its Members' individual or coalition interests, and subsidy control is based on complaints and retaliation.

7.2 THE EU'S REGULATORY RESPONSE TO GLOBAL COMPETITION

7.2.1 Beware of the Subsidy Race! Functioning Internal Market vs Global Competition Challenges

Is EU state aid control too strict? Does it limit the ability of EU industries to compete with foreign industries that are not subject to the same regulatory standards? This leads to the question: Should the EU-internal state aid regime be softened in order to retain high-value product development and manufacturing in the EU? To put it more strikingly: Should the EU care less about internal market distortions in order to stand up to global market distortions beyond its control?

State intervention to promote R&D&I illustrates this dilemma: it is the sole area where the EU provided for a 'matching clause' – that is the possibility to grant aid that matches aid for competitors abroad and thus goes beyond the levels permitted in the EU:

> In order to address actual or potential direct or indirect distortions of international trade, higher intensities than generally permissible under this framework may be authorised if, directly or indirectly, competitors located outside the Union have received in the last three years or are going to receive aid of an equivalent intensity for similar projects. However, where distortions of international trade are likely to occur after more than three years, given the particular nature of the sector in question, the reference period may be extended accordingly. Where possible, the Member State concerned will provide the Commission with sufficient information to enable it to assess the situation, in particular the need to take account of the competitive advantage enjoyed by a third country competitor. Where the Commission does not have evidence concerning the awarded or proposed aid, it may also base its decision on circumstantial evidence.[30]

---

[30] Point 92 of the R&D&I Framework.

The matching clause was first introduced in 1996. It has never been invoked by Member States, nor has the Commission applied it on its own initiative. In the first place, this may suggest that the level of support allowed under the normal R&D&I-aid rules is sufficient. It may however also suggest that the burden of proof is too heavy. Notably, such a clause does not exist in EU state aid rules for investment aid for manufacturing, which in the EU is allowed if it helps the development of disadvantaged regions.

The supranational legislator has three options for addressing third-country subsidies granted outside the EU: first, he could reduce the burden of proof; secondly, he could admit that would-be beneficiaries propose a 'counterfactual scenario' on the location of R&D activities, including scenarios with aid received outside the EU; thirdly, he may extend the matching clause to regional investment aid and thus to manufacturing.

Would either of these options, or two of them or all combined, be a wise choice?

Lowering the burden of proof would not avail much, as subsidies outside the EU are largely non-transparent. The second alternative means that the supranational EU legislator would allow a Member State to grant aid with the sole purpose of retaining a project in the EU that the beneficiary would otherwise carry out more efficiently abroad, or – and that is possible – with foreign subsidies. In the latter case, the supranational legislator would be dragged along by policy choices – or even alleged policy choices – taken abroad.[31] Thereby, the supranational legislator would silently abandon its authority to safeguard the integrity of the internal market. The 'market failure' as a core criterion that justifies aid would be replaced by the 'regulatory failure' of the international community of nations, namely to agree on a transparent and non-discriminatory subsidisation order.

Moreover, those two options and the third option of extending the matching clause to regional investment aid would very likely translate into windfall profits to mobile investors at the expense of state interventions that would be in the common interest. In fact, state aid seems to be of marginal importance for location decisions, which, as a rule, are of a strategic nature. Location decisions are rather based on factors such as pre-existing production at the selected location, availability and cost of

[31] In that sense Flett *et al.* (n. 14), 462.

the labour force, proximity to raw materials, availability of land and other soft location factors.[32]

This could have long-term negative effects on cohesion within the EU, as richer regions would be in a better position to out-bid the poorer ones and attract investment with matching aid if they wanted to.

Moreover, the granting of even higher aid in competition with third countries would not only stoke the EU-internal and the global subsidy race but could also make hitherto unquestioned EU aid the object of WTO complaints. As was described above, statistics indicate that the EU is the most generous granter of subsidies. Although the notion of 'subsidy' is broader than the notion of 'state aid', and although the lack of transparency in other jurisdictions may lead to distorted statistics, the figures are public. The risk is that WTO Members outside the EU might then take legal action and that competitors inside the EU would no longer enjoy legal certainty of protection against disproportionate state aid. Hence, the EU should rather take a defensive position and not give in to the lure of 'matching aid'.

To conclude, the matching clause is well-placed in the field of R&D&I-aid, a field that does not reach into manufacturing which is so close to export, the WTO's sensitive spot.

There is only one way to enable would-be beneficiaries and aid-granting authorities to legitimately invoke the matching clause in R&D&I aid. It is again about transparency and the availability of meaningful information. In the absence of reliable WTO notifications and transparent national subsidy regimes, reliable evidence on foreign subsidies to competitors can only be gathered by extensive market investigation. Much more than private-market beneficiaries and individual governments, a supranational executive is able to do that effectively. Recently, the European legislator vested the Commission with such market investigation powers.

> For the purpose of assessing the compatibility of an aid measure after the initiation of the formal investigation procedure, in particular as regards technically complex cases subject to substantive assessment, the Commission should be able, by simple request or by decision, to require any Member State, undertaking or association of undertakings to provide all market information necessary for completing its assessment, if the information provided by the Member State concerned during the course of the preliminary

[32] *Ex-post* evaluation of the Regional Aid Guidelines 2007–2013: final report, Report commissioned by the European Commission, 5, 6.

examination is not sufficient, taking due account of the principle of proportionality, in particular for small and medium-sized enterprises.[33]

7.2.2 Promoting Transparency (and Using Some Other Tools)

Looking at the WTO's and the EU's subsidies/state aid regulatory objectives above, we found that EU regulation is more ambitious and transparent. True, the EU is committed to strengthening the competitiveness of its industry. Nevertheless, supranational state aid control must keep competition distortions at bay. This also means that state intervention is permitted despite its distortive effect only if it helps competitiveness or other EU objectives that go beyond competitiveness – such as sustainable development or regional and social cohesion. Hence, competition and trade must be regarded as a mere tool to achieve common objectives, not as an end in itself. This goes far beyond what the global trade community was able to agree on: the principles enshrined in the WTO's SCM Agreement do not go beyond prohibiting specific categories of subsidies and allowing legal action, or retaliation, against other subsidies. Obviously, the lowest common denominator is 'no unfair subsidisation and if necessary – retaliation'. Interestingly, the only manifestation of a common goal that reaches beyond that lowest common denominator has disappeared from the SCM Agreement: WTO Members could not bring themselves to extend the exemption from legal action of research aid, regional development aid and environmental aid (non-actionable subsidies) beyond 1999.

It is becoming obvious that the world's nations are caught in a prisoner's dilemma. Presently, the WTO is driven – or blocked – by its Members' individual or coalition interests, and subsidy control is based on complaints and retaliation, and transparency cannot be enforced. In order to overcome that prisoner's dilemma, that system would have to be replaced by a treaty that defines all Members' interests and provides for supranational regulation that gives life to prohibitions and exemptions. It would certainly be foolhardy to believe that third countries would adopt a state aid discipline comparable to the EU's rules, let alone a utopian 'World Treaty'. Here, a rather formal common denominator comes into play – 'transparency'. Enhancing transparency might be impossible at the multilateral level but seems achievable at the bilateral level. That is why

---

[33] Recital (10) of Council Regulation (EU) No 2015/1589 of 13.07.2015 laying down detailed rules for the application of Article 108 of the Treaty on the Functioning of the European Union, OJ EU 2015 L 248/9; material provisions are set out in Art. 7 of that Regulation.

the EU should not only project its values in bilateral and multilateral agreements but also should advocate for transparency provisions. It has been successful in including transparency provisions for subsidies in the FTAs with Ukraine, South Korea and Singapore, Central America, Colombia and Peru. For instance, the EU-South Korea Free Trade Agreement provides for some basic understanding on subsidies: Article 11.9 of that agreement stipulates that:

> The Parties agree to use their best endeavours to remedy or remove through the application of their competition laws or otherwise, distortions of competition caused by subsidies in so far as they affect international trade, and to prevent the occurrence of such situations.

That FTA refers to subsidies in the sense of the SCMA but also – and that can be described as 'WTO-plus' – defines transparency criteria although these provisions are quite weak as regards contentious areas of services, fisheries and agriculture.

> Article 11.12
>
> Transparency
>
> 1. Each Party shall ensure transparency in the area of subsidies. To this end, each Party shall report annually to the other Party on the total amount, types and the sectoral distribution of subsidies which are specific and may affect international trade. Reporting should contain information concerning the objective, form, the amount or budget and where possible the recipient of the subsidy granted by a government or any public body.
>
> 2. Such report is deemed to have been provided if it is sent to the other Party, or if the relevant information is made available on a publicly accessible Internet website, by 31 December of the subsequent calendar year.
>
> 3. Upon request by a Party, the other Party shall provide further information on any subsidy schemes and particular individual cases of subsidy which is specific. The Parties shall exchange this information, taking into account the limitations imposed by the requirements of professional and business secrecy.

In negotiations with the US on the Transatlantic Trade and Investment Partnership (TTIP), the EU wants to:

- build on the effective EU–US cooperation agreement to enforce competition laws;
- further develop rules on competition and cooperation, including with other countries;

- ensure that SOEs with monopoly powers or special rights do not discriminate against private companies;
- agree rules on transparency for subsidies to companies supplying industrial goods and services.[34]

> **FURTHER READING**
>
> The EU-South Korea Free Trade Agreement: http://eur-lex.europa.eu/legal-content/EN/TXT/?uri=uriserv:OJ.L_.2011.127.01.0001.01.ENG&toc=OJ:L:2011:127:FULL.
>
> Explanatory paper focusing on the practical aspects of the EU-South Korea Free Trade Agreement in practice: http://trade.ec.europa.eu/doclib/docs/2011/october/tradoc_148303.pdf.
>
> Inside TTIP – An overview and chapter-by-chapter guide in plain English: http://trade.ec.europa.eu/doclib/docs/2015/july/tradoc_153635.pdf.

It goes without saying that apart from this modest yet potentially quite effective transparency initiative, the EU should make pro-active use of trade defence instruments, namely the WTO dispute settlement procedure or countervailing duties as provided for in the SCMA. Thereby, the EU could at least attempt to correct future trade-distortions. Recall the EU defensive interests discussed above.

7.3 CONCLUSION – OBJECTIVES NOBLER THAN TRADE DEFENCE

The above discussion shows that loosening state aid rules would torpedo the internal market from within, and with it achievements that go beyond fair competition.

The EU's alleged weakness, namely its commitment to controlling Member States' state aid, is in fact strength, because Member State interventions are thereby bound to redistribute wealth for common sustainable development objectives such as training, innovation, the environment, mobility or infrastructure.

One example is the shipbuilding industry: Europe's once dominant shipbuilding industry came under pressure as manufacturers from Japan (in the 1950s) and South Korea (in the 1970s) entered the market and

[34] European Commission, 2015, Inside TTIP – An overview and chapter-by-chapter guide in plain English, 44.

grew rapidly. The Commission released a number of state aid measures to lessen the blow but did so only as a transitory measure. The sector was able to adapt and now the EU is specialised in manufacturing ships that require a high degree of specialisation, such as cruise ships (99 per cent market share) or offshore vessels while the production of large container ships has been almost completely abandoned.

The EU, thereby, because it is more than just a trading bloc, is in a far better position than single nations or trade-focused alliances to prepare its industry, regions and people for the economic challenges of global competition. State aid that has a real incentive effect, tackles market failures and is proportionate, can accompany change and help companies face globalisation. It can take the form of regional, restructuring, training or employment aid, or aid for R&D&I or risk financing to help companies stay at the competitive edge. 'Trade may provide a superficially attractive veneer for development, but capitalism requires the development of human resources and effective domestic institutions through access to education, infrastructure, and above all legal protections, all of which require an effective state.'[35]

[35] Scott, Capitalism: Its Origins and Evolution as a System of Governance, 23.

8. Where we are going to …

The EU set out to become more democratic – or so it seems: '*Democratic Change – Making the EU more democratic*' is among the European Commission's top ten priorities for its current term (2014–19). A 'European Spring'? Democratic change claimed by disgruntled citizens – or rather prescribed by bureaucrats? Is there a 'democratic deficit' in the first place and, if so, could it be remedied by better regulation?

After all, regulation remains what it is, namely ordinary law that should always be adopted and enforced on the basis of democratic principles. Those principles limit executive power, guarantee the rights of individuals and prescribe a democratic process. They are enshrined in constitutions. 'Constitutions bring legitimate government into existence and formulate the conditions for the exercise of public power. They thus antedate government and are not at its disposal.'[1] How can it then be that the European Commission as an executive body could 'democratise' the European Union? The response lies in the peculiar position and structure of EU law, which is between international law and the law of a federal state, and which contains both, genuinely constitutional and ordinary provisions.

In this chapter, we will first retrace the EU regulator's actual course in the internal market, wealth, and competition policies. The questions and particularities outlined above are central to that discussion – they are about the EU's navigation chart. In particular, we will discuss how far the EU regulator is sailing on the most fundamental bearing: the democratic principle. Then, we will look at the EU's current attempts to 'make the EU as a whole more democratic', to cut red tape and to improve the quality of legislation. We will also make proposals on how to effectively control and limit the regulator.

---

[1] Grimm, The Democratic Costs of Constitutionalisation: The European Case, 462.

8.1 SUPRANATIONAL REGULATION AND THE LEGITIMACY ISSUE

8.1.1 The Democratic Principle in the EU

Whenever the EU intervenes – directly or through its Member States – in market allocations, in order to direct market behaviour towards the public interest, the question of economic justification and democratic legitimisation arises. We have already dealt with the economic justification of regulation, in particular in Chapters 4, 5, and 6. Now, the question of democratic legitimisation of EU-driven public intervention in market allocations and market behaviour comes to the fore. If regulation prescribes official methods and standards to which market behaviour *must* adhere, any such imperative must be democratically legitimate.

According to one theory, legitimacy can be found in the extent to which EU policy 'outputs' protect and possibly expand the welfare of European citizens ('government *for* the people'). This theory holds that such 'output legitimacy' is a more appropriate concept for a complex reality such as the EU, which cannot receive 'input legitimacy' from a 'European' constituency ('government *by* the people').[2] Indeed, 'output legitimacy' seems an appealing enough concept to give EU regulators peace of mind. After all, the EU is politically fragmented and its integration process is not likely to be reinforced anytime soon. That legitimacy concept however necessitates that the common good – or, in the EU's terminology, 'the general economic interest' or 'the common interest'[3] – is defined in a way that is permanently in line with the implicit preference of an imaginary European constituency. This would be 'enlightened government'. Such 'enlightened government' – which in fact is 'enlightened dictatorship' – would in practice have to define concrete policy objectives in the common interest, e.g. in the fields of transport, energy, research, regional policy, or the environment, and then the market failures that prevent results in the common interest, as well as the interventions and incentives necessary to overcome such market failures. This however requires decisions that are eminently political, rather than technocratic in the sense that some democratically pre-defined

---

[2] Discussion of 'input' and 'output legitimacy' in Hallerberg/Marzinotto/Wolff, An Assessment of the European Semester, 34 *et seq.*; with reference to Scharpf, Interdependence and democratic legitimation, MPIfG Working Paper, No 98/2, September 1998.

[3] In the EU's rules on competition: Arts 106(2) and 107(3) b), c), d) of the TFEU.

goals are merely filled with life and implemented. Achieving this means that certain interest groups, i.e. industries or regions, are favoured over others.

This is the reality of EU-supranational regulation of the internal market, competition, and state intervention in markets. In order to better understand that legal reality, and its legitimacy and effects, we need to look at the EU's constitutional frame. First of all, there is no EU constitution as such. Rather, the EU was built on a body of treaties under international law. Its Member States' governments, in turn, have legitimacy on the basis of national constitutions. Even the unsuccessful 'Treaty Establishing a Constitution for Europe' – the project was dropped as the text had not been ratified by all Member States – despite its label was still a treaty under international law. In reality, though, the current Treaties fulfil many of a constitution's typical functions: they specify the purposes of the EU, establish its organs, determine their powers and procedures, frame the relationship with the Member States, and contain a charter of fundamental rights just as constitutions do.[4] The EU's supranational judiciary interprets the Treaties and controls the EU's organs as well as the Member States.

FURTHER READING – THE EUROPEAN COURT, DIRECT EFFECT OF EU LAW, AND 'THE PEOPLES OF EUROPE'

The shift of the EU Treaties from a compact between nations towards a quasi-constitutional frame that constitutes rights and obligations for individual EU citizens commenced in the 1960s, several years after the Treaties of Rome were signed on 25 March 1957, to establish the EU's predecessor, the European Economic Community (EEC).

In a judgment on the direct applicability of European supranational law in Member States, the European Court of Justice found that:

> The objective of the EEC Treaty, which is to establish a Common Market, the functioning of which is of direct concern to interested parties in the Community, implies that this Treaty is more than an agreement which merely creates mutual obligations between the contracting states. This view is confirmed by the preamble to the Treaty which refers not only to governments but to peoples. It is also confirmed more specifically by the establishment of institutions endowed with sovereign rights, the exercise of which affects Member States and also their citizens. Furthermore, it must be noted that the nationals of the states brought together in the Community are called upon to

[4] Grimm (n 1), 265.

> cooperate in the functioning of this Community through the intermediary of the European Parliament and the Economic and Social Committee.[5]

The Court then says that Member States, through the Treaty, had tasked the European Court of Justice with securing the uniform interpretation of the Treaty by national courts and tribunals, and thus acknowledged that Community law has an authority which can be invoked by their nationals before those courts and tribunals, the most significant and interesting reason being that:

> the Community constitutes a new legal order of international law for the benefit of which the states have limited their sovereign rights, albeit within limited fields, and the subjects of which comprise not only Member States but also their nationals. Independently of the legislation of Member States, Community law therefore not only imposes obligations on individuals but is also intended to confer upon them rights which become part of their legal heritage.[6]

This must have sounded quite revolutionary in 1963, when governments thought in terms of international law, national prerogatives and, at best, a very limited cessation of sovereign rights as long as this obviously prevents international conflict or serves economic interest. The Court then concluded that the implementation of clear and unconditional EU rules is not conditional upon a positive legislative measure enacted under national law.

With that judgment, two things became obvious: first, the European supranational judiciary was going to interpret EU law assertively and in light of the effect it has on citizens, not only on contracting states. Secondly, supranational law is even applicable where Member States fail to transpose it into national law.

With another landmark judgment, the Court went even further, as it then confirmed not only the direct effect of European supranational law but also its supremacy over national law:

> The integration into the laws of each Member State of provisions which derive from the Community, and more generally the terms and the spirit of the Treaty, make it impossible for the states, as a corollary, to accord precedence to a unilateral and subsequent measure over a legal system accepted by them on a basis of reciprocity. Such a measure cannot therefore be inconsistent with that legal system. [...] The precedence of Community law is confirmed by Article 189, whereby a regulation 'shall be binding' and 'directly applicable in all Member States'. This provision, which is subject to no reservation, would be quite meaningless if a state could unilaterally nullify its effects by means of a legislative measure which could prevail over Community law. It follows from all these observations that the law stemming from the Treaty, an independent source of law, could not, because of its special and original nature, be overridden by domestic legal provisions, however framed, without being deprived of its character as Community law and without the legal basis of the Community itself being called into question. The transfer by the states from their domestic legal system to the Community

[5] ECJ, judgment of 05.02.1963, C-26/62 – *Van Gend en Loos*.

[6] Ibid.

> legal system of the rights and obligations arising under the Treaty carries with it a permanent limitation of their sovereign rights, against which a subsequent unilateral act incompatible with the concept of the Community cannot prevail.[7]

The point is, however, that the EU Treaties, contrary to any genuine constitution, do not only 'bring legitimate government into existence and formulate the conditions for the exercise of public power'.[8] They also contain rules that are eminently political. In the field of the internal market and competition, these are rules that prohibit cartel agreements between market operators which restrict competition, the abuse of market power, and state aid unless that cannot be justified by reasons of general economic development. A host of secondary hard and soft law spells out detailed rules of application that interpret and implement the 'quasi-constitutional' basis.

The field of competition law illustrates the EU's constitutional peculiarity: EU secondary law can be political and prescriptive but, to a large extent, is outside the political debate and left to the interpretation of both the European executive and the Court of Justice. This is the consequence of the quasi-constitutional status of EU primary law. EU competition law was enshrined in the Treaties, replacing national competition law. EU competition law provides for a wide margin of interpretation. That margin needs to be filled with practicable secondary law. At the EU supranational level, such legislation can be adopted with varying degrees of legitimacy: either by the Parliament together with the Council (co-decision), or by the European Commission as empowered by the Council, or by the Commission alone.

As EU primary law in competition matters is enshrined in a quasi-constitutional frame, it is interpreted by the European Court and the European Commission.

The European Commission as an executive body enjoys a broad margin of discretion. For example, when assessing the compatibility of state aid with the internal market on the basis of soft law adopted by the European Commission, that same executive body enjoys a wide margin of discretion which, according to the European Court of Justice, 'involves complex economic and social assessments which must be made in a European Union context'.[9] Economic and social assessments are indeed

---

[7] ECJ, judgment of 15.07.1964, C-6/64 – *Costa v E.N.E.L.*

[8] Grimm (n. 1).

[9] ECJ, judgment of 14.02.1990, C-301/87 – *France v Commission* ('*Boussac*'), para. 49.

at the heart of the 'balancing test' the Commission has to make when comparing the positive and negative effects of state intervention in the markets in order to find out if such an intervention can be justified with the common European interest. An example where the Council, i.e. the representation of democratically elected Member State governments, left the Commission with a broad margin of discretion is the regulation of cartel fines.[10] The Commission adopted Guidelines on the method of setting fines.[11] That method however is highly relevant for the parties concerned, i.e. convictable cartels.

Title II (*Provisions on Democratic Principles,* Articles 9–12 TEU) of the Lisbon Treaty pursues a (badly structured) merger of various democratic components such as the principles of representation and participation, political equality, transparency, openness, and good governance.[12] However, the Lisbon EU Treaty deliberately avoids any reference to a (in fact non-existent) European People. When evoking 'an ever closer union', the Treaty means union 'among the peoples of Europe'. As the EU is a federation of nation states, 'peoples' comprise the Member States' nationals. The Treaty brings these nationals together in the EU and calls upon them to cooperate in its functioning, through the intermediary of the European Parliament and the Economic and Social Committee. Reference to 'peoples' distinguishes that Treaty from classic international treaties among nations. It directly confers obligations and rights on individual citizens.[13]

What is more, the Lisbon Treaty does not stipulate that all power comes from the People. Instead, the Treaty proclaims a Union of citizens and Member States whose 'functioning shall be founded on representative democracy' (Art. 10(1) TEU). Whereas the Member States are represented by virtue of their role as democratic rulers in the European

---

[10] Council Regulation (EC) No 1/2003 of 16.12.2002 on the implementation of the rules on competition laid down in Articles 81 and 82 of the Treaty, OJ EU 2003 L1/1, 04.01.2003.

[11] Recital 2 of Guidelines on the method of setting fines imposed pursuant to Article 23(2) a) of Regulation No 1/2003, OJ EU 2006 C 210/2, 01.09.2006; with reference to ECJ, judgment of 28.06.2005, joined cases C-189/02 P, C-202/02 P, C-205/02 P to C-208/02 P, C-213/02 P – *Dansk Rørindustri and others v Commission*, para. 172; discussion of the democratic legitimacy of these Guidelines in Weiβ, Das Leitlininen(un)wesen der Kommission verletzt den Vertrag von Lissabon.

[12] Cuesta Lopez, The Lisbon Treaty's Provisions on Democratic Principles, 127.

[13] To this effect ECJ, judgment of 05.02.1963, C-26/62 – *Van Gend en Loos*.

Council and the Council of the EU, the European Citizens are 'directly represented at Union level in the European Parliament' (Art. 10(2) TEU).

FURTHER READING

The **European Council** consists of the heads of state or government of the EU's Member States, together with its President and the European Commission President. It defines the EU's general political direction and priorities.

The **Council of the EU** represents the Member States' governments. Also informally known as the EU Council, it is the organ where national ministers from each EU Member State meet to adopt laws and coordinate policies.

The **European Parliament** acts as a co-legislator, sharing with the Council the power to adopt and amend legislative proposals and to decide on the EU budget. It also supervises the work of the Commission and other EU bodies and cooperates with national parliaments of Member States to get their input.

The *representatives of the Union's citizens* (Art. 14(2) TEU) in the European Parliament (EP) are selected in direct European elections, in which the Union's citizens enjoy an equal right to vote and to stand as candidates. Under the Lisbon Treaty, the lawmaking role of the EP has been enhanced by the extension of co-decision procedure (between the EP and the Council of the EU) to new policy areas and new powers over the EU budget and international agreements. Democratic legitimisation of EU legislation rests on the following three pillars:

(1) the Union's citizens exercise representative democracy in the EP;
(2) Member States are represented in the European Council by their respective heads of state or government, as well as in the Council by their governments, which are in turn democratically accountable either to their national parliaments, or to their citizens;
(3) national parliaments or, according to their respective national constitutions, citizens by means of national referendums need to give green light for ratification of EU Treaties.

Some authors criticise the architecture of EU democracy as '*chaotic*' due to its 'uneasy combination of several models and inputs'.[14] Among the

[14] Closa, European Citizenship and New Forms of Democracy, in Genèse et destinée de la Constitution Européenne: commentaire du Traité établissant une Constitution pour l'Europe à la lumière des travaux préparatoires et perspectives d'avenir, 1050, (1057).

critics the German Federal Constitutional Court voiced its strong concern about the EU's democratic legitimisation as follows:

> The extent of the Union's freedom of action has steadily and considerably increased, not least by the Treaty of Lisbon, so that meanwhile in some fields of policy, the European Union has a shape that corresponds to that of a federal state, i.e. is analogous to that of a state. In contrast, the internal decision-making and appointment procedures remain predominantly committed to the pattern of an international organisation, i.e. are analogous to international law; as before, the structure of the European Union essentially follows the principle of the equality of States. [...] Due to this structural democratic deficit, which cannot be resolved in an association of sovereign national states (*Staatenverbund*), further steps of integration that go beyond the status quo may undermine neither the States' political power of action nor the principle of conferral. The peoples of the Member States are the holders of the constituent power. [...] The constitutional identity is an inalienable element of the democratic self-determination of a people.[15]

Other authors put forward a more differentiated approach to EU democracy, warning about exaggerated and inappropriate understandings of democratic legitimisation of the EU which is – in the absence of a European People – not founded on the principle of the People's sovereignty, i.e. a concept confined to the democratic nation state inspired by social contract philosophies.[16] Instead, the exercise of EU powers is embedded within the diversity of already existing and consolidated democracies of its Member States.

All this is symptomatic of the fact that there is no 'European People' that could provide the EU legislative process and its regulators with genuine legitimacy. Rather, the European integration process was exactly to create a union among different European Demoi, a process far removed from a nation-building exercise.[17]

Thus, it is contradictory to, on the one hand, demand democratic legitimacy according to nation state standards and, on the other hand, deny the development of the EU towards statehood. There is a need for an adjusted understanding of supranational democracy, in particular, to

---

[15] *German Federal Constitutional Court – Press office, 30.06.2009,* press release No 72/2009; ECJ, judgment of 30.06.2009 *(Press release).*

[16] von Bogdandy, A Disputed Idea Becomes Law: Remarks on European Democracy as a Legal Principle, in *Debating the Democratic Legitimacy of the European Union*, 35.

[17] Discussion in Hallerberg/Marzinotto/Wolff (n. 2) with reference to Weiler, European Neo-Constitutionalism: in Search of Foundations for the European Constitutional Order.

the EU's constitutional reality. In that reality, supranational power and lawmaking is limited by the principle of conferral: the Union shall act only within the limits of the competences conferred upon it by the Member States in the Treaties to attain the objectives set out therein, all other competences remaining with the Member States (Art. 5 TEU). The Member States – and they alone – confer on the Union parts of their sovereign powers.

Democratic nation states rest on a different concept of 'democratic principle' than a union of such states. According to the democratic principle under the nation state concept, the parliament has the supreme role as a lawmaker. By contrast, in the EU, lawmaking is allocated to an institutional compromise that has a tendency to swing to the parliament's benefit each time the constitution of the EU is revised. However, traditionally the European Communities have been built upon rather strong pillars of the ministerial executive of the Member States. Therefore, each treaty revision has to balance lawmaking between the EP and the Council, i.e. the representation of democratically elected Member States' governments. Thus, the democratic checks and balances of the EU's constitutional systems relies heavily on striking a balance between the EP and the Council.

To sum up this highly constitutional debate on the EU, we should not expect 'the emergence of a new democratic unit, a European demos'.[18] As the former Advocate General of the Court of Justice of the EU, Maduro, has aptly put it, the European Union must not pretend a popular *pouvoir constituant*, because 'it would entail replacing the national polities for the European polity and it could destroy the present plural relationship between the European and national constitutions'.[19]

8.1.2 EU Hard Lawmaking – Surrender of a Transparent Legislative Process?

The EU's body of rules comprises *primary law* and *secondary law*. The Treaty on (establishing) the European Union (TEU) and the (more mechanical) Treaty on the Functioning of the European Union (TFEU) are primary law and constitute the above-discussed constitutional framework. The general competition rules under Articles 101–109 TFEU (see Chapter 3), and the rules on the free movement of goods (Arts 28 *et seq.*

[18] Cuesta Lopez, (n. 12), 128.
[19] Maduro, How Constitutional Can the European Union Be?, 38.

TFEU) and services (Arts 56 *et seq.* TFEU), i.e. the essential toolkit for the functioning of the internal market, are thus part of EU primary law.

The body of EU secondary law is then formed by EU directives and regulations which are binding on Member States. In the area of competition, these acts for instance relate to specific sectors, such as telecommunications, postal services, energy, railways, or financial markets as discussed in Chapter 6, or regulation that exempts broad categories of state interventions from the general prohibitions on state aid. These secondary legal acts implement a system of sustainable competition in order to achieve economic and social justice. Secondary lawmaking is limited by the principle of conferral (Art. 5 TEU): all EU regulations, directives and decisions must be derived from the competences conferred upon the EU legislator under the Treaties (TFEU or TEU).

The principal lawmaking procedure is provided by the *Ordinary Legislative Procedure* under Articles 289 and 294 TFEU, where the procedure is precisely defined. Under the Ordinary Legislative Procedure (aptly labelled 'co-decision'), legislation is passed jointly by the EP and the Council. During multistage parliamentary reading and conciliation committee's proceedings, the directly elected EP adopts EU legislation together ('co-decision') with the Council (the representation of the 28 Member States' governments) upon the European Commission's drafts.

So far so good. The bad news is that co-decision is construed in such extremely complicated procedural steps between the EP and the Council that outside observers – even professors of European law – often feel lost in the legislative labyrinth, so euphemistically labelled the *Ordinary Legislative Procedure*. However, this legislative labyrinth is the result of the fundamental constitutional compromise inherent in each treaty revision in order to balance lawmaking between the directly elected EP and the Council, i.e. the representation of democratically elected Member States' governments.

In the area of EU state aid law, however, the EP is not involved in decision-making but is merely 'consulted'. Indeed, Article 109 TFEU stipulates that the Council, on a proposal from the Commission and after 'consulting' the EP, may make any appropriate regulations for the application of Articles 107 and 108, i.e. the core state aid rules of the TFEU. It is unsurprising that the EP in a resolution regrets that this legal base for new proposals provides only for consultation, not co-decision in line with other areas of market integration and economic regulation. The EP also criticises that this democratic deficit cannot be tolerated where the proposals shape the means the Commission has to oversee decisions and acts of nationally and locally elected authorities. With that resolution, the EP proposes that this deficit be overcome through interinstitutional arrangements and corrected in any future Treaty change.[20]

The current state of balancing lawmaking between EP and the Council is codified in the convoluted wording of Article 294 TFEU under the Lisbon Treaty *signed in 2007* by the Heads of Member States, which entered into force as late as *2012 due to national* constitutional (democratically founded) difficulties in some Member States and only after completion *of the national ratification* process of all Member States.

Article 294 TFEU

1. Where reference is made in the Treaties to the ordinary legislative procedure for the adoption of an act, the following procedure shall apply.

2. The Commission shall submit a proposal to the European Parliament and the Council.

First reading

3. The European Parliament shall adopt its position at first reading and communicate it to the Council.

4. If the Council approves the European Parliament's position, the act concerned shall be adopted in the wording which corresponds to the position of the European Parliament.

5. If the Council does not approve the European Parliament's position, it shall adopt its position at first reading and communicate it to the European Parliament.

6. The Council shall inform the European Parliament fully of the reasons which led it to adopt its position at first reading. The Commission shall inform the European Parliament fully of its position.

Second reading

7. If, within three months of such communication, the European Parliament:

(a) approves the Council's position at first reading or has not taken a decision, the act concerned shall be deemed to have been adopted in the wording which corresponds to the position of the Council;
(b) rejects, by a majority of its component members, the Council's position at first reading, the proposed act shall be deemed not to have been adopted;
(c) proposes, by a majority of its component members, amendments to the Council's position at first reading, the text thus amended shall be forwarded to the Council and to the Commission, which shall deliver an opinion on those amendments.

---

[20] European Parliament resolution of 17 January 2013 on state aid modernisation (2012/2920(RSP)).

8. If, within three months of receiving the European Parliament's amendments, the Council, acting by a qualified majority:

(a) approves all those amendments, the act in question shall be deemed to have been adopted;
(b) does not approve all the amendments, the President of the Council, in agreement with the President of the European Parliament, shall within six weeks convene a meeting of the Conciliation Committee.

9. The Council shall act unanimously on the amendments on which the Commission has delivered a negative opinion.

Conciliation

10. The Conciliation Committee, which shall be composed of the members of the Council or their representatives and an equal number of members representing the European Parliament, shall have the task of reaching agreement on a joint text, by a qualified majority of the members of the Council or their representatives and by a majority of the members representing the European Parliament within six weeks of its being convened, on the basis of the positions of the European Parliament and the Council at second reading.

11. The Commission shall take part in the Conciliation Committee's proceedings and shall take all necessary initiatives with a view to reconciling the positions of the European Parliament and the Council.

12. If, within six weeks of its being convened, the Conciliation Committee does not approve the joint text, the proposed act shall be deemed not to have been adopted.

Third reading

13. If, within that period, the Conciliation Committee approves a joint text, the European Parliament, acting by a majority of the votes cast, and the Council, acting by a qualified majority, shall each have a period of six weeks from that approval in which to adopt the act in question in accordance with the joint text. If they fail to do so, the proposed act shall be deemed not to have been adopted.

14. The periods of three months and six weeks referred to in this Article shall be extended by a maximum of one month and two weeks respectively at the initiative of the European Parliament or the Council.

Special provisions

15. Where, in the cases provided for in the Treaties, a legislative act is submitted to the ordinary legislative procedure on the initiative of a group of Member States, on a recommendation by the European Central Bank, or at the request of the Court of Justice, paragraph 2, the second sentence of paragraph 6, and paragraph 9 shall not apply.

In such cases, the European Parliament and the Council shall communicate the proposed act to the Commission with their positions at first and second

> readings. The European Parliament or the Council may request the opinion of the Commission throughout the procedure, which the Commission may also deliver on its own initiative. It may also, if it deems it necessary, take part in the Conciliation Committee in accordance with paragraph 11.

Last but not least, the Ordinary Legislative Procedure also allows for non-binding 'opinions' by the Member States' national parliaments, the EU Economic and Social Committee (ESC, Art. 304 TFEU) and/or the Committee of the Regions (CoR, Article 307 TFEU).

As already mentioned, lawmaking under the Ordinary Legislative Procedure reflects the changing democratic checks and balances of the EU's constitutional systems. It is precisely this permanent strife for democratic checks and balances in the EU during each Treaty revision yielding the legislative labyrinth, which is simplified in Figure 8.1 below.

Besides the principal Ordinary Legislative Procedure (co-decision), which puts the EP on an equal footing with the Council, there also exist Special Legislative Procedures, which apply only in exceptional and rare cases where the EP has only a consultative role. For instance, the EP gives only an advisory opinion (the 'Consultation Procedure') on certain issues of taxation. If the treaty provides explicitly that the EP's consultation is obligatory under the rare Consultation Procedure, the legislative proposal will not enter into force unless the EP has delivered its opinion. However, it has to be kept in mind that the *Art of Regulation* within the EU internal market by virtue of secondary law legislation, e.g. by EU directives and regulations on telecommunications, postal services, energy, railways, or financial markets (see Chapter 6), is subjected to the principal Ordinary Legislative Procedure (co-decision).

FURTHER READING

On the EU's law-making procedures: http://www.europa.eu/eu-law/decision-making/procedures/index_en.htm.

On the EP's and the Council's legislative powers within the respective law-making procedures: http://www.europarl.europa.eu/aboutparliament/en/20150201PVL00004/Legislative-powers.

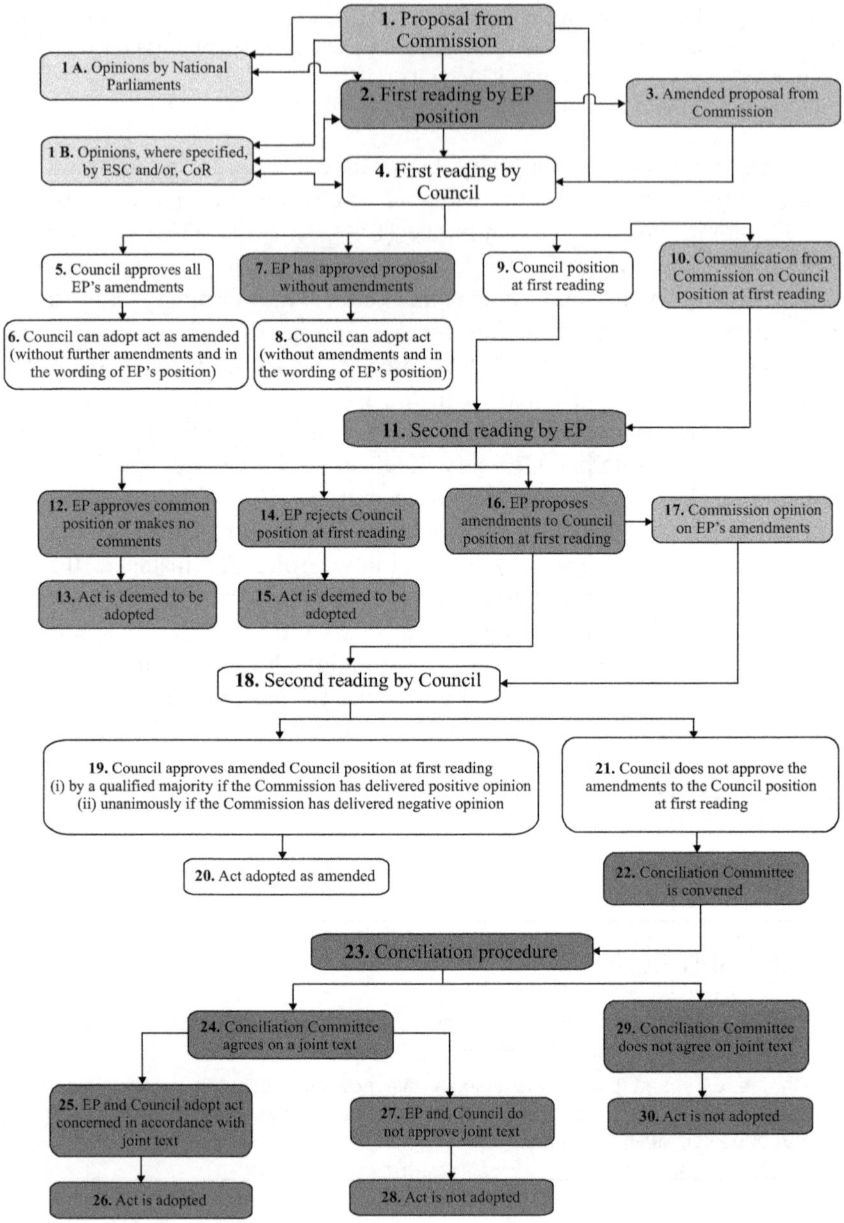

Source: European Commission.

Figure 8.1 Ordinary Legislative Procedure

8.1.3 EU Soft Law-making – 'Structuring Effect' or Violation of Democratic Principles?

Above, we explained that Member States transferred powers to the EU and that the EU legislative process involves democratically legitimated and accountable national governments and parliaments and also the EP. There are two reasons why the Treaty confers wide ranging and interim powers to the EU's executive body, i.e. the Commission: first, the generic character of EU Treaty provisions that have to be given life by practicable rules; second, the complexity and time-consuming nature of the supranational lawmaking process.

FURTHER READING – THE EUROPEAN COMMISSION AS THE EU'S EXECUTIVE BODY

The European Commission, with its headquarters in Brussels, Belgium, is often referred to as the 'Guardian of the EU Treaties'. Its role is comparable to a government with ministries for each area of competence. Its main roles are to propose legislation, to manage and implement EU policies and the EU budget, and to represent the interests of the EU, e.g. when negotiating trade agreements with other countries.

Article 17(1) TFEU:

> The Commission shall promote the general interest of the Union and take appropriate initiatives to that end. It shall ensure the application of the Treaties, and of measures adopted by the institutions pursuant to them. It shall oversee the application of Union law under the control of the Court of Justice of the European Union. It shall execute the budget and manage programmes. It shall exercise coordinating, executive and management functions, as laid down in the Treaties. With the exception of the common foreign and security policy, and other cases provided for in the Treaties, it shall ensure the Union's external representation. It shall initiate the Union's annual and multiannual programming with a view to achieving interinstitutional agreements.

The Commission consists of a College of 28 Commissioners including the President and Vice-Presidents. Each Commissioner is from one of the EU's 28 Member States. Officially though, neither the President nor any Commissioner 'represents' Member States in the Commission.

The nomination of the Commission's President – whose position can be compared to that of Prime Minister – has received greater democratic legitimacy lately: now, the European Council, i.e. Member State governments, can no longer expect to have its candidate – chosen behind closed doors – to be rubber-stamped by the Parliament but must take into account the elections to the EP. In 2014, for the first time, the Commission President was a candidate overtly nominated by Parliament, not by Member State leaders.

> The Commission President is then elected by the EP by a majority of its component members (which corresponds to at least 376 out of 751 votes). The President-elect selects the 27 other members of the Commission, on the basis of the suggestions made by Member States. The final list of Commissioners-designate then needs to be agreed upon between the President-elect and the Council. The Commission as a whole needs the Parliament's consent. Prior to this, Commissioners-designate are assessed by the EP committees.

The establishment and functioning of the internal market is an EU objective enshrined in Article 3(3) TEU. In the field of state interventions in the market, for instance, Article 107(1) TFEU defines a general prohibition of state aid. Article 107(3) however also provides for quite generic exceptions from the general prohibition. Such exceptions are laid down in secondary legal acts that provide for specific compatibility criteria which the Commission uses to assess the compatibility of state aid with the internal market. Examples are Guidelines on Research and Development and innovation aid, risk finance aid, environmental and energy aid, or regional aid, to name a few. Such rules lay down compatibility rules whereby the Commission can test state aid measures in certain areas or sectors against Treaty provisions, in particular by balancing the positive effects of aid against its negative effects. This is a concretisation of the principles enshrined in Article 107(3) c) TFEU.

Article 108 TFEU sets out the Commission's exclusive competence over state aid control, with the exception of the very limited circumstances when the Council may act. The EU has exclusive competence to establish the competition rules necessary for the functioning of the internal market, pursuant to Article 3(1) b) TFEU. Hence, the Commission has the right, and even the obligation, to adopt secondary law in the domain of state aid.

What would happen in the absence of any such unilateral regulatory action? The compatibility of state aid would have to be assessed directly on the basis of the TFEU, on a case-by-case basis. This situation would lead to vastly reduced legal certainty and predictability. It would also likely result in longer procedural durations, since assessment criteria would not be codified, but would permanently evolve in a diverse body of individual case law.

The principal question is: is such law really 'soft', or is its soft shell hiding a hard core? As an example, we refer to state aid rules. As was already explained above, the Commission has a wide margin of discretion when applying exemptions from the general prohibition of state aid. Soft law defines the Commission's margin of discretion in assessing the compatibility of state aid with the internal market under Article 107(3)

TFEU. It has binding effect only on the Commission in that the Commission must approve state aid that is in line with the applicable soft-law criteria. Such law is 'soft' in the sense that it does not legally bind Member States.

There is however a soft law/hard law ambiguity: formally, this soft law binds only the Commission itself; in practice, however, it defines positive criteria for national state aid policies compatible with the common market and leaves little room for Member States' aid policies which deviate from these criteria.[21] This, in turn, drives Member States to design and implement industrial policy measures in line with state aid frameworks or guidelines, e.g. by granting state aid only for certain activities and within aid limits as permitted by such 'soft law'. Thereby, soft law develops a strong structuring effect and, consequently, is not at all as 'soft' as it pretends to be.

FURTHER READING – THE HARD 'STRUCTURING EFFECT' OF SOFT LAW IN THE AREA OF SMALL-BUSINESS FINANCING

In the late 1990s the European Commission developed policies that favour small- and medium-sized enterprises (SMEs). In particular, the Commission wanted to create a climate that is favourable for risk finance investment in early-phase SMEs, as such enterprises do not find easy access to equity and quasi-equity investments, loans, or guarantees. In 2001, the Commission adopted first 'soft-law' compatibility criteria for state aid in the form of risk capital for SMEs. Since then, the Commission has repeatedly assessed the market failures that prevent SMEs from adequate access to risk finance. It is the magnitude of the market failures as perceived by the Commission that determines the scope of state aid that can be permitted 'in the common interest'.

Comparing soft law from 2008 with soft law from 2014 exposes the structuring effect of the Commission's market-failure appraisal: in 2008, the Commission generally acknowledged the existence of a funding gap of the size of €2.5 million over a year for predominantly equity and quasi-equity investments. Moreover, the Commission decided that Member States could only provide risk finance aid predominantly in the form of equity and quasi-equity capital, while debt-financing aid instruments could only constitute up to 30 per cent of an aid measure. Member States then designed their SME start-up aid accordingly.

In 2014, the Commission found that the funding gap that start-up SMEs cannot cover with market financing could be significantly higher, in the range of €10–15 million. Furthermore, the Commission realised that debt instruments such as sub-commercial loans with no or little collateral or convertible bonds are

[21] Terpan, Soft Law in the European Union – The Changing Nature of EU Law, 85.

often combined with equity investments or loans at market-rates. The previous 30 per cent upper limit for debt-financing aid could thus have prevented debt/equity combinations that eligible start-up SMEs really needed and that were attractive enough for private investors to join the state investment. Lastly, the Commission found that not only early-stage SMEs but also larger 'mid-caps' may be facing market failures that hamper access to finance.[22]

The main results of that reassessment of the venture capital market failure and the resulting financing gap were that the Commission since 2014 has permitted higher aid amounts, a wider range of public financial instruments, and a wider range of eligible companies and also less rigid rules for minimum private-investor participation. It is obvious that the Commission made an effort to align risk finance aid rules with market practice. Again, Member States are structuring their small-business support instruments accordingly.

- European Commission, Impact Assessment Accompanying the document Communication from the Commission Guidelines on State aid to promote risk finance investment, SWD(2014) 6, http://ec.europa.eu/smart-regulation/impact/ia_carried_out/docs/ia_2014/swd_2014_0006_en.pdf.
- General Block Exemption Regulation, in particular Aid for access to finance for SMEs, Article 21 *et seq.*, OJ 2014 L 187/1; Guidelines on State aid to promote risk finance investments, OJ 2014 C 19/4.

EU soft lawmaking epitomises the welfare paradox of supranational regulation: the fact that an administrative body throughout decades has adopted rules of high relevance for the welfare of half a billion citizens did not help raise the acceptance of EU lawmaking among citizens or companies. This brings us back to the concept of output legitimacy. The question arises: Who defines welfare standards in the 'common European interest' and the 'right' output of EU legislation to achieve those standards legitimately? Is 'enlightened executive' the answer?

It is true that the European Commission is making some efforts to keep the soft-legislative process transparent but it is also true that this is a voluntary transparency and does not exclude that predisposed conclusions are drawn (we will discuss democratisation and transparency efforts in the section on good governance further below). That system has some output legitimacy in the sense that it is acting in the common interest and increases social welfare. The weak points of that system however are that first, it is subject to interpretation by the Courts rather than open political debate, second, that there is no precise definition of 'social welfare' for EU policy purposes, and third, that the executive (technocratic) body has

[22] Discussion of market failure assessments and Commission risk finance policy in von Wendland, in Säcker/Montag, European State Aid Law, 2016, Section 3 – Aid for access to finance for SMEs.

a wide margin of discretion, as confirmed by the Courts, when balancing and assessing complex economic matters 'in the common European interest'. Although there is a resemblance to an 'enlightened' process (the Commission consults stakeholders and publishes questionnaires), at the end of the day, Commission soft law is adopted by bureaucrats and not by democratically elected officials. Nevertheless, the technocratic input principle is rather dominant.

Instead of democracy there is a technocratic super nanny. Is this a bad thing?

In Chapter 6 we dealt with the art of steering sector-specific regulation in the internal market. We observed, for instance, under the EU framework of telecommunication regulation that the European Commission subtly steers and supervises the Member States' National Regulatory Authorities (NRAs) within the Body of European Regulators for Electronic Communications (BEREC). And according to Regulation (EC) No 1211/2009, NRAs 'have to take utmost account' of any opinion, recommendation, guidelines, advice, or regulatory best practice adopted by BEREC. Another example, within the telecommunication sector, is the implementation of Commission Recommendation 2009/396/EC, of 7 May 2009, on the regulatory treatment of fixed and mobile termination rates in the EU,[23] according to which NRAs '*should*' set symmetric termination rates based on the costs incurred by an efficient operator by the end of 2012. Not all Member States have, in fact, applied this so-called pure LRIC (only long-run incremental costs may be priced) method to their cost modelling. According to the Commission the effect has been to distort competition between Member States. The differences of mobile termination rates may cause higher costs for network operators in other Member States:

> Significant divergences in the regulatory treatment of fixed and mobile termination rates create fundamental competitive distortions. (…) Where termination rates are set above efficient costs, this creates substantial transfers between fixed and mobile markets and consumers. In addition, in markets where operators have asymmetric market shares, this can result in significant payments from smaller to larger competitors. (…) High termination rates tend to lead to high retail prices for originating calls and correspondingly lower usage rates, thus decreasing consumer welfare.[24]
>
> 1. When imposing price control and cost-accounting obligations in accordance with Article 13 of Directive 2002/19/EC on the operators designated by

---

23 OJ EU 2009 L 124/67.

24 Recommendation 2009/396/EC recital 3.

> National Regulatory Authorities (NRAs) as having significant market power on the markets for wholesale voice call termination on individual public telephone networks (hereinafter referred to as 'fixed and mobile termination markets') as a result of a market analysis carried out in accordance with Article 16 of Directive 2002/21/EC, NRAs should set termination rates based on the costs incurred by an efficient operator. This implies that they would also be symmetric. In doing so, NRAs should proceed in the way set out below. (…)[25]

Structuring regulation and the *ex-ante* exercise of the Commission's wide margin of discretion by virtue of its 'soft law' is not subject to parliamentary control. Instead, institutional checks and balances are realised, in particular, by proceedings brought before the EU Court of Justice. However, these proceedings have to be anchored always on binding legal acts of the EU (hard law) to which the Commission's 'soft law' refers. For instance, the Court interprets aforementioned Article 13 of Access Directive 2002/19/EC in light of Commission Recommendation 2009/396/EC on fixed and mobile electronic communication termination rates. Thereby, the Court exercises *indirect* (but not direct) control over recommendations, i.e. 'soft law', within its annulment or preliminary proceedings. Therefore, the EU's institutional checks and balances follow a different path compared to parliamentary systems according to Member States' constitutions. Even if these supranational checks and balances might appear strange to ingrained constitutional lawyers, EU's institutional checks and balances are in our opinion perfectly in line with the very rationale of its founding EU Treaty. Thus, it is highly exaggerated and inappropriate to condemn the structuring effect of the Commission's frameworks, guidelines, or recommendations as a surrender of EU democracy!

The structuring effect is a result of the EU's political reality: the fragmentation of power at the EU level generates political incentives for EU policymakers to craft detailed, action-forcing legislation and to put in place provisions that can be readily enforced in court.[26]

EU soft law indeed has a hard core – and it has teeth. Some complain about the lack of democratic legitimacy, and they are right. Nevertheless, soft law is adapted to the reality of a legal order of its own kind – that is a hybrid between an international treaty and a constitution, conceived for a polity stuck on its way from a confederation of nations towards a nation. Apparently there is no viable alternative, because the Treaties –

---

25 Ibid., para. 1.

26 Kelemen, *Eurolegalism*, 43.

the EU's quasi-constitution – have proved so difficult to amend towards stronger political integration. After all, it is the peoples of EU Member States – the EU's fragmented *demoi* – who are not ready to build a nation.

8.1.4 Regulatory Checks and Balances Exercised by the Court of Justice of the EU

Another technique of subtly steering Member States' regulation of market areas which still remain in Member States' competencies (due to a lack of EU secondary law harmonisation), such as gambling laws, is to put pressure on Member States by the Commission launching infringement procedures, or threatening to do so (Arts 258, 260 TFEU) and, in particular, by preliminary proceedings on referral of a national court (Art. 267 TFEU) before the Court of Justice.

The Court interacts as an interpretational authority which often comes to the fore when European treaty provisions or secondary legal acts are either unclear or have regulatory gaps, or, in particular, in the absence of EU secondary law harmonisation. Often, in the absence of EU secondary law the internal market freedoms, in particular the free movement of goods (Arts 28 *et seq.* TFEU) and services (Arts 56 *et seq.* TFEU), apply however as EU primary law; for instance, the free movement of services can be invoked by EU providers of transborder online gambling (online sports bets, online poker). In the absence of EU harmonisation the Court of Justice often refers to the principle of coherency (consistency) of Member States' regulation[27] under the internal market freedoms:

> 53 The Court has held that, by reason of the primacy of directly applicable EU law, national legislation concerning a public monopoly on bets on sporting competitions which, according to the findings of a national court, comprises restrictions that are incompatible with the freedom of establishment and the freedom to provide services, because those restrictions do not contribute to limiting betting activities in a consistent and systematic manner, cannot continue to apply during a transitional period.[28]

The national lawmaker is able to fill gaps faster where the Court of Justice exercises the institutional function to bring coherency (consistency) into non-harmonised Member States' legislation under the four

---

[27] See ECJ, judgment of 08.09.2010, C-409/06 – *Winner Wetten*, para. 69; and ECJ, judgment of 24.01.2013, ECLI:EU:C:2013:33 – *Stanleybet International and Others*, para. 38.

[28] ECJ, judgment of 04.02.2016, C-336/14 – *Ince*, paras 53–55.

freedoms in order to remedy regulatory shortcomings. Again, the EU is far from the traditional dichotomy of legislature and judiciary under the concepts of the democratic nation state. The EU Court of Justice is not confined to act as a mere *'bouche de la loi'* ('mouth of law', Montesquieu, l'Esprit des Lois, 1777). Rather, the Court acts as an institutional balancing agent between the EU and its Member States in pursuit of filling regulatory gaps which can harm the welfare of the Union's citizens protected, in particular, with the internal market freedoms, environmental, health or social sustainability objectives under the TFEU.

8.2 REGULATION AND THE QUEST FOR DEMOCRACY

8.2.1 Regulatory Policy and Democratisation – Pragmatism or False Labelling?

In the preceding sections we discovered the reality of the EU legal order and found that there may be a democratic deficit in the sense that the European executive has wide discretion in adopting rules that are legally and economically very relevant. The executive regulator, though, is not democratically accountable. Nevertheless, since the regulator is obliged to act 'in the common interest' and, more specifically, to promote social welfare, there is a point for 'output legitimacy'. Contenting oneself with that form of legitimacy however requires great confidence in seemingly 'non-political' bureaucrats who, through soft law, shape the future of Europe's wealth. Better regulation and transparency are a means to create a stronger sense of legitimacy. Regulatory policy and good governance could thus help creating a more palpable perception of the European legislator, reducing reservations amongst citizens who often find the EU opaque and confusing. This could be a first, very small step on the long march towards real political integration and a European identity.

FURTHER READING – REGULATORY POLICY AND REGULATORY GOVERNANCE

'**Regulatory policy** refers to the set of rules, procedures and institutions introduced by government for the express purpose of developing, administering, and reviewing regulation (both primary and subordinate).' (OECD, Government at a Glance, p. 124)

'**Regulatory governance** is grounded in the principles of democratic governance and engages a wider domain of players including the legislature, the judiciary, sub-national and supranational levels of government and international standard setting activities, including those of the private sector.' (OECD, Recommendation of the Council on Regulatory Policy and Governance, OECD 2012, p. 22)

The OECD's 2012 *Recommendation on Regulatory Policy and Governance* recommends that OECD member countries 'commit at the highest political level to an explicit whole-of-government policy for regulatory quality'. The 'whole-of-government' concept focuses on aspects such as the confidence of citizens in their national government, the rule of law, income redistribution, and broad measures of public sector efficiency (output-based) and cost effectiveness (outcome-based). According to the OECD's 2015 report *Government at a Glance*, the EU had adopted an explicit 'whole-of-government' policy for regulatory quality (Government at a Glance, p. 125).

Government at a Glance: http://www.oecd-ilibrary.org/governance/government-at-a-glance-2015_gov_glance-2015-en.

Recommendation on Regulatory Policy and Governance: http://www.oecd.org/governance/regulatory-policy/2012-recommendation.htm.

In 2012, the European Commission started a new regulatory policy initiative – the Regulatory Fitness and Performance Programme (REFIT). The objective of that current initiative is to make EU legislation 'even more effective and efficient in achieving its public policy objectives: demonstrating clear added value, delivering full benefits at minimum cost and respecting the principles of subsidiarity and proportionality. The final result must be a simple, clear, stable and predictable regulatory framework for businesses, workers and citizens'.[29]

Among the European Commission's top ten political priorities – as no. 10 – is 'Making the EU as a whole more democratic'. The Commission's sole initiative under that heading is REFIT. The term 'Democracy', however, has never entered the REFIT vocabulary.

The 2014–2019 Commission's political priorities are set out in Political Guidelines written by its President:

1. Competitiveness and investment that creates jobs
2. A 'connected digital single market'
3. Less energy dependency and better energy efficiency
4. The completion of the internal market with a strengthened industrial base
5. Deeper and fairer economic and monetary union
6. A 'reasonable and balanced' free trade agreement with the US
7. Upholding EU-values, the rule of law and fundamental rights
8. Migration policy

[29] European Commission, Communication 'Regulatory Fitness', 12.12.2012, 3.

9. Becoming a stronger global actor
10. Making the EU as a whole more democratic

Jean-Claude Juncker, A New Start for Europe: My Agenda for Jobs, Growth, Fairness and Democratic Change, Political Guidelines for the next European Commission, 15.7.2015. https://ec.europa.eu/priorities/sites/beta-political/files/juncker-political-guidelines_en.pdf.

With REFIT, the Commission rather seems to mention areas where it is feasible to create a better image of legitimacy and accountability, and to heighten citizens' confidence. This is pragmatic, given the Commission's portfolio of fragmented competencies and its weak administrative and enforcement powers. Hence, the closest thing to augmenting legitimacy is augmenting transparency and bringing the legislative process closer to citizens. This is quite evident from a paper the Commission published within the REFIT process:

> Dialogue with citizens, social partners and other stakeholders in business and civil society helps to make sure that EU law making is transparent, well targeted and coherent. The consultation of social partners and other stakeholders is enshrined in the Treaties and is particularly important in relation to detecting issues of proportionality and subsidiarity.[30]

The Commission seems rather content with the regulatory quality in the field of competition policy: the Commission applauds that the competition rules are constantly monitored and evaluated with a view to refine the legal framework when gaps or scope for improvement are identified. The Commission recalls its strong enforcement role in that field for which specific tools had been developed to ensure that decisions are fit for purpose. These include, inter alia, measures to ensure transparency and interaction with parties at different stages of the procedure, over and above the legal right to be heard, as well as 'market testing', and *ex-post* monitoring of the correct implementation of state aid approval decisions. Legislative reforms, e.g. so-called block-exemptions, had significantly reduced administrative burden for Member States, businesses, and the Commission. All this would have allowed the Commission to focus its resources on serious competition problems.[31]

---

[30] Communication 'Regulatory Fitness and Performance Programme (REFIT): State of Play and Outlook, 18.06.2014, 14.

[31] European Commission, Staff Working Document 'Regulatory Fitness and Performance Programme (REFIT): Initial Results of the Mapping of the Acquis', 01.08.2013, 27 *et seq.* on competition policy.

In conclusion, REFIT is a worthy regulatory policy effort and fits into the bigger scheme of things, in particular the OECD's recommendations. That effort is however restricted to bureaucratic and secondary legislative procedures to enhance the quality and transparency of legislation, and to reduce administrative costs. Hence, any such regulatory improvement cannot be 'democratisation' as such. Promoting it under the democratisation flag rather is pragmatic false labelling; it can only be the first step on the long march towards democratisation, in the sense that slowly, and in the long run, European citizens gain confidence in supranational legislators, then enter into a European political debate on substance, not dominated by national particular interests, thereby discovering their European identity. First and timid steps towards ... a European *Demos*.

8.2.2 'The European Semester'

When discussing soft law and governance in the EU, another quite unique instrument of economic governance must be mentioned: the 'European Semester'. This annual cycle of economic policy guidance and supervision aims to detect, prevent, and correct problematic economic trends such as excessive government deficits or public debt levels in the Member States.

Each year, the Commission undertakes a detailed analysis of EU Member States' plans of budgetary, macroeconomic and structural reforms and provides them with country-specific recommendations for the subsequent cycle of 12 to 18 months.

The EU is making an effort to give this governance process a democratic face: as regards the 'Democratic legitimacy and accountability', the European Commission declares that 'effective democratic legitimacy and accountability is crucial for strengthening ownership of the European Semester process'. It then refers to dialogue with national stakeholders (governments, parliaments, social partners, civil society) and the EP, early publication of the country reports, increasing involvement of national parliaments, and close involvement of social partners.[32]

Interestingly, the European Commission intends to instrumentalise EU state aid rules for budget surveillance under the European Semester, and thus for purposes other than protecting fair competition in the internal market:

---

[32] European Commission, Communication '2016 European Semester: Country-specific recommendations', Brussels, 18.05.2016, 7.

> Other elements also buttress the need for a broad modernisation package for EU State aid policy as a whole: [...] the strengthening of the economic and budgetary surveillance system under the EU semester. [...] By putting an emphasis on the quality and the efficiency of public support, State aid control can also help Member States to strengthen budgetary discipline and improve the quality of public finances – resulting in a better use of taxpayers' money. It is particularly important in order to achieve smart fiscal consolidation, reconciling the role of targeted public spending in generating growth with the need to bring budgets under control. There is therefore also a need to embed State aid control and more general competition concerns in the EU Semester procedure.[33]

The 'European Semester' is both ambitious and ambiguous. It exemplifies the dilemma of an institution with fragmented competencies and weak enforcement capabilities: obviously, the Commission wants to use its exclusive competition policy competence to reign in free-spending Member States who usually insist on their budgetary and industrial-policy prerogatives. Such 'encroachment' is certainly done with a welfare rationale, and thus has 'output legitimacy'. Highly transparent legislative processes in the state aid field as well as independent non-political regulators are needed to make such 'enlightened encroaching' palatable to national governments and legislators. Otherwise, they might use such EU policy initiatives against political integration.

The EP's Committee on Economic and Monetary Affairs commissioned a study on the European Semester's effectiveness and legitimacy. In essence, the study found that the legitimacy of that major governance initiative was not fully ensured from the beginning but had to be enhanced by the EP together with national parliaments. Here, we cannot discuss the report's many policy recommendations; however, one of the report's conclusions is highly relevant for the discussion of legitimacy and the Art of Regulation. It does not only apply to the European Semester, which is only one specific governance initiative; it applies to all EU secondary lawmaking that is outside the democratically legitimate process. Instead of 'European Semester' read 'European Project':

> Public awareness of the process is important not only because it increases the legitimacy of the process but it also strengthens ownership of the process at the national level and thereby increases effectiveness. Our media discourse analysis showed that the European Semester receives moderate media coverage. Yet, public discourse is of central importance to fostering ownership of reform processes. All actors in the European Semester should increase their

---

[33] European Commission, Communication 'EU State Aid Modernisation (SAM), 2012, cf. points 7 and 14.

efforts to communicate on the results of the Semester and more importantly justify the need for action due to the large connections among EU economies.[34]

8.3 HOW TO REGULATE THE REGULATOR?

8.3.1 The European Commission: A Regulatory 'Dark Knight'?

So far, we discovered that the European Commission is the supranational key player omnipresent in sector-specific regulation. Furthermore, the Commission operates a general regulatory (horizontal) safety net in the internal market through the enforcement of general EU competition rules (Chapter 3), in particular Article 101 TFEU (cartel prohibition), Article 102 TFEU (abuse of a dominant position), the Merger Control Regulation, Article 106 TFEU (exclusive and special rights), and Articles 107 and 108 TFEU (state aid).

Under Competition Regulation 1/2003, in particular, the Commission enjoys far-reaching investigating, decision-making, and sanctioning powers against infringements of EU competition rules.

In the *Cimeteries CBR* case two parties argued that the principle of impartiality was violated on the ground that the same Commission official carried out the investigations, acted as rapporteur, drew up the Statement of the Objections and prepared the draft decision. The Court of First Instance (CFI; now General Court of the European Union), however, upheld the contested decision as legally (formally) impartial:

> The contested decision was not taken by the official to whom the parties refer, but by the college of Commissioners. What is more, the procedural guarantees provided for by Community law do not require the Commission to adopt an internal organization precluding the same official from acting as investigator and rapporteur in the same case.[35]

Furthermore, the European judiciary relies strongly on its *judicial self-restraint* as evidenced in the standing case law of the Courts of the EU with regard to economic and regulatory assessments contained in the decision making by the Commission. In state aid case *Niki Luftfahrt*,[36] the claimant brought an annulment action (Art. 263(4) TFEU) before the

---

[34] Hallerberg/Marzinotto/Wolff (n. 2), 83.

[35] ECJ, judgment of 15.03.2000, T-25/95 – *Cimenteries CBR v Commission*, para. 721.

[36] ECJ, judgment of 13.05.2015, T-511/09 – *Niki Luftfahrt v Commission.*

General Court against the Commission's decision declaring the state aid for rescuing and restructuring of Austrian Airlines group compatible in light of the latter's privatisation process. The Commission's approval decision was taken on the basis of its guidelines on state aid for rescuing and restructuring firms in difficulty. The General Court refused to review the Commission's economic and regulatory assessments on the merits for the following grounds, which likewise apply in all areas of complex internal market interventions carried out by the Commission:

> However, when conducting such a review, the Courts of the European Union must not substitute their own economic assessment for that of the Commission. The review by the Courts of the European Union of the complex economic assessments made by the Commission is necessarily limited and confined to verifying whether the rules on procedure and on the statement of reasons have been complied with, whether the facts have been accurately stated and whether there has been any manifest error of assessment or misuse of powers [...].[37]

Even if the EU Courts act quite often and more or less extensively as an institutional balancing agent between the EU and its Member States to fill regulatory gaps, the same European judiciary exercises strong judicial self-restraint with regard to economic and regulatory assessments underlying the decision-making by the Commission in limiting its judicial review 'to verifying whether the rules on procedure and on the statement of reasons have been complied with, whether the facts have been accurately stated and whether there has been any manifest error of assessment or misuse of powers'.

Under these terms of the Courts' judicial self-restraint with regard to economic and regulatory assessments contained in the decision making by the Commission, the multitasking roles of the Commission as a lawmaker, policeman, investigator, prosecutor, judge and jury[38] raise questions on its independence as a controller and regulator, even if cleared by the judiciary. Thus, the ultimate two questions are: Who controls the controller on the merits? How to regulate the regulator?

As enlightened as the controller or regulator may be: if it is not subject to independent and efficient supervision, it risks being perceived as a regulatory Dark Knight or Darth Vader. Such dark characters might be a staple in the eternal battle between good and evil in space and other operas. However, under the highly complex conditions of the internal

---

37 *Ince* (n.27), para. 126.
38 Jones and Sufrin, EC Competition Law, 1055.

market, even the most enlightened unchecked regulator is prone to regulatory failures.

On a positive note, the Commission's Directorate-General for Competition (DG COMP) has increasingly improved its internal decision-making process during the last decade. In particular, DG COMP has enhanced decision making on the basis of scientifically driven economic and regulatory assessments on the merits carried out by a Chief Economist and his staff since 2003. The Chief Economist encourages DG COMP to handle competition cases independently from other policy considerations by providing economic input to policy discussions within the Commission and by training in economics for DG COMP's staff.[39]

Ultimately, however, the Commission, i.e. the college of Commissioners, is not independent in the final decision making despite the solemn affirmation in Article 245(1) TFEU.[40] Risks of policy influence, in particular by Member States' governments or political parties, are inherent due to the decisive role of Member States in the appointment of each Commissioner under Article 244 TFEU ('the Members of the Commission shall be chosen on the basis of a system of rotation established unanimously by the European Council').

8.3.2 Proposal for an Independent EU Supervisory Competition and Regulatory Authority Far from Political Realities

How to enhance regulatory independence in the EU? How to heighten confidence in the regulator? The straightforward answer is: by adding 'technocratic input legitimacy'. To achieve this, these authors propose ... an independent EU Supervisory Competition and Regulatory Authority (EUSCRA) with a board of directors appointed for only one office term of at least eight years by the EP from a list of internationally prominent experts in the diverse areas of internal market regulation. This list of experts should be drawn up by the European Council on the basis that each Member State submits a proposal of two experts, renowned in the fields of competition and multisector regulation, who are *not* nationals of the respective Member State. EUSCRA should act primarily as an independent administrative appeals body to which appeals can be lodged

---

[39] Van de Gronden/de Vries, Independent Competition Authorities in the EU, 38.

[40] Article 245(1) TFEU: 'The Members of the Commission shall refrain from any action incompatible with their duties. Member States shall respect their independence and shall not seek to influence them in the performance of their tasks.'

by natural or legal persons who are individually (not necessarily directly) affected by the Commission's decisions, directives, regulations, but as well as by frameworks, guidelines, communications or recommendations. EUSCRA's appeals decisions should be based on full economic and regulatory assessments on the merits of each appealed Commission's act without any 'appeals body self-restraint'. Of course, EUSCRA's appeals decisions would be subject to judicial review by the EU Courts.

In addition, EUSCRA should have the power to issue (non-binding) *supervisory standards on good regulation* which should be taken into account by the Commission, the National Regulatory and Competition Authorities, and last but not least by market participants in order to enhance predictability of EUSCRA's appeals decisions.

The European Commission could only adopt secondary legislation after taking into account EUSCRA's expertise. Where the Commission does not follow EUSCRA's advice, this must be justified and noted transparently, e.g. in the legal act and the impact assessment that accompanies it.

Taking due account of the ECJ judgments in *Meroni*[41] and *Alliance for Natural Health*,[42] the EU is not allowed to delegate discretionary powers to bodies other than those established by the Treaties itself. Therefore, the establishment of EUSCRA would be subject to treaty revision by the Member States.

These authors are well aware that such a proposal for an independent EU Supervisory Competition and Regulatory Authority might be perceived politically as a 'bridge too far'.[43] However, the argument that under the present institutional structure the EP can still control the Commission enforcing EU law, including the regulatory and competition rules, falls short of political realities. The same holds true with regard to the realities of judicial review. After all, standing case law of the Courts of the EU with regard to economic and regulatory assessments by the Commission underlying its decision making relies strongly on judicial self-restraint.

Although the proposal might resemble the platonic idea of an enlightened kingdom of philosophers far from political realities, it is worth dreaming about at least in the learned discourse between authors and appreciative readers.

---

41 ECJ, judgment of 13.06.1958, C-9/56 – *Meroni v High Authority.*

42 ECJ, judgment of 12.07.2005, C-154/04, C-155/04 – *Alliance for Natural Health and Others.*

43 Van de Gronden/de Vries (n. 38), 66; van Miert, The proposal for a European competition agency, 1996 EC Competition Policy Newsletter, No 2.

8.4 THE STAGE IS SET

Our journey through regulated Europe is coming to an end. We are warily gazing at the horizon. Beyond it, new resources, fresh potential, and tough challenges are waiting to be discovered. For regulators, businesses, and consumers, this new frontier is *big data*. Pioneers venturing into this territory must be careful and attentive. Above all, they must free themselves from conditioned patterns of classical 'one-fits-all economics' that worked so well in the old offline world.

Is the supranational regulator able to comprehend the big data phenomenon, avert its risks, and fully use its potential?

Regulators are certainly bureaucrats but they are nevertheless human. Perceiving new phenomena according to the patterns of the known and trying to learn from the past is a quite human trait. When legislators, regulators, welfare policy agents, lawyers, business strategists, and economists are caught in the past, social welfare is in danger. Unable to handle inconsistencies between prior attitudes and the present, individual agents get stuck in those prior positions and tend to defend these positions even more vigorously. Psychologists name the intellectual phenomenon the *cognitive dissonance paradox*. The crux of cognitive dissonance can be observed well beyond pathological patterns of human behaviour exposed to emerging information and challenges inconsistent with prior experiences, attitudes, or beliefs.[44] Failure to perceive and understand fresh potentials and risks inherent in any moment of new opportunity however leads to opportunity costs that have negative welfare effects.

Hence, knowledge, theory, learned patterns, formats, or techniques must be first understood and then processed most attentively in the awareness that even the most recent insights are necessarily conditioned by the (recent) past and might not fit the very present moment and momentum.[45]

---

[44] Cooper, Cognitive Dissonance: 50 years of a Classic Theory; Festinger/Riecken/Schachter, When Prophecy Fails: A Social and Psychological Study of a Modern Group That Predicted the Destruction of the World, 1956, were the first who described the psychological mechanisms of disconfirmed expectations; Harmon-Jones, A Cognitive Dissonance Theory Perspective on Persuasion, in *The Persuasion Handbook: Developments in Theory and Practice*, 101.

[45] The Indian thinker Jiddu Krishnamurti (1895–1986) explained the intellectual traps of conditionings from the past in his various published speeches and writings, i.e.: Freedom from the Known (1969); The Awakening of Intelligence (1973); The Urgency of Change (1970); The Flame of Attention (1984); The

Governments or EU agents, lawyers, judges, and regulators are prone to be trapped by conditionings from the past: they are trained and bound by the rule of law and its inherent principles of legal certainty and predictability, building on long-standing legal practice. Attentiveness and awareness of the present moment and momentum however enables these agents to make full use of their margins of discretion which they enjoy, even under laws conditioned by the past. The global financial and sovereign debt crisis has served as a perfect laboratory for understanding how to use these legal margins and how to catch the momentum by *ad hoc* regulation in order to find the balance between safeguarding financial institutions' systemic functions and competition rules on state aid (Chapters 6.3.1 and 6.3.11). During the financial crisis, the EU Commission together with the Member States' governments have illustrated that good regulation is not an accumulated trend of past normative decisions, but rather an economic and policy-driven public enforcement in order to save inclusive welfare under the rule of law.

With regard to big data, EU competition commissioner *Vestager* stressed the need for an open-minded perception of risks as well as of welfare potentials to identify appropriate regulatory remedies:

> Very few people realize that, if you tick the box, your information can be exchanged with others. [...] Actually, you are paying a price, an extra price for the product that you are purchasing. You give away something that was valuable. I think that point is underestimated as a factor as to how competition works. [...] The more data you can collect, the more you know, the better product you can provide, but also the more powerful will you be towards others. It's very important for us to be able to say what is competition-related and what is an issue of privacy, ownership, data, and how you can be as secure on the net as you can be in the physical world.[46]

Still, legislators, regulators, businesses, and consumers seem to be wary of the big data potential. Remaining conditioned only to the trodden paths of welfare from the past, our society would however miss great opportunities for innovation implied in the new resources. Europe and its traditional industries have been caught repeatedly in the cognitive paradox: ailing industries plagued by overcapacity, e.g. coal, textile and steel,

---

Network of Thought (1982); according to Krishnamurti human perception is largely shaped by concepts already established in formatted consciousness. Freedom from this mere formatted consciousness can be obtained by clear observation, attentiveness and awareness.

[46] Cowen, Big Data as a Competition Issue: Should the EU Commission's Approach Be More Careful?, 15.

were kept alive by state aid in order to save jobs instead of shifting public resources to more research, development, and innovation and thereby exploring new resources. Member States' monopolies in the supply of telecommunication, postal, and railway services or energy deprived consumers of exercising their freedom of choice. Consumers' bondage within state monopolies resulted in poor quality of service, obsolete product designs, and much higher prices, e.g. for telecommunication services, compared to liberalised markets outside Europe (Chapter 6). The discovery of data as the currency paid by consumers and traded as goods by services that are otherwise free of charge is a tremendous driver of transactions and knowledge and, in principle, of welfare. But if consumers pay with their personal data, privacy as a human right is at stake.

This is where the supranational legislator and controller must step in. These authors propose to establish a European Data Networking Agency (EDNA). That body would give advice to NRAs as well as to the European Commission in matters of big data mining and processing, their respective market power aspects, and data privacy. That advisory agency could balance the risks and the potentials of big data.

Such an institution could help develop an integrated approach within the scope of EU competition law, taking due account of privacy-related concerns flowing from increased concentrations of data. Competition law provides for sufficient margins of appreciation, proportionality, and discretion to consider privacy-related concerns. In the authors' view, the open formula of '*any abuse* by one or more undertakings of a dominant position' [emphasis added] under Article 102 TFEU invites the Commission to take due account of privacy concerns against critical activities of dominant undertakings.

This applies as well to merger control, being the *ex-ante* equivalent to cartel and market abuse control (see Chapter 3.2.3 and 3.6). By clearing Facebook's acquisition of WhatsApp, the Commission took the contrary stance, stating: 'Any privacy-related concerns flowing from the increased concentration of data within the control of Facebook as a result of the transaction do not fall within the scope of EU competition law'.[47] The German competition agency recently delved into this field, opening an

[47] Commission, press release from 03.10.2014 in Case *M.7217 – Facebook/ WhatsApp*, http://europa.eu/rapid/press-release_IP-14-1088_en.htm, 06.07.2016.

investigation about a possible infringement of data protection by Facebook under competition rules.[48] The discussions about the role of competition and regulatory agencies in the age of big data have been triggered in Europe only five minutes to twelve.

These new frontiers of market regulation deserve a head-on approach. Innovative regulation also serves as the bridge over troubled water caused by waves of 'aggressive' businesses challenging structural European conservatism. Regulation has to keep pace with innovative and even revolutionary business strategies be they driven by big data or bitcoins. Just warily gazing to the horizon will set Europe aside from the global club of innovators.

The stage is set for the next act.

Europe will need to keep its eyes and mind wide open.

48 Bundeskartellamt, press release from 02.03.2016, http://www.bundeskartellamt.de/SharedDocs/Meldung/EN/Pressemitteilungen/2016/02_03_2016_Facebook.html, 06.07.2016.

9. Epilogue – the European Cause after the British referendum

Warily … the EU is standing at a historic junction. The very day the manuscript of this book was being finalised, the EU woke up to learn that it will soon lose a Member State – the United Kingdom. The British EU referendum in essence was about the perceived legitimacy of supranational legislation and regulation. The referendum showed that the welfare objective of EU-driven regulation was less appealing than the sentiment of liberating oneself from what was perceived as a 'foreign rule' of an elite technocracy rather than legislation with representation.

Europe may be wary concerning its future but it is still wealthy. The source of Europe's wealth is its vast internal market. That source, however, will remain plentiful only as long as intelligent supranational regulation prevents some – be it with political or economic intentions – from abusing it. Nevertheless, the EU learned today that a horn of plenty, and the rules to protect it, may also be the mountain that hides very fundamental principles – democracy and the rule of law. As long as EU citizens do not see and comprehend every day that EU-driven regulation stands firmly on the principles of democracy and the rule of law, even the most legitimate regulatory welfare objective – and ultimately the wealth of Europe – may be standing on feet of clay.

The British referendum certainly has taught Europe and the world many lessons, for example, about the lure of sticking with the devil you know best, the power of demagoguery, and growing alienation from 'big politics'. For this epilogue, though, one point seems most relevant: The 'Art of Regulation' will fail if its methods and objectives are not fully embraced by those whom it serves. So, in order to secure and improve the wealth of Europe, EU leaders must reflect now on how to effectively instil more democratic legitimacy to EU regulation. In other words – they must move a mountain.

Since the death of Helen Joanne 'Jo' Cox on 16 June 2016, this is not only a political obligation but also an eminently moral one. We have dedicated this piece to her outstanding service for the European Cause as a Member of Parliament for the Batley and Spen constituency in Northern England.

Bibliography

Amato, G./Bribosia, H./de Witte, B. (eds.), Genèse et destinée de la Constitution Européenne: commentaire du Traité établissant une Constitution pour l'Europe à la lumière des travaux préparatoires et perspectives d'avenir, 2007.

Bartsch, G./Scirankova, D., Large differences in regional labour markets show asymmetric impact of the economic crisis, Eurostat, 2012, http://ec.europa.eu/eurostat/documents/3433488/5585556/KS-SF-12-054-EN.PDF/0d04dc75-d1ba-4896-ac07-2b9a13231517.

Buttarelli, G., Privacy and Competition in in the Digital Economy, 21 January 2015, https://secure.edps.europa.eu/EDPSWEB/webdav/site/mySite/shared/Documents/EDPS/Publications/Speeches/2015/15-01-21_speech_GB_EN.pdf.

Capobianco, A./Christiansen, H., Competitive Neutrality and State-Owned Enterprises: Challenges and Policy Options, OECD Corporate Governance Working Papers, No. 1, 2011, http://dx.doi.org/10.1787/5kg9xfgjdhg6-en.

Christiansen, H., The Size and Composition of the SOE Sector in OECD Countries, OECD Corporate Governance Working Papers, No. 5, 2011, http://www.oecd-ilibrary.org/governance/the-size-and-composition-of-the-soe-sector-in-oecd-countries_5kg54cwps0s3-en%3Fcrawler%3D true.

Cisneros, M., *The role of EU State Aid Law in promoting a Pro-innovation Policy*, Intersentia, 2014.

Clarke, C., *The Iron Kingdom – The Rise and Downfall of Prussia*, 1600–1947, Penguin – Allen Lane, 2006.

Cooper, J., *Cognitive Dissonance: 50 Years of a Classic Theory*, Sage Publications, 2007.

Cowen, T., Big Data as a Competition Issue: Should the EU Commission's Approach Be More Careful?, *European Networks Law & Regulation Quarterly* (ENLR), 1/2016.

Crane, D. A. /Hovenkamp, H., *The Making of Competition Policy: Legal and Economic Sources*, Oxford University Press, 2013.

Cuesta Lopez, V., The Lisbon Treaty's Provisions on Democratic Principles: A Legal Framework for Participatory Democracy, *European Public Law* No. 1, Vol 16, 2010, http://ec.europa.eu/dgs/secretariat_general/citizens_initiative/docs/cuesta_victor_3_en.pdf.

Dee, M., The European Union in a Multipolar World, World Trade, Global Governance and the Case of the WTO, 2015.

Deutsche Bank Research, Regionalflughäfen politisch und wirtschaftlich unter Druck, 2015.

Dillard, J. P./Pfau, M. (eds), *The Persuasion Handbook: Developments in Theory and Practice*, Sage Publications, 2002.

Einav, L./Levin, J., The Data Revolution and Economic Analysis, 2014, paper published by the National Bureau of Economic Research (NBER; 978-0-226-16540-0/2014/2014-0001), http://web.stanford.edu/~jdlevin/Papers/BigData.pdf.

Festinger, L./Riecken, H./Schachter, S., When Prophecy Fails: A Social and Psychological Study of a Modern Group That Predicted the Destruction of the World, 1956.

Flett, J./Jessen, A. C./Talabér-Ritz, K., *The Relationship between WTO Subsidies Law and EC State Aid Law, EC State Aid Law*, Chapter 21, Kluwer Law International, 2008.

Flyvbjerg, B., What You Should Know About Megaprojects And Why: An Overview, *Project Management Journal,* 2014, http://papers.ssrn.com/sol3/papers.cfm?abstract_id=2424835.

Gesterkamp, S./Hellstern, M./Koenig, C., Wettbewerbsschutz gegen Quersubventionen im Rahmen von Rekommunalisierungsstrategien am Beispiel des Abfallrechts, Wettbewerb in Recht und Praxis, 8/2011.

Grimm, D., The Democratic Costs of Constitutionalisation: The European Case, *European Law Journal*, Vol. 21, No. 4, 462, 2015.

Hallerberg, M./Marzinotto, B./Wolff, G. B., An Assessment of the European Semester, Study for the European Parliament, Brussels, September 2012, http://www.europarl.europa.eu/meetdocs/2009_2014/documents/econ/dv/studybruegel_/studybruegel_en.pdf.

Honoré-Gabriel Riquetti, Comte de Mirabeau, De la Monarchie Prussiennne sous Frédéric le Grand, vol. 3, 1788.

Jones, A./Sufrin, B., *EC Competition Law*, Oxford, 2004.

Kelemen, R. D., *Lessons from Europe? What can Americans learn from European Public Policies*, Thousand Oaks, CA: Sage, 2015.

Kelemen, R. D.,*The Rules of Federalism: Institutions and Regulatory Politics in the EU and Beyond*, Harvard University Press, 2012.

Kelemen, R. D., *Eurolegalism: The Transformation of Law and Regulation in the European Union*, Harvard University Press, 2011.

Khan, N./Borchardt, K.-D., The Private Market Investor Principle: Reality Check or Distorting Mirror? EC State Aid Law, Liber Amicorum Francisco Santaolalla Gadea, International Competition Law Series Vol. 36, Kluwer Law International, 2008.

Koenig, C./Bartosch, A./Braun, J.-D./Romes, M. (eds.), *EC Competition and Telecommunications Law*, 2nd ed., Kluwer Law International, 2009.

Kohler-Koch, B./Rittberger, B. (eds), *Debating the Democratic Legitimacy of the European Union*, Lanham: Rowman & Littlefield, 2007.

Kowalski, P. et al., State-Owned Enterprises: Trade Effects and Policy Implications, OECD Trade Policy Papers, No. 147, OECD Publishing, 2013, http://dx.doi.org/10.1787/5k4869ckqk7l-en; http://www.oecd-ilibrary.org/docserver/download/5k4869ckqk7l.pdf?expires=1451467071&id=id&accname=guest&checksum=8BF3E4664F0B55819BA6173CC6DA5A33.

Lerner, A. V., The Role of 'Big Data' in Online Platform Competition, 2014, http://papers.ssrn.com/sol3/papers.cfm?abstract_id=2482780.

Maduro, M. P., How Constitutional Can the European Union Be? The Tension between Intergovernamentalism and Constitutionalism in the European Union, Jean Monnet Working Paper 5/04, 2004.

Manzella, G. P./Mendez, C., The turning points of EU cohesion policy, Working Paper Report to Barca Report, 2009, http://ec.europa.eu/regional_policy/archive/policy/future/pdf/8_manzella_final-formatted.pdf.

Morse, H., Product Market Definition in the Pharmaceutical Industry, *Antitrust Law Journal* No 2, Vol. 71, 633, 2003.

Nicolaidis, P., The Incentive Effect of State Aid: Its Meaning, Measurement, Pitfalls and Application, *World Competition* 32, No 4, 2009.

OECD, Guidelines on Corporate Governance of State-Owned Enterprises, 2005.

Price, A. H et al., Money for Metal – A Detailed Examination of Chinese Government Subsidies to its Steel Industry, prepared for the American Steel Institute, the Steel Manufacturers Association, the Specialty Steel Industry of North Amercia and the Committee on Pipe and Tube Imports, 2007, http://www.steelnet.org/archive/20070730.a.pdf.

Säcker, F. J./Montag, F. (eds), *European State Aid Law*, Hart Publishing, 2016.

Scott, B. R., *Capitalism: Its Origins and Evolution as a System of Governance*, Springer, 2011.

Smith, Adam, The Theory of Moral Sentiments, 1759.

Terpan, F., Soft Law in the European Union – The Changing Nature of EU, *European Law Journal*, Vol. 21, No. 1, 2015.

Van de Gronden, J. W./de Vries, S. A., Independent Competition Authorities in the EU, *Utrecht Law Review*, Volume 2, Issue 1, 2006, https://www.utrechtlawreview.org/articles/abstract/10.18352/ulr.16/.

Varian, H. R., Big Data: New Tricks for Econometrics, 2014, http://people.ischool.berkeley.edu/~hal/Papers/2013/ml.pdf.

Weiβ, W., Das Leitlininen(un)wesen der Kommission verletzt den Vertrag von Lissabon, Europäisches Wirtschafts- und Steuerrecht, Vol. 21, N° 7, 2010.
Wellford, H. B./Tucker, D. S., Big Mistakes Regarding Big Data, 2014, http://papers.ssrn.com/sol3/papers.cfm?abstract_id=2549044.
von Wendland, B., New Rules for State Aid for Research, Development and Innovation 'Not a Revolution but a Silent Reform', EStAL 1/2015.
Wilson, 'The State – Elements of Historical and Practical Politics', 1889.
WTO, International Trade Statistics, 2015.
Zahariadis, N., *State Subsidies in the Global Economy*, Palgrave, 2008.

Index